CANADIAN ETHNOGRAPHY SERIES VOLUME 3

Ta'n Teli-ktlamsɨtasit (Ways of Believing)

MI'KMAW RELIGION IN ESKASONI, NOVA SCOTIA

Series Editors:
Bryan D. Cummins
MCMASTER UNIVERSITY

John L. Steckley
HUMBER COLLEGE

ANGELA ROBINSON
St. Thomas University

PEARSON
Education
Canada

Toronto

National Library of Canada Cataloguing in Publication

Robinson, Angela, 1957–
    Ta'n teliktlamsitasit (Ways of believing) : Mi'kmaw religion in Eskasoni, Nova Scotia / Angela Robinson.

(Canadian ethnography series ; v. 3)
ISBN 0-13-177067-5

    1. Micmac Indians—Nova Scotia—Eskasoni—Religion. 2. Micmac Indians—Religion. 3. Eskasoni (N.S.)—Religion. I. Title. II. Title: Ways of believing. III. Series.

E99.M6R663 2005   299.7'8343'0097169   C2004-901394-7

ISBN 0-13-177067-5

Vice President, Editorial Director: Michael J. Young
Executive Acquisitions Editor: Christine Cozens
Marketing Manager: Ryan St. Peters
Associate Editor: Patti Altridge
Production Editor: Martin Tooke
Copy Editor: Colleen Ste. Marie
Proofreader: Maryan Gibson
Production Manager: Wendy Moran
Page Layout: Laserwords
Art Director: Julia Hall
Cover Design: Miguel Acevedo
Cover Image: Photodisc

30 16

This book is dedicated to the Mi'kmaw people, for whom I have the utmost respect and admiration and who have enriched my life with many gifts.

Welali'oq aqq nemu'ltes.

Contents

Preface

Canadian Ethnography Series

The Canadian Ethnography Series is intended to familiarize undergraduate students with the background and recent history of some of the diverse cultures that make up this country. While the series has as its primary audience students taking courses in anthropology, the monographs will be useful to students of Canadian studies, indigenous studies, sociology, and history.

The series of monographs will examine the distinct histories and contemporary experiences of some of the diverse cultures that make up Canada. The ethnographies will look at a variety of themes, such as indigenous rights, multiculturalism, and socio-economic development. While some of the topics may resemble those covered by sociologists or historians, each book in our series will provide a first-hand, detailed description of a particular Canadian culture based on personal experience. It is our belief that good case studies are critical for a better understanding.

Through ethnographies, students get to know a people in greater depth. To enhance this experience, each of the ethnographies in our series will be supported by the use of some pedagogical features. Each book in the series will be short, fewer than 200 pages, and will include learning objectives, key terms with glossary, and content questions. The series is intended to be accessible to today's post-secondary students.

Acknowledgments

This book is based on fieldwork conducted between July 1997 and September 2001. From this project's inception up to its conclusion I have sought and received advice, guidance, and support from many individuals. To the following I am particularly grateful: Dr. Ellen Badone, my mentor and friend, whose encouragement and support helped make this project a reality. I would also like to thank Drs. Trudy Nicks and Travis Kroeker, whose advice and assistance proved invaluable.

I am also thankful to Dr. Bern Francis, Helen Sylliboy, the extended members of the Sylliboy family, Dr. Margaret Johnson and her family, especially Joan Marshall and Elizabeth Ryan Paul, Caroline and Roddy Gould, Marjorie Gould, Bessie and Wilfred Prosper, Murdena and Albert Marshall, and the many Mi'kmaw "relatives" and friends who generously shared thoughts, ideas, and conversations, and who welcomed me into their hearts and homes.

I would like to acknowledge the helpful suggestions and comments offered by Drs. Bryan Cummins and John Steckley and the editorial staff at Pearson Education for their invaluable input in the production of this work.

Of course, I am eternally grateful to my family and personal friends, who sustain me in ways too numerous to mention.

Angela Robinson, 2004

chapter one

Introduction

Throughout the world, indigenous peoples have had to reckon with the forces of "progress" and "national" unification. Many traditions, languages, cosmologies, and values are lost, some literally murdered, but much has simultaneously been invented and received in complex, oppositional contexts. If the victims of progress and empire are weak, they are seldom passive. It used to be assumed that conversion to Christianity . . . would lead to the extinction of indigenous culture rather than to their transformation. Something more ambiguous and historically complex has occurred.

James Clifford (1988: 16)

LEARNING OBJECTIVES

After reading this chapter, students should be able to:

- Identify and distinguish among the three religious groups of the Mi'kmaq.
- Contrast a traditional approach with a modern approach to ethnography.
- Identify the main ideas and issues presented in this ethnography.
- Describe the functions of salites in contemporary Mi'kmaw culture in Eskasoni.
- Discuss the importance of Mi'kmaw religion and spirituality in constructing personal and social identity.

INTRODUCTION

On a warm day in late July 1999, a group of 600 or 700 people gathered at Holy Family Church in Eskasoni, Nova Scotia. The crowd was unusual for this time of year. For by mid-July the **Mi'kmaq** of this predominantly Roman Catholic Aboriginal community have already moved to Chapel Island (Potlotek)[1] for the annual St. Anne's Mission (*Se'tta'newimk*). On this particular occasion, however, people had either stayed in or returned to the community to attend the funerals of two of the community's residents who had tragically drowned. Mali,[2] a friend of mine, who was a family member of one of the victims, invited me to attend the funeral mass, as well as the feast and *salite* (auction) immediately following internment of the deceased. The *salite* is a "local" (Christian 1981a) funerary ritual that is not part of mainstream Roman Catholic practice. However, it is also a ritualistic expression of specific beliefs and values that help to illuminate various features of **Mi'kmaw** religion, culture, and tradition.

I watched as a man strode between the dining tables in the church hall holding a set of books high over his head. "Any offers?" he asked. No offers came, so he set the bidding at $40. In a very short time the price was well over $100. Mali, seated next to me, became more and more agitated as the bids rose. "They're my father's books," she said with tears welling up in her eyes. "I offered them for the salite because I knew they would get a good price. But, Angela, I can't afford to buy them back. I'm broke." I felt totally at a loss. For, as much as I wanted to help, I could not afford to match the bids being offered. Mali's sister approached the table and was told that the books being auctioned belonged to the family. Mali was even more upset than before and said with resignation, "Father's books are gone now and I can't do anything about it." Her sister left immediately. So bids started coming from other family members, but they could not compete with the bids of the other interested parties.

The parcel up for auction was a set of Mi'kmaw prayer books. Some were written (using the Roman alphabet) in the Mi'kmaw language and some in Mi'kmaw hieroglyphics. The editions offered for sale were old and difficult to obtain. Most were out of print. Among the Mi'kmaq, books such as these are highly prized items, not simply because of their rarity but also because of their social and personal significance. As well as historical artifacts, such books are usually family heirlooms that are often passed on to a relative when the owner dies. Mali had obtained the prayer books in this manner upon her father's death.

As the bids steadily rose Mali became more and more upset. By the time the final bid was submitted and accepted, she was devastated and in tears, with her face buried in her

Box 1.1	Naming the Mi'kmaq

Mi'kmaq (plural) and *Mi'kmaw* (singular) are spelled in compliance with the Smith-Francis orthographic system. The adverbial and adjectival forms usually appear as *Mi'kmaw*, as in references to the Mi'kmaw language or the Mi'kmaw flag. The term *Mi'kma'ki* refers to the traditional lands of the Mi'kmaq, which include portions of New Brunswick, Nova Scotia, Prince Edward Island, Newfoundland and Labrador, and northeastern Quebec.

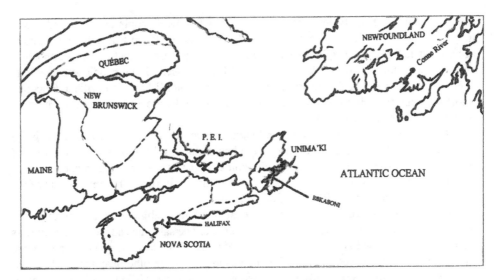

This map includes provincial territories and Mi'kmaw political units. The territory labelled **Unama'ki** refers to the region of Cape Breton Island.

hands. It was heart-wrenching to watch. As I was trying to comfort Mali I noticed that the lady who had purchased the books was approaching our table. She came up to where we sat and placed the books in front of Mali, astonishing her. Then she said, "Now let this be a lesson—don't you ever do that again." "*O' wela'lin, wela'lin t'us*" ("Oh, thank you, thank you daughter"),[3] said Mali, hugging the woman while trying to restrain her tears. This gesture was one of the most moving I have ever witnessed. In the space of 20 minutes I watched Mali's anguish as she saw an heirloom slip out of her hands with the prospect of being lost to her family forever, contrasted with her overwhelming joy when the coveted objects were returned with simplicity and generosity. I was soon to learn that such unselfish and considerate acts are commonplace among the Mi'kmaw people.

Typically, the family, friends, and acquaintances of the deceased assemble after the funeral mass for a communal "feast" and the auction of sundry items. Among the Mi'kmaq the term *feast* is used to refer to a special meal, usually shared communally by a large number of people. Normally, feasts are part of ritual celebrations, like funerals, Treaty Day celebrations, clan gatherings, birthdays, or any special occasion where a large number of people gather for a common purpose. Typically, traditional foods, such as salmon, lobster, eel, deer, moose, and bear are served on these occasions, but non-traditional foods, such as chicken, lamb, beef, pork, and turkey may also be included. Whatever food is served is usually in abundance.

On a social level, the feast and salite provide people with the opportunity to share food, swap stories, and visit with friends and family. However, both the feast and the salite also have spiritual and practical dimensions. Their essential purpose is to celebrate the life of the deceased and to help the grieving family financially and emotionally. Salites are not sombre affairs: there is much laughter and conversation. Sometimes the bidding for desired items enters into friendly competition. The items sold at the salite are provided by friends and family of the deceased. Quite often an inexpensive but treasured item sells for a price far beyond its retail value. For example, a $2 mug purchased locally might sell for $80 and might appear again in future salites, becoming a standing joke. The exorbitant prices paid for salite items are actually donations to the grieving family. If people cannot afford to participate in the auction they refrain from bidding. Typically, those whose budgets cannot accommodate the amounts of money required for the purchase of auction items contribute whatever they can afford to help the family of the deceased. Some people are unable to attend either the wake or the funeral mass. However, most Mi'kmaq do make a concerted effort to attend the salite because it is considered to be the most practical and important way to help the grieving family.

The salite also has social and cultural significance, for, as I was often told, "It is the Mi'kmaw way." On a personal level, it is the beginning of a healing process; on a social level, it is the way in which the community comes together to help those in need of emotional support and to help offset funeral costs. For many Mi'kmaq, the salite is one of the most important features of Mi'kmaw funerary ritual.

As mentioned, the salite is a feature of "local" Mi'kmaw religious expression that does not conform to mainstream Roman Catholic practice. The salite has added significance as a communal gathering that encourages a sense of unity with which many Mi'kmaw people identify, to varying degrees and for different reasons. However, other features of Mi'kmaw religious practice promote conflict and dissent. Although the Mi'kmaq, like many other Aboriginal groups, are confronted with the daunting task of maintaining personal and social identities, there are diverse, and often competing, understandings of how to accomplish this task. Conflict surrounds the use of religion in the daily ordering and reordering of Mi'kmaw social life. This conflict is due, in part, to the diversity of religious and spiritual values and rules of conduct that influence social organization. Because Mi'kmaw identity is at issue, some Mi'kmaq reject the Catholic Church entirely, associating it with colonialism and the demise of Aboriginal culture. Others, however, hold that the Church is as legitimately traditional as many of the newly imported and recently adopted Aboriginal religious traditions. Yet again, there are many Mi'kmaq whose religious beliefs and practices combine features of Christian and non-Christian Aboriginal traditions. For the Mi'kmaq of Eskasoni, religion is not strictly confined to institutionalized religion, such as Roman Catholicism. It is informed by both Christian and non-Christian influences, from which a diversity of religious expressions emerges.

This book focuses on three issues related to the points discussed above. First, I discuss the reciprocal nature of the exchange between Christian and Mi'kmaw religious beliefs, values, and expressions. Second, I address the various religious or spiritual orientations that individuals may either invoke or subvert in the process of constructing a positive Mi'kmaw personal and social identity. Third, and more generally, I look at how religion functions in the day-to-day lives of the Mi'kmaw people.

CONTEXT AND METHODOLOGY

Located on the Bras D'Or Lake in Cape Breton, Nova Scotia, Eskasoni is home to nearly four thousand Mi'kmaq. It is the largest Mi'kmaw community and the only Aboriginal Roman Catholic parish in Nova Scotia. The remaining Mi'kmaw communities in the province are served by the Catholic mission church system. Eskasoni residents are predominately Christian with approximately 95 percent claiming affiliation with the Roman Catholic Church. But "affiliation" does not necessarily imply that the relationship with the Church is a close one. Of those who are baptized into Catholicism, many are nominally Catholic and participate in church activities, such as funerals and christenings, often only perfunctorily.

The remaining 5 percent of the population are either **Traditionalists**, of which there are about 100, or practitioners of the Baha'i faith,[4] which claims a membership of 30 to 40 people. For the Mi'kmaq, the term *Traditionalist* is laden with meaning. While for the most part it refers to someone who subscribes exclusively to a non-Christian, Aboriginal religion, such a definition is misleading. Several variant meanings of the term are offered in the chapters that follow.

These simple statistics obscure the distinctiveness and creativity of Mi'kmaw beliefs and expressions. Currently we lack data about the religious affiliation of Aboriginal Canadians in general, as sociologist James S. Frideres states:

> According to present statistics, 46 percent of Indians in Canada are Catholics ... Protestants make up another 36 percent, while "no religion" adds another 17 percent. The second largest Indian religious group is Anglican, with 18 percent. Another 10 percent of Indians belong to the United Church, and the remaining 8 percent are distributed among the other Christian churches in Canada. This information is based on official government statistics. However, no information has been gathered regarding the extent to which Aboriginal people still adhere to pre-Christian religious beliefs. Apparently, a significant number of Aboriginal persons have retained their indigenous religious beliefs.

> *(Frideres 2001: 88–89)*

Even though these figures are based on "official government statistics," as the author points out, we must question the degree to which Christianity predominates Aboriginal religious affiliations in Canada.

To date, much of the scholarship concerning Mi'kmaw religious life deals exclusively with either Roman Catholicism or non-Christian traditionalism. However, through this tendency to essentialize (i.e., to emphasize one aspect of culture over and above all others), specific aspects of Mi'kmaw belief and expression have been ignored. Little attention has been paid to the ways in which features of both Roman Catholic and non-Catholic religious systems are evident in "local" religious expression. My research clearly indicates that what is understood as Mi'kmaw spirituality or culture informs the way in which Roman Catholicism is believed and practised. As in most societies, among the Mi'kmaq there is no single, comprehensive definition that encompasses the many individualistic and subtly different understandings of what it means to be spiritual. However, generally speaking, the Mi'kmaw people do not think of spirituality as an abstract entity. Spirituality is not something that one *has*. Rather, it is something that one *does* every day. Accordingly, Mi'kmaw spirituality must be embodied in real people and in real contexts. Because spirituality is perceived to be evident and expressed in everyday life, spirituality and culture are often inextricably intertwined for the Mi'kmaq. As a result, Mi'kmaw religion cannot be confined within the dogma and ritual of the Catholic Church, but must be understood in more comprehensive terms and must be recognized as playing a role in all aspects of Mi'kmaw social life. While Catholic teachings and practices are clearly a part of Mi'kmaw daily life, at the same time there are commonly and continually practised elements of Mi'kmaw spirituality that are separate from the teachings and beliefs of the Roman Catholic Church. However, these Mi'kmaw spiritual and religious teachings do not necessarily negate those of the Church. There are both points of convergence and points of departure between Catholicism and non-Christian Mi'kmaw faith.

THE ETHNOGRAPHIC PROCESS: CONDUCTING FIELD RESEARCH

Between July 1997 and April 2000, I conducted three separate periods of participant-observation research in Cape Breton. My first two visits were spent mostly on the island of Potlotek, where I attended the annual St. Anne's Mission in July of 1997 and again in 1998. The third period of research was between April 1999 and April 2000. During my preliminary research periods at Potlotek, I sought to determine whether or not my research on Mi'kmaw religion was feasible and whether the Mi'kmaw people themselves were receptive to this study. I found that not only were many Mi'kmaw people receptive, but most with whom I spoke were excited about the idea. Several made the point that Mi'kmaw religion is an important aspect of Mi'kmaw culture and society that had never been adequately addressed by social-scientific researchers.

In addition to attending the St. Anne's Mission at Potlotek for three consecutive years, at Eskasoni I attended funerals, weekly masses, special liturgical celebrations—such as the Good Friday pilgrimage "up the mountain"—and the masses for Thanksgiving, Memorial Day, Christmas Eve and Christmas Day, New Year's Eve, Candlemas Day, and Ash Wednesday. I also attended a powwow, a **sweat**, and several "prayer" or sacred circles held by a group of Mi'kmaw Traditionalists. In addition, I had the privilege of being invited to share in numerous feasts and celebrations, specifically those associated with baptisms, anniversaries, weddings, clan gatherings, salites, and birthday parties.

As part of my field research, I also conducted 42 open-ended formal interviews with members of the Eskasoni community and with several former clergy, as well as the priest and nuns who now reside in Eskasoni. The interviews sought to elicit personal reflections on and interpretations of Mi'kmaw religious life.[5] For the most part, those interviewed were men and women between the ages of 40 and 85, from diverse economic and educational backgrounds, and from different religious affiliations. Initially, I had intended to interview people from a broader age range. However, soon after beginning my research I realized that the members of the 40- to 85-year-old demographic group had lived in Eskasoni for all or most of their lives. These people had consequently witnessed significant changes both in the Catholic Church and in the ways in which non-Christian traditional beliefs and expressions have persisted and evolved. This made them especially fruitful sources of information. My research was not, however, restricted solely to this age group. I also had the opportunity to hold a number of informal interviews and conversations with children and young adults and to observe people of all ages in a variety of social settings, both formal and informal.

As a discipline, ethnography demands a wide variety of sources and contexts in order to give depth and breadth of meaning to the study of culture in its many dimensions. Ethnography is a discipline that has gone through a series of growing pains since its inception in the latter part of the 19th century. Since the mid-1980s, ethnographic research and writing has been subject to a series of critiques, sometimes characterized as a "crisis of representation" (Marcus and Fischer 1986: 8). In classical ethnography, the **monologic** authority of the author mediated the voices of the "informants" by speaking *for* them and by concealing the construction of the **"Other"** by an invisible anthropological self. Ethnographers, by removing themselves from their texts, attempted to impart an objective view of the cultures under study. However, in the final decades of the 20th century, this objective ideal was abandoned by many ethnographers (e.g., Badone 1989; Clifford and Marcus 1986; Danforth 1982, 1989; Geertz 1973; Jackson 1996, 1998; Narayan 1989; Rosaldo 1989; Tedlock 1983) who adopted a **reflexive** approach to the ethnographic process that embraced **multivocality**—the inclusion of many voices—as a central feature of ethnographic writing and research. Multivocality is now necessary to the enterprise of ethnography because it recognizes and allows the participants' voices to be heard on both individual and collective levels.

As James Clifford suggests, the inclusion of multiple voices is crucial to the study and interpretation of culture, for "culture is **contested, temporal** and **emergent**. Representations and explanation—both by insiders and outsiders—are **implicated** in this emergence" (Clifford and Marcus 1986: 19). *Contested* means that not everyone in the society agrees that "this is how this is done" or "this is how that is interpreted." Imagine Canadians commenting on the role of hockey in their culture or discussing whether or not fighting in hockey is a good or bad thing. You would need to hear the voices of a large number of Canadians before you could develop an informed opinion about hockey in Canada. And no one person would hold that view. *Temporal* refers to aspects of a culture connected with a particular point in time, what was traditionally referred to by anthropologists as a particular "ethnographic present." The importance of the temporal can be illustrated with the use of slang terms by Canadian teenagers. Think of how inaccurate you would be if you said that *hip, fab,* and *groovy* were slang terms used by contemporary Canadian teenagers! *Emergent* culture means that the discussion of a culture emerges or develops out of a particular people who either belong to or are outside of the culture and who participate in that discussion. It is the participants themselves who, in cooperation with the author, lend intricacy, complexity, and breadth to ethnographic research and writing. *Implicated* means that those representing or explaining the culture, both insiders and outsiders, have a personal or individual effect on the resulting description of the culture.

While multivocality is currently promoted as a necessary component of responsible anthropological scholarship, the visibility of the subjective component—that is, the viewpoint or voice of the author—is also accepted and encouraged in the production of ethnographies. As mentioned, the authors of classical ethnographic texts were usually invisible authorities, who, in an attempt to maintain subjectivity, remained obscurely remote from the text. Anthropologists George Marcus and Dick Cushman point out that "While the use of the omniscient [all-knowing] author heightens the sense of scientific objectivity projected by the text, such usage also helps to sever the relationship between what the ethnographer knows and how he [she] came to know it" (Marcus and Cushman 1982: 32). Within the social sciences, it is now well accepted that the subjective experience of the researcher/author in the field is a continually negotiated and interpreted performance that must be acknowledged and addressed in the course of "writing culture." After all, as Mary Pratt informs us, ethnography is not "a neutral, tropeless discourse," free from "our own values and interpretive schema" (Pratt 1986: 27). Ethnographers should not hide behind a mask of objectivity in their texts. Instead, an awareness of the subjective positional nature of the authorial voice and the need for reflexivity are considered necessary features of research analysis and text production.

There has been a tendency for anthropologists to locate and study "exotic others" whose cultures are remarkably different from their own. This trend is particularly evident in North America, where Aboriginal American groups have been the subject of anthropological study for generations. However, anthropologists have also been taken to task for "essentializing" Aboriginal cultures and constructing too radical a dichotomy between "Them" and "Us." As Johannes Fabian points out, this criticism is not groundless:

> Anthropology contributed above all to the intellectual justification of the colonial enterprise. It gave to politics and economics—both concerned with human Time—a firm belief in "natural," i.e., evolutionary Time. It promoted a scheme in terms of which not only past cultures, but all living societies were irrevocably placed on a temporal slope, a stream of Time—some upstream, some downstream . . . A discourse employing terms such as primitive, savage . . . does not think, or observe, or critically study, the "primitive"; it thinks, observes, studies *in terms* of the primitive. *Primitive* being essentially a temporal concept, is a category, not an object, of Western thought.
>
> *(Fabian 1983: 17-18)*

In an attempt to establish social and cultural differences, some researchers have stumbled into the pitfall of temporally and spatially dislocating Aboriginal groups, isolating them into convenient cultural enclaves that somehow elude the passage of time. James Clifford comments on the situation of the Wampanoag people of Mashpee, Massachusetts:

> Indians have always filled a pathetic imaginative space for the dominant culture; they were always survivors noble or wretched. Their cultures had been steadily eroding, at best hanging on in museum like reservations. Native American societies could not by definition be dynamic, inventive, or expansive.
>
> *(Clifford 1988: 284)*

Ethnographers are now called to be aware of and receptive to divisions of time and space, as these are perceived and understood within the society being studied.

While the description and interpretation of social and cultural differences are at the heart of the anthropological enterprise, in my experience as a field researcher it is the Mi'kmaw people themselves who wish to establish their distinctiveness as a group. Many Mi'kmaq not only wish to establish the uniqueness of their culture and society from that of non-Aboriginals, but also want to emphasize their distinctiveness relative to other Aboriginal groups. The Mi'kmaq, like most Aboriginal peoples, are no longer spatially isolated from the dominant non-Aboriginal society. Most Aboriginal communities now have many of the technologies and modern conveniences available to other North Americans in the 21st century. However, there is also a perceived need to establish and maintain a certain amount of community insularity, whereby the community becomes an instrument for the preservation of Aboriginal culture and society. For instance, in 1980 the Mi'kmaq of Eskasoni managed to gain control of the local educational system to ensure that Mi'kmaw culture and language would be taught as part of the core curriculum.

Oftentimes, claims of "otherness" on the part of Aboriginal groups have serious social, political, and cultural implications. In terms of locating or relocating themselves historically, Aboriginal groups have been accused of resurrecting aspects of the past to further specific political agendas, such as land claims settlements, control of natural resources, or increased political autonomy. Anthropologist Tord Larsen wrote about the Mi'kmaq in the mid-1980s:

Indians employ elements in their universe—among other things, elements of their aboriginal culture, the history of Indian/White relations, the ways in which they see themselves different from whites—in order to construct a statement which is intended to make whites see things differently. In doing so, Indians give new import to old facts, juxtapose ideas that have not been related previously and endow forgotten events with new significance.

(Larsen 1983: 39)

Using the past for political gain is, however, only part of the overall picture. Also included in how the past is discussed are issues of cultural integrity and social and personal identity. References to the past may also be an Aboriginal response to colonialism (both historical and current) and the contemporary trend toward globalization, both of which contribute to the possible erosion of indigenous societies. The recognition of connections to an Aboriginal past does not mean that Aboriginal peoples are not part of the 21st century or that they are somehow buried in the past. In contemporary societies, intermingling influences of the past and present shape the ways in which Aboriginal peoples relate to the world around them.

MI'KMAW CULTURE AND SOCIETY IN ACADEMIC CONTEXTS

The confluence of present and past traditions, world views, and modes of religious expression provide a portrait of Mi'kmaw society that is far more complex and varied than most scholars have previously suggested. In the study of Mi'kmaw religion, researchers have often privileged non-Christian religious practices over those of Christianity while failing to consider the influence of the latter. Conversely, other researchers have failed to recognize that institutionalized religion, such as Roman Catholicism, has been influenced by non-Christian Aboriginal religious traditions and ideologies. In the case of Mi'kmaw religion, a clean separation of non-Christian Aboriginal practices from those associated with Christianity cannot be easily made. Part of the problem with earlier treatments of Mi'kmaw religion was the tendency to subject the Mi'kmaq to investigation and analysis informed by the cultural categories of the dominant society. Since the 1980s, however, research on Aboriginal religion has moved away from **assimilationist** models that interpret the relationship between Christian and non-Christian Aboriginal practices from the perspective of the dominant Euro-American, Christian culture (Barker 1998; Grant 1984; Morinis 1992; Watanabe 1990).

This book draws on current studies of Aboriginal-Christian interaction that highlight the reciprocal nature of the exchange between Aboriginal and Christian values, beliefs, and practices. Works relevant to this project include those that consider the Aboriginal voice a primary source of information (Axtell 1985; Brown 1996; Dickason 1984; Henderson 1997; Warkentin 1996); those that discuss the effects of cross-cultural exchange (Barker 1998; Chute 1992; Goulet 1982; Hulkrantz 1979; Kan 1991; Morrison 1990; Steckley 1992; Stirrat 1992); those that discuss the persistence of non-Christian Aboriginal practices (Barker 1998; Blanchard 1982; Dusenberry 1962; Goulet 1982; Kan 1991; Morinis 1992; Morrison 1981, 1990); and those that consider the role of religion in the formation of individual and collective Aboriginal identities (Chute 1992; McMillan 1996; Preston 1987; Reid 1995; Slaney 1997; Watanabe 1990).

Of the last-mentioned category, Jennifer Reid's book, *Myth, Symbol, and Colonial Encounter*, is one of the most significant ethnohistorical works on the role of religion in the shaping of Mi'kmaw identity. Reid astutely points out that human religiosity gives meaning to history. Reid argues that in the construction of a British colonial identity, the Mi'kmaq served as a counter-identity, whereby the Christianity and civility of British colonials was held up against the savagery and heathenism of indigenous peoples. Reid does not consider Aboriginal religion in terms of Christian categories and ideologies but suggests that sacred beliefs, like "rootedness" in the land, were conveniently denied and ignored to serve British interests (Reid 1995: 101–102). This point is significant, since it seems that we have inherited the tendency to understand Aboriginal religion in terms of Euro-American ideologies and perspectives. This work will serve as a partial corrective to such approaches, in that it uncovers and recognizes how Mi'kmaw understandings of the sacred inform current religious beliefs and expressions.

The relationship between indigenous peoples and Christianity is an area of scholarship that currently receives considerable attention. However, scholarship on Mi'kmaw Catholicism is practically nonexistent, with the exception of several short articles (Brooks 1986; Campbell 1998; Chute 1992; Krieger 1989); Bock's 1966 ethnography of the Mi'kmaq of Restigouche, New Brunswick; Anne-Christine Hornborg's 2001 historical study of the Mi'kmaq; and Leslie J. McMillan's research on the Grand Council. While some ethnographic works (Hoffman 1946; McGee 1974; Wallis and Wallis 1955) exist, these studies deal primarily with premissionary Mi'kmaw religious practices. They pay little attention to the role of Catholicism in Mi'kmaw life.

In the discipline of anthropology, the move away from viewing a specific social system or culture as a functionally integrated whole has been prompted by the realization that social and personal identities are not guided by one single world view or by one homogenous set of collective values. Anthropologists now commonly hold that social systems are in a continual state of flux and that conflict and negotiation are at the heart of social and cultural dynamics (Asad 1993; Kapferer 1997; Morrison 1990; Turner 1969). For the most part, however, past scholarship concerning Mi'kmaw religion has not adequately reflected such understandings.

TERMINOLOGY

Although it would be easy, and perhaps convenient, to consider Mi'kmaw life perspectives as relics or survivors of the past, to do so would be negligent. Conversely, to ignore the pervasive influences of Euro-American institutions, laws, and ideologies on the lives of the Mi'kmaw people would be equally remiss. Present-day Mi'kmaw culture and social organization, like that of most Aboriginal peoples, are drawn from both Western and non-Western contexts. These organizations are influenced by the world views within Western thought and also by the views that emerge from indigenous understandings of the world. Thus, when we speak in terms of spirituality, religion, and tradition within Mi'kmaw society, we must do so with the understanding that such references may or may not hold the same intentional meanings as they do within Western society at large.

In 1691, the Récollet priest, Father Chrétien Le Clercq, wrote about the Indians of Gaspesia[6]:

> I should never finish if I wished to report to you here all the traits of superstition of these barbarians. That which I have said thereon is enough to make you see the extent

of the error and the simplicity of this blind people, who have lived in the shades of Christianity without law, without faith, and without religion.

(Le Clercq 1968 [1691]: 233)

Of course, the charges of being "blind" and in "error" can also be applied to those on the opposite side of early Aboriginal–European encounters. The religious predispositions of early European visitors, combined with their lack of knowledge and understanding of indigenous languages, lifeways, and systems of belief, precluded a recognition of religion when it presented itself in unfamiliar forms and contexts. Instead, indigenous religions were often perceived as "superstition" and have been variously described by such pejorative terms as "jugglery," "devil worship," or simply "nonsense" (Le Clercq 1968 [1691]: 216, 221). Such terms are now recognized as the products of a less enlightened era and have fallen into general disuse. However, the residual effects of the ideology of European dominance remain with us. Kenneth Morrison suggests that the inability of early ethnographers and historians to recognize and appreciate the complexity of precontact indigenous religions emerges "from an outdated effort to classify religious practices on some evolutionary scale of institutionalized expression" (Morrison 1981: 237). Thus, when we speak of religion we may refer to institutionalized religion alone. However, if we understand the concept of religion to include aspects of religion that are non-institutionalized, then many Aboriginal traditional religious practices can be included under the general category of "religion." This understanding is particularly important when referring to non-Christian practices that do not conform to Western models of religion.

The term *religion* also poses a number of problems because many aspects of Mi'kmaw beliefs and values are not easily categorized. I use the term *belief system* wherever possible, but completely avoiding the term *religion* is impractical. The operational understanding of religion in this book is broadly defined. In keeping with Clifford Geertz, I understand religion to be a meaningful "system of symbols" that serves to establish powerful "moods and motivations," which in turn give rise to a vision of a "general order of existence" for the society in which it functions (Geertz 1973: 90). Moreover, following Talal Asad, I understand the concept of *symbol* to mean not simply "an object or event that serves to carry a meaning but a set of relationships between objects or events uniquely brought together as complexes or as concepts, having at once an intellectual, instrumental, and emotional significance" (Asad 1993: 31). Accordingly, the process of constructing, appropriating, and utilizing symbols takes place in response to the economic, political, and social milieux from which these symbols emerge and in which they exist and operate. Thus, the public and private uses of religious symbols may be imbued with diverse meanings depending on the contexts in which they occur. As a case in point, among the Mi'kmaq of Eskasoni, the appropriation and use of Christian and non-Christian religious symbols is often idiosyncratic and is largely dependent on one's particular orientation. In Eskasoni, the creative use of symbolism is especially notable when elements of Catholic and non-Catholic traditions are combined.

MI'KMAW BELIEF SYSTEMS

There are three prominent and immediately identifiable religious groups in the community of Eskasoni: Traditionalists (or **neo-Traditionalists**), **Catholics,** and **Catholic-Traditionalists,** all three of which are not rigidly bounded categories. Rather, these groups refer to the specific religious orientations that are made up of individuals who participate to different degrees in these religious affiliations. For instance, a Catholic-Traditionalist may prefer regular church services to occasional sacred circles or, conversely, may prefer noninstitutionalized practices to routine church services.

Traditionalism is an ambiguous term among the Mi'kmaq of Eskasoni. For some Mi'kmaq, tradition, spirituality, and religion are discrete terms. However, for many others these three specific facets of Mi'kmaw culture are not unrelated categories but fluid concepts that are often intertwined and open to interpretation. At base, the perception of what it means to be Mi'kmaq, as in personal and social identity, influences religious affiliation. Many Eskasoni residents use the term *Traditionalist* to refer to specific persons or groups of people within the community who subscribe to what are considered to be authentic, pre-Christian religious practices exclusive of Catholicism. However, among Catholic Mi'kmaq is the understanding that someone can be a lower-case traditionalist in another sense of the term. A person can uphold Mi'kmaw culture and tradition while accepting Catholicism as a primary religious orientation.

Throughout this text, I use the term *neo-Traditionalist* to refer to a particular religious orientation: that is, Mi'kmaq who espouse specifically non-Christian practices believed to have their origin in "authentic" precontact Mi'kmaw religion. However, since many aspects of original or authentic Mi'kmaw religion fell into disuse, current practices associated with Traditionalism have been primarily re-created from orally transmitted texts and etymological analysis of the Mi'kmaw language. I use the terms *neo-Traditionalist/Traditionalism* and *Traditionalist/Traditionalism* interchangeably. Traditionalism (with a capital *T*) refers to a specific religious orientation employed by the Mi'kmaw people themselves and appears throughout this work in reference to direct quotations. The instances where *traditionalism* (lower case *t*) is used is in reference to the socio-cultural, rather than strictly religious, sense of the term. Similarly, anthropologist Thomas Parkhill claims that "the process of reclaiming ways began in the late 1970s among Micmac and Abenaki people, and that devout Micmac Catholics refer to *their* religion as 'traditional,'" (Parkhill 1997: 135). Parkhill also uses the term *neo-traditionalism* to refer to recently formed "traditional" religions and to distinguish these particular religious orientations from "traditional" Catholicism.

Among Mi'kmaw Catholics, those who consider themselves Traditionalists assert that since most of "authentic" Mi'kmaw religion has been lost to posterity and since Catholicism is an ancestral religion, Traditionalism is a legitimate form of Mi'kmaw religious tradition. Conversely, many non-Christian Mi'kmaq who espouse decolonizationalist views seek to forge a Mi'kmaw identity quite separate from dominant Euro-American ideologies and institutions that they perceive as formidable and continual threats to the preservation of Mi'kmaw society and culture. Of course, such an orientation demands an outright rejection of Catholicism. The third group, Catholic-Traditionalists, are those whose beliefs allow for the incorporation of elements of both religious affiliations in a variety of public and private devotional practices. This group is quite diverse with respect to individual religious understandings and practices, especially in terms of its relationship to the creation and maintenance of personal and social identities. Of these three groups, the last-named is possibly the least recognized category among the Mi'kmaw people. It seems that individual religious expression is condoned by most Mi'kmaq as long as tradition in its broadest sense is upheld, meaning that Catholicism, along with other traditional beliefs, is respected.

TRADITIONALISM

Many Mi'kmaw people are seriously concerned with retaining, reclaiming, and re-creating Mi'kmaw culture, and a return to non-Christian Traditional religion is one feature of culture that is of fundamental importance in the reconstruction and maintenance of Mi'kmaw personal and social identity. The more formalized and regulated forms of religious expressions found in Mi'kmaw Catholicism are generally accepted and upheld. Increasingly, however, a growing number of Mi'kmaq find that the less structured and more individualized forms of neo-Traditionalism offer a viable means of reclaiming self-identity and self-expression.

Stating that neo-Traditional religion is less structured than Catholicism essentially means that non-Christian Traditional practice and belief are nondogmatic, lack a formal institutional context and liturgy, and have no "canon." While many people participate in specific non-Christian neo-Traditional rituals, such expressions are not governed by any central authority that provides specific rules, regulations, and guidelines. The manner in which these practices are performed and the frequency and degree to which they are conducted are left to the individuals themselves.

The types of rituals commonly practised within neo-Traditionalism include powwows, **prayer in the four directions**, sacred (or prayer) circles, **smudges**, sweats, sunrise ceremonies, and drumming, chanting, and dancing.

Sweats require a lot of preparation. Normally sweat lodges are dismantled at the end of the lunar year and are rebuilt during the next lunar month. The lodges used by the Mi'kmaq are dome-shaped structures built low to the ground and constructed almost entirely from indigenous materials. The construction of a sweat lodge begins with the digging of a circular pit. Saplings are gathered and are lashed to a dome-shaped frame with red ties made from leather or other suitable materials. The lodge is completed by covering the frame with blankets or furs in order to prevent steam from escaping. The only "imported," or nonindigenous, materials used in the construction of a lodge are the blankets.

Sacred, or prayer, circles are events that are frequently practised among the Mi'kmaq. These occasions are essentially noncalendrical and tend to be performed in response to individual or group requests. Sacred circles involve smudging as a form of purification, often led by a **pipe-carrier**. The smudge is followed by **prayer in the four directions**, which may or may not include Christian prayers. Prayer in the four directions and smudging are the most frequently performed rituals because they are usually included as important elements of most ritual gatherings. Smudging is a purification ritual involving the burning of sweetgrass,[7] tobacco, sage, cedar, or any combination of these materials in a small vessel, usually a mollusc shell or an earthenware pot. For larger events, such as powwows or sweats, smoke from a sacred fire is used for smudging. The smoke produced in the process of smudging serves to purify or cleanse persons and ritual items that will be involved in the ceremony to follow. Typically, before a sacred circle ceremony commences, the various items to be used in the ceremony are purified by being passed over the smoke from the smudge. Likewise, in the case of a powwow or a sweat the persons and items involved in the ceremony will be "smudged" or purified with smoke from the sacred fire. For powwows, the dancing circle and the arbour where the chanters and musicians are housed are also smudged. Usually the fire-keeper fashions a torch that is lit from the sacred fire and is carried to the powwow grounds, where purification takes place. For sweats, the sacred fire is used to heat the stones for use in the sweat lodge and is also used to smudge all participants and the

various items to be carried into the lodge. For instance, the pipe, the various salves and oint-
ments, and the water to be used in the sweat are purified with smoke before the ceremony
can commence.

Prayer in the four directions is an important feature of most ritual ceremonies, including smudges, sweats, sacred circles, and sunrise ceremonies. Prayers offered in the four
directions differ from person to person and are often customized to suit the occasion. For
instance, the prayers said for a deceased person and those offered for the birth of a child vary
greatly. However, while there are differences in content, the form remains much the same:
prayer is offered first to the east, then, moving in a clockwise direction, the one offering the
prayer directs it to the south, next to the west, and ends with a prayer to the north.

Sweats, sacred circles, and sunrise ceremonies can be conducted to venerate the dead,
to appeal for spiritual or emotional healing, and to seek help for physical or emotional hardship. Traditional rituals can also be celebratory. They may welcome a new family member
or offer thanks for spiritual, emotional, or physical nourishment. Typically, the person who
offers ceremonial prayers at ritual events is a pipe-carrier. This means that a person who
has gone through a period of initiation to "earn" his or her pipe and, having done so, is recognized as a sacred person by Traditionalists and by some Mi'kmaw Catholics. To be a pipe-
carrier is a great honour for a Traditionalist. It may take years to acquire a sacred pipe. It is
only given to a Traditionalist who has advanced through various devotional levels, including intensive sweats and prolonged fasts. Although there no formal rules that generally apply
to obtaining the status of pipe-carrier, most agree that the recipient has to have withstood at
least one fasting period of seven days or more.

Sunrise ceremonies and sacred circles are usually intimate events. As the name suggests,
sunrise ceremonies are initiated at dawn and involve prayer in the four cardinal directions.
These ceremonies are often performed on an individual basis, and the prayers involved are
usually of a highly personal nature. These prayers may include expressions of thankfulness
to the Creator for the sustenance and nourishment found in all of creation. Depending on the
participants, sunrise ceremonies may involve the use of a sacred pipe. However, sacred circles are often led by a pipe-carrier and are normally done in a small group, typically involving smudging, prayer in the four directions, and drumming and chanting.

EXPRESSIONS OF NEO-TRADITIONALISM, CATHOLIC-TRADITIONALISM, AND MI'KMAW CATHOLICISM

The degree to which Traditional rituals are practised and accepted as legitimate religious
devotions ultimately depends on religious orientation. In order to illustrate how different
religious orientations influence Mi'kmaw devotions, I have selected three profiles that I
feel clearly express the diversity and creativity of Mi'kmaw religious beliefs and expressions:
Tumas (pronounced Dumas) is a self-professed Traditionalist, Piel (pronounced Biel) is a
Catholic-Traditionalist, and Nora claims Catholicism as her religious affiliation.

Tumas: A Traditionalist

Tumas, a man in his early 50s, is a former Catholic who became involved in neo-
Traditionalism during the early 1980s. He conducts sweats both on and off the reserve and
holds sunrise ceremonies on a regular basis. Tumas is also a former student of the

Shubenacadie residential school, which was located in the town of Shubenacadie, Nova Scotia, approximately 270 kilometres from Eskasoni. The school, called "Shubie" by many Mi'kmaq, operated for 37 years. It was closed in 1967 in the midst of much controversy relating to charges of physical, mental, and sexual abuse of Aboriginal children by the nuns and priests who ran the institution. Owing to his negative experiences there, Tumas harbours a deep resentment toward the Catholic Church. As far as Tumas is concerned, the Church is the source of many of the problems affecting Mi'kmaw society, beginning with the abuses at the residential schools. Tumas feels these abuses continue because of the Church's failure to properly compensate the Mi'kmaw people for the past wrongs inflicted upon them. Tumas refuses to participate in Catholic ceremonies of any kind and is openly critical of the Church:

> The Church is responsible for allowing the abuse at Shubie to happen. They sent us a bunch of criminals. People who did things wrong wherever they were before and this was their punishment—send them to the Indians! No one knows what some of those people did before. They weren't fit for regular society so they pawned them off on us—a bunch of misfits and criminals sent to teach the Indian children. They're all responsible. They should just settle with us now and fight between themselves later, who pays for what. All the former residents are paying now in their own way. We all have our stories.

> *(Fieldnotes Book V: 940)*

Tumas is also perturbed by subsequent actions of the Catholic Church. He said that "since the Pope's visit [1984], the Church has been intruding into 'Traditionalism' because the Pope said it was OK. Now, the Church uses sweetgrass, drumming and chants, and the [eagle] feather, but I don't think the Church respects it . . . How would the Church react if I started holding confession and passing around [Communion] wafers in the sweat lodge?" He added jokingly, "There'd be Hell to pay!"

According to Tumas the Church has lost a lot of Mi'kmaw people, and the use of Traditionalism is "an attempt to stop the bleeding." Clearly, Tumas sees the Church's use of Traditional symbols and rituals as superficial—as a means to appease the discontented. In Tumas's opinion, the Church does not accept Traditional practices as legitimately religious. However, Piel, who openly practises Catholicism and neo-Traditionalism, holds a markedly different view of the Church.

Piel: A Catholic Traditionalist

Piel, another of my respondents in his 50s, is deeply devoted to the Church, but incorporates features of neo-Traditionalism in his regular devotions. In addition to attending weekly Mass and other Church functions, Piel conducts sweats and smudges and is a pipe-carrier. Piel is usually the person called upon to perform non-Catholic Aboriginal rituals in the local church on special occasions. He told me that the Church attempts to accommodate Traditional ceremonies but that this process did not begin until 1984 after Pope John Paul II's visit to Canada. Piel recalls that it was as late as 1992 when the first pipe ceremony was conducted in the Church during a general absolution ceremony.

When asked about the resurgence of Traditionalism in Eskasoni, Piel suggested that as a result of their negative experiences at residential school, many former residents have turned to Traditionalism for healing. Neither Piel nor his wife attended the Shubenacadie school:

> I don't think it was too good. There's a lot of pain associated with it [the school]. I also think that's why a lot of people turned to Traditionalism for healing. That's not why I did it, but I can see why people become fanatics about their traditional culture. I'm a Traditionalist, but I'm not a fanatic. I try to strike a balance between culture, religion and the material aspect [of culture]. I have all three . . . When you look at it everything is three, the Holy Trinity is three.

(Fieldnotes Book IV: 800–801)

When I asked Piel about prayer in the four directions, I was quite unprepared for the response I received. Piel explained that the east is represented by the colour red: it "can represent the blood of Christ that was spilt to save us. The south is yellow. It indicates warmth, summer, growth . . . It's mother's warm bread. When you think of it you can see Mary kneeling at the foot of the cross [south being the foot of the cross] . . . The west is black—the spirit world. Jesus bowed his head toward the west when he died . . . The north is white—good medicine, healing, purity, Jesus' soul. So, we were praying the cross even before Jesus was crucified." For Piel then, Traditionalism is part of what makes him Mi'kmaw. Neo-Traditional religion is important to him, but Catholicism is of greater importance, since Aboriginal Traditional practices and beliefs only become religiously meaningful for him when they are interpreted within a Christian frame of reference.

Nora: A Catholic

Finally, there is Nora, a middle-aged woman whose concept of what is sacred extends beyond what is typically identified as Roman Catholic. While Nora incorporates features of both neo-Traditionalism and Catholicism into her religious life, she does not refer to herself as a Traditionalist. She is a self-proclaimed Catholic. Like many Mi'kmaw people, Nora has a

Box 1.2	The Four Basic Elements

There are a number of items used in different rituals that represent the four basic elements. Typically, for most ceremonies the fanning of an eagle feather is used to represent air. In sacred circles participants are ceremoniously sprinkled with water that has been smudged. This sacred water is never thrown away, but is used to clean the smudge pots and shells and may be used again in future ceremonies.

Earth can be represented in a number of ways, but is often symbolized by stone or sand. Many Mi'kmaq carry small stones in *wijipoti* (medicine bags). Fire is used for smudging. In many neo-Traditional ceremonies, such as powwows and sweats, a fire-keeper is assigned to keep watch over the sacred fire to ensure that it remains lit for the duration of the ceremony.

personal altar at home. What is most striking about this altar is the way in which Traditional sacred objects are mixed with Catholic icons and iconography. The various objects placed on the altar, such as holy water, blessed candles, rocks, *wijipoti* (medicine bag), and eagle feathers may appear to be an eclectic and odd grouping, but for Nora they are not. They are highly symbolic. To anyone familiar with Catholic iconography and sacred items, the holy water and candles can be readily identified as part of Catholic tradition, but here they become infused with added meaning. The rocks, feathers, candles, and holy water also represent for Nora the four basic elements of earth, air, fire, and water, respectively. These four elements are also symbolically represented in numerous neo-Traditional rituals, including powwows, sacred circle ceremonies, sunrise ceremonies, and sweats.

Nora is not actively involved in ceremonies such as powwows and sweats, but on occasion she attends sacred circle ceremonies where she participates in chanting, smudging, and praying in the four directions. However, Nora interprets and understands these ceremonies differently than Piel does. She accepts them as part of Mi'kmaw culture, but also views them as legitimate religious rituals *in and of themselves*. Nora approaches Catholic and neo-Traditional expressions of faith with the same devotional zeal. She sees both as opportunities to worship the divine. For Nora, importance is not placed on the actual expression but on the sincerity of devotion. Any expression of faith is legitimate—a prayer is a prayer, a meditation is a meditation.

CONCLUSION AND DISCUSSION

The preceding narratives are a small but telling sample of the diversity and creativity of Mi'kmaw practices. These narratives illustrate that in the process of constructing Mi'kmaw social and personal identity, meaning can be derived from Christian and non-Christian views of the sacred. In Tumas's case, the practice of Traditionalism is closely linked with his identity as a Mi'kmaw person, and Catholicism is viewed as a threat to that identity. However, for Piel and Nora, Catholicism provides a formal religious structure that does not preclude their involvement in neo-Traditional religion. Non-Christian devotions are also predominant features of their respective religious and cultural identities. Like Tumas, Piel, and Nora, there are many Mi'kmaq who, to varying degrees, accept features of either Catholicism or neo-Traditional religion or both as legitimate and meaningful expressions of faith.

CONTENT QUESTIONS

1. Identify the three main points of this book.
2. Outline the ethnographic methodologies used in this monograph.
3. Distinguish between Traditionalist and neo-Traditionalist in Mi'kmaw religion.
4. Contrast traditional and more recent ethnographic research concerning the presumed objectivity/subjectivity and invisibility/visibility of the ethnographer.
5. Explain why the term *religion* is a problematic one for anthropologists.
6. Describe the functions of salites in contemporary Mi'kmaw culture in Eskasoni.

ENDNOTES

1. The island of Potlotek (Chapel Island) shares its name with a neighbouring Mi'kmaw community. The Mi'kmaw term *Potlotek* is used throughout this book to refer to the island that hosts the annual St. Anne's Mission (*Se'tta'newimk*), and Chapel Island is used to refer to the nearby Mi'kmaw community.

2. Unless otherwise noted, the actual names of respondents will not be used in this book for reasons of privacy.

3. Here, *t'us* ("daughter") is meant as a term of endearment and should not be taken literally. It should also be noted that in Mi'kmaq *wela'lin* means "you do me well" but is often used as the functional equivalent to the English "thank you."

4. A religion founded by Baha'ullah in the 1860s, governed by an elected body—the Universal House of Justice. The Baha'i faith is monotheistic but claims that God is completely transcendent and unknowable. Baha'ism has no official priesthood; administration rests with locally and nationally elected councils. The unity and equality of all peoples and religions is the central focus of the faith.

5. I usually opened an interview by asking the interviewee to tell me about Mi'kmaw Catholicism, Christian-Traditionalism, or neo-Traditionalism, depending on his or her religious affiliation. Interviews were, for the most part, open-ended to avoid restricting the type of information gathered and to prevent overly directed questions from shaping interviewees' responses. The term *neo-Traditionalism* is defined in detail below.

6. *Gaspesia* refers to the general area of Quebec and the Atlantic provinces. The indigenous peoples inhabiting Gaspesia, the modern-day Mi'kmaq and Maliseet, were once called Gaspesians.

7. Sweetgrass is a long, grass-shaped plant that grows near swampy areas. Each year it is harvested by the Mi'kmaq to be used in making crafts and for ceremonial purposes like those described. Among the Mi'kmaq, the sweetgrass used for ceremonial purposes usually comes in braided form and is rarely, if ever, sold on the open market. However, sweetgrass used in the production of crafts is sold in bundles of loose blades.

chapter two

The Mi'kmaq:

An Ethnohistorical Overview

...culture is precisely the organization of the current situation in terms of a past.

Marshall Sahlins, *Islands of History*, 1987

LEARNING OBJECTIVES

After reading this chapter, students should be able to:

- Describe the precontact subsistence patterns of the **Mi'kmaq**.
- Identify present-day problems that confront the Mi'kmaq.
- Outline aspects of pre- and postcontact religion.
- Identify the significant changes in culture that have taken place in the postcontact era.
- Identify forms of **Mi'kmaw** resistance to colonialism.

INTRODUCTION

The Mi'kmaq are an Algonquian people. They reside throughout Mi'kma'ki on the East Coast of Canada in the provinces of New Brunswick, Newfoundland, Nova Scotia, and Prince Edward Island, and on the Gaspé Peninsula, Quebec. According to archaeological findings at the Debert and Red Bank sites in Nova Scotia, the Mi'kmaq have inhabited these regions for well over 10 000 years. One interpretation of the terms *Mi'kmaq* (plural; in the past, often referred to as "Micmac") and *Mi'kmaw* (singular) is that they are derived from *no'kmaq*, meaning "all my relations." Oral tradition suggests that early visitors to Mi'kma'ki mistook *Mi'kmaq* as a reference to the Aboriginal inhabitants. According to Mi'kmaw oral history, the term *L'nu*, meaning "the people," is the proper referent. However, the latter term rarely appears in common usage except to mean *L'nu'sinej*—literally "let's speak L'nu [Mi'kmaq]"—and *L'nu'ktat*—"she, he, or it is wearing L'nu [Mi'kmaw] clothing."

Eskasoni, the principal research site for this study, is located on the Bras D'Or Lakes in the region of Cape Breton, Nova Scotia, approximately 400 kilometres northeast of the capital city of Halifax. Eskasoni is the largest Mi'kmaw community, with a population of close to 4000 residents, or approximately 20 percent of the estimated Mi'kmaw population of 20 000. In 1610, Grand Chief Membertou remarked that the Mi'kmaq were once "as thickly planted as the hairs upon his head" (Thwaites, *Jesuit Relations* 1: 177). However, in the postcontact era (i.e., after European contact) numbers were drastically reduced, due to the adoption of the "bad habits" of the French with respect to food and drink (Thwaites, *JR* 3: 105–107); imported diseases, such as smallpox and influenza; the disruption and eventual eradication of traditional subsistence strategies; and war with the British Crown.

MI'KMAQ IN THE PRECONTACT PERIOD

Subsistence Patterns

Prior to European contact, the Mi'kmaq depended on foraging as a subsistence strategy. Most scholars believe that the Mi'kmaq followed a seasonal migration pattern, travelling extensively throughout Mi'kma'ki, availing themselves of the bounty provided by indigenous flora and fauna. Hunting and fishing practices of the Mi'kmaq were based on the principle of *netukulimk* ("we hunt in partnership"). This concept acknowledges the reciprocal environmental relationship that exists among all creatures, and that ultimately supports the well-being of all. Humans are not placed at the centre of this world order. Rather, they are seen as part of a web of life in which plants, animals, humans, and the four elements (earth, air, fire, water) are interdependent.

During the spring and summer months, the Mi'kmaq gathered in large social groups of up to several hundred individuals. These groups resided in Atlantic coastal regions, where abundant seasonal resources were available. During the fall and winter months, the Mi'kmaq divided into smaller migrational groups, usually consisting of extended family members. These smaller groups headed inland to more sheltered regions, where they hunted various game animals. In 1616, Jesuit missionary Father Pierre Biard described Mi'kmaw subsistence patterns in detail:

[I]n January they have the seal hunting . . . In the months of February and until the middle of March, is the great hunt for Beavers, otters, moose, bears (which are very good), and for the caribou . . . If the weather is then favourable, they live in great abundance, and are as haughty as Princes and Kings . . . In the middle of March fish begin to spawn, and come up from the sea in certain streams . . . Among these fish the smelt is the first . . . After the smelt comes the herring and at the end of April: at the same time bustards, sturgeon, and salmon, and the great search through the Isles for [fowl] eggs . . . From the month of May up to the middle of September, they are free from all anxiety about their food; for the cod are upon the coast, and all kinds of fish and shellfish . . . our savages in the middle of September withdraw from the sea, beyond the reach of the tide, to the little rivers, where the eels spawn, of which they lay in supply . . . In October and November comes the second hunt for elks [moose] and beavers; and then in December comes a fish called by them ponanmo, which spawns under the ice.

(Thwaites, JR 3: 79–83)

Although they depended on a variety of natural resources for subsistence, the Mi'kmaw gathered the largest percentage of their diet from the sea. They used a number of technologies to harvest seafood, including harpoons, weirs, traps, and the hook and line (McMillan 1995: 51). Historian Alan McMillan notes that while hunting occupied less time and contributed far less to the Mi'kmaw diet it was a more prestigious activity closely associated with personal knowledge, skill, and achievement. According to Mi'kmaw oral history, the ability to contribute to the well-being of the band by providing food, especially in winter, established successful hunters as valued members of the group.

Social and Political Organization

As with most hunter/gatherer societies, the Mi'kmaw social structure was organized around small groups, or bands, usually comprising extended family members. Politically, the Mi'kmaq were subdivided into regional and local groups, with each unit recognizing a **Saqamaw**, or "Chief," and the larger group paying allegiance to a *Kji-saqamaw*, or "Grand Chief." *Mi'kma'ki* was the name given to the area covered by the seven main hunting districts[1] shared by the Mi'kmaw people. A local Saqamaw and the Kji-saqamaw managed each of these districts: Unama'ki (Cape Breton); *Kespékewaq* (Gaspé region); *Sipekni'kati* (the general area of the New Brunswick–Nova Scotia border); *Kespukwi* (southern Nova Scotia); *Eskikewa'ki* (eastern mainland Nova Scotia); *Epekwit aq Piktu* (Prince Edward Island/Pictou); and *Siknikt* (northern Maine and southwest New Brunswick). Traditionally, the Saqamaw and Kji-saqamaw were male. Women were given different sets of responsibilities within the band. A modified version of Mi'kmaw political organization remains intact today in the form of the *Sante' Mawio'mi*, or "Grand Council" (described in chapter 5). The traditional role of the Kji-saqamaw was to call group meetings of Mi'kmaw leaders and elders to discuss matters of economic, political, and social concern. Although most decisions were made through group consensus, one of the main tasks of the Kji-sakamow was the allocation of hunting and fishing territories to Mi'kmaw families. Prior to European contact, land ownership was a foreign concept to the Mi'kmaq. Bands were not granted exclusive rights to a hunting area but managed resources on the principle of stewardship. Throughout Mi'kma'ki, any individual could gain access to resources in any territory but was required to ask permission of the stewards overseeing the area in order to do so. These regulations were put in place in the interest of maintaining an ecological balance. The allocation of specific areas of land was enforced in order to ensure that resources, upon which the survival of the prey species depended, would neither be placed under stress nor seriously depleted. Even with these regulations in place, the Mi'kmaq were sometimes subjected to near starvation when winters were particularly harsh and access to game was severely limited.

Labour among the Mi'kmaq was divided between women and men. As noted, men were primarily responsible for procuring game and other foodstuffs as well as overseeing band territories. Women's roles were more closely associated with the day-to-day operations of the camp. Women typically nursed the ill, cared for children, prepared food, and conducted various other tasks associated with general household maintenance. The manufacture of clothing was also the responsibility of Mi'kmaw women, who were trained from early childhood to perform this essential function. Whitehead comments that 17th-century Mi'kmaw girls "were required to complete an entire outfit for their fiancés, as evidence of their proficiency" (Whitehead 1980: 11).

The women made clothing from the skins and sinew of animals, and often decorated clothing with paintings and dyed porcupine quills. During warm weather, the men typically wore loincloths, to which they added fur or hide robes during cooler periods. The women, described as being modest in their dress, wore moose skin dresses that extended down below the knees (Denys 1908 [1672]: 407). Women and men wore leggings, moccasins, and medicine pouches made of moose or seal skin. Mi'kmaw clothing was highly ornamented. The traditional symbols and motifs were not simply decorative but usually had specific meanings for the wearer. These symbols were often seen as sources of power (Whitehead 1980: 11). The various designs used to embellish pre- and postcontact traditional clothing also appear as decorative features of Mi'kmaw baskets, quill boxes, religious items, jewellery, and personal adornments.

In keeping with hunter/gatherer technologies, Mi'kmaw houses were temporary yet sturdy. Ease of construction and transportability were important features of the Mi'kmaw *wikuom*, or "wigwam." These cone-shaped structures were constructed of birch-bark and wooden, upright poles. Catholic missionary Father Chrétien Le Clerq describes the wikuom as being "so light and portable that our Indians roll them up like a piece of paper and carry them thus upon their backs wherever it pleases them, very much like the tortoises that carry their own houses" (Le Clerq 1968 [1910]: 100).

The Mi'kmaq possessed extensive knowledge of their territory and the natural resources found within it. The subsistence strategies used in the precontact period indicate that the Mi'kmaq were well adapted to the environment in which they lived. Incidences of scarcity, when they did occur, were not detrimental to the overall survival of the group. The Mi'kmaq did not truly fall on hard times until colonialism completely took hold.

Religion: Shamans and Storytellers

Most of the literature pertaining to precontact Mi'kmaw religious beliefs and practices comes from two sources: early travellers to New France—particularly Catholic clergy—and Mi'kmaw oral tradition. Although historians often document that the Mi'kmaq believed in a supreme being, it is unclear whether this was truly the case. Because many of those writing about religion were Christian, any form of religious practices and beliefs that did not conform to those of the writer was open to misinterpretation and misrepresentation. Unfortunately, much of the information contained in early historical documents has been accepted without question. For instance, Le Clerq states that "they [the Mi'kmaq] say that when the sun, which they have always recognized as their God, created all this great universe, he divided the earth immediately into several parts, wholly separated from one another by great lakes: that in each part he caused to be born one man and one woman, and they multiplied and lived a long time ..." (Le Clerq 1910: 84–85). However, some Mi'kmaq believe that this interpretation of the sun as a deity was propagated by Catholic missionaries in the attempt to establish the Mi'kmaq as pagans or worshippers of false gods (Fieldnotes May 1999; Jan. 2000).

Le Clerq's description, which conforms to decidedly Western concepts of God/Creator and the process of creation, differs from a number of teachings found within Mi'kmaw oral tradition. For instance, the notion that *Kji-kinap*, or "great power," made the world is included in the story of *Kluscap*—a Mi'kmaw religious figure (Whitehead 1988: 3). Mi'kmaw linguist Bern Francis informs us that the Mi'kmaw language conceptualizes God as an active entity, as in the verb form *kisu'lkw*—"she/he/it who creates us" (Francis, personal interview).

Additionally, Mi'kmaw oral tradition informs us that the sun, or *na'ku'set*, in combination with the moon, *tepkunaset*, was acknowledged as "the one who creates." From this perspective, na'ku'set and tepkunaset are not to be understood as gods but recognized as forces that contribute to the continuous cycle of creation, decline, and renewal. Missionaries, in their attempts to convert and "civilize" the Mi'kmaq, quite possibly assumed that the Mi'kmaw concepts of the Creator and creation were equivalent to those found within Christian teachings. Such observations may, in fact, be erroneous assumptions based upon strictly Western categories of interpretation. Both oral tradition and several concepts inherent in the Mi'kmaw language suggest that, even though some commonalities may exist between precontact understandings about the Creator and creation and those found within Christian teachings, there are also fundamental differences. The beings described within Mi'kmaw oral tradition are more appropriately described as spiritual guides whose teachings express specific ideas about the nature of existence. There is no clear indication that these beings were recognized as deities or that they were worshipped as such.

The European endeavour to convert the Mi'kmaq to Christianity also involved the subversion and demonization of many aspects of precontact Mi'kmaw religion. Most Europeans, and the missionaries who spearheaded the conversion process, considered the Mi'kmaq to be without any "real" religion. As a result, Mi'kmaw religious shamans were not recognized as religious leaders but were referred to as "jugglers" and devil worshippers (Le Clerq 1968 [1910]: 210, 221). Religious rituals were generally referred to as "diabolical ceremonies" (Thwaites, *JR* 28: 53). Similarly, the figure of *Kji-mntu* (also *Kji-manitou*), or "great power"—recognized by the Mi'kmaq as a spiritual life force—was understood within Christian contexts as a heathen notion inconsistent with church teachings of "the one true God." As a result, Kji-mntu—"great power/life force"—became associated with idolatry. At present, the term is equated with the Christian notion of the devil.

MI'KMAQ IN THE POSTCONTACT PERIOD

Economies

From the early stages of European contact in the 17th to the late 18th centuries, there was a gradual yet dramatic change in Mi'kmaw culture. The arrival of French trappers, traders, and missionaries in the 17th century greatly influenced traditional Mi'kmaw subsistence strategies and social organization. The European demand for furs, seal oil, and fish transformed band structures and seriously disrupted Mi'kmaw territorial and resource management.

During the early phase of contact (early 17th to mid-18th centuries), travellers to New France were primarily concerned with the extraction of resources. European trappers and traders set up working partnerships with the Mi'kmaq. The Mi'kmaq became interested in acquiring foreign trade goods, particularly guns, knives, metal pots and pans, blankets, coloured glass beads, and, later, alcohol, which were traded for pelts, seal oil, and guide services. The switch from hunter/gatherer to increasingly market-dependent enterprises had a devastating effect on Mi'kmaw culture and well-being. The traditional stewardship associated with Mi'kmaw subsistence strategies was uprooted in favour of more market-driven interests that transformed hunting and fishing practices and placed stress on available resources.

The arrival of the British and the initiation of the colonialist project caused the Mi'kmaq to lose control over most of their traditional lands and severely restricted their access to resources. The intrusion of the British onto Mi'kmaw lands did not come without resistance. Both the Mi'kmaq and the French, who had established lucrative trade agreements with the Mi'kmaq, resisted incursions into Mi'kmaw territory. Warfare between the allied forces of the French and Mi'kmaq and the British over the disputed territories eventually resulted in the expulsion of the French Acadians. In 1713 Britain and France signed the Treaty of Utrecht, which granted the lands within Nova Scotia (Acadia) and Newfoundland to Great Britain. However, the signing of this treaty did not put an end to disputes over the lands. Between 1713 and 1749, the Mi'kmaq and French continued to resist British control. With the loss of the fortress of Louisbourg (a French military base located in Cape Breton) in 1745, the French began to lessen their support of the Mi'kmaq. After the founding of Halifax in 1749, the British began colonization in earnest. In the same year, the arrival of Governor Edward Cornwallis and 2500 new settlers in Halifax marked the beginning of a series of aggressive attacks on the Mi'kmaw population. Continued Mi'kmaw resistance to British control prompted Cornwallis to offer £10 for every Mi'kmaw scalp or prisoner. In 1750 the scalp price was raised to £50. Cornwallis's campaign against the Mi'kmaq was so successful that it almost eradicated the entire Mi'kmaw population. It is estimated that by the close of the 18th century the Mi'kmaq numbered about 3000, down from a precontact population of approximately 30 000.

Historical evidence suggests that the adversarial relationship between the Mi'kmaq and the British was never fully resolved. Both oral and written histories also suggest that there was a marked difference between the Mi'kmaw relationship with the French and the Mi'kmaw relationship with the British. Chief Louis Algimou describes the nature of these differences in a speech given to the Legislative Assembly of Prince Edward Island in 1831:

Fathers: Before the white man crossed the great waters, our Woods offered us food and clothes in plenty—the waters gave us fish—the woods game—our fathers were hardy, brave and free—we knew no want—we were the only owners of the Land. Fathers: When the French came to us they asked for land to set up their Wigwam we gave it freely—in return they taught us new arts—protected and cherished us—sent holy men amongst our fathers—who taught us Christianity—who made books for us—and taught us to read them—that was good and we were grateful. Fathers: When your [British] fathers came and drove away our French Fathers—we were left alone—our people were sorry, but they were brave—they raised the war cry—and took up the tomahawk against your fathers. The fathers spoke to us—they said, put up the axe—we will protect you—we will become your Fathers. Our fathers and your fathers had long talks around the Council fire—the hatchets were buried and we became friends. Fathers: they promised to leave us some of our land—but they did not—they drove us from place to place like wild beasts—that was not just.

(Whitehead 1991: 207–208)

Between 1725 and 1779, the Mi'kmaw nation and the British Crown settled on a series of treaties that recognized specific rights and privileges of the Mi'kmaq, including entitlement to land (Marshall 1991: 35). However, by the time Halifax was established in 1749, the Mi'kmaq were divested of most of their lands and were relocated into wilderness areas considered unsuitable for development by European settlers. Many of the prime farming and residential areas were granted to British subjects by the Crown. Historian Leslie Upton notes that at the turn of the 19th century the Mi'kmaq could not get title to lands. Rather, they were granted "licenses of occupation during pleasure" on reserves—that is, on lands owned by the Crown and *reserved* for use by a particular Aboriginal band (Upton 1977: 70, 82). In 1822, Walter Bromley reported on the condition of the Mi'kmaq in Chedabucto Bay, Nova Scotia:

[W]here the indians have been in constant fishing and supplying their manufacture of peltry & c. for several years, they have been expelled in the most brutish manner from the fishing ground by the white people, who entered their camps, defiled their women, abused and beat the men, and, in fact, conducted themselves in such a manner as to prevent the possibility of their remaining there any longer.

(Bromley 1822: 9)

By the 1790s, the Mi'kmaq could no longer follow their traditional means of subsistence. In order to make a living, the Mi'kmaq engaged in the production of items, such as "baskets, axe-handles, shingles and staves," that were easily marketed to European immigrants. However, the sale of these goods could not meet the subsistence needs of the Mi'kmaq. From the middle of the 18th century and on, the Mi'kmaq experienced widespread and continuous impoverishment. In 1800, the government of Nova Scotia established a Committee for Indian Affairs, which issued a "Plan of Relief of the Indians." However, the plan to offset Mi'kmaw privation was inconsistently and inadequately applied and did little to improve conditions for the Mi'kmaq. In 1800, one government agent stated that, despite the distribution of goods, many of the Mi'kmaq in Antigonish, Nova Scotia, were without clothing and were in a "miserable condition" (Miller 1982: 112).

In 1807, Nova Scotia was divided into 12 districts, with a part-time Indian agent assigned to each. In addition to reporting on the condition of the Mi'kmaq, agents were responsible for handling grievances and issuing relief goods. In 1819, agents were asked to identify tracts of land still frequented by the Mi'kmaq. These tracts of land were to become reserves. However, the agents did little to protect reserve lands from European encroachment. In 1845 an Indian commissioner acknowledged that "it will not be easy for any Commissioner holding a seat in the Nova Scotia Legislature . . . to do justice to the Indians, and to retain the goodwill of his [white, voting] constituents . . ." Four years later, in an attempt to appease white constituents, the Committee for Indian Affairs suggested that "[Indian] lands which had been trespassed upon be sold to the violators" (as quoted in Prins 1996: 182–183). Subsequently, in order to justify pauper relief expenditures, the provincial government offered

Mi'kmaw lands for sale, leaving only a small portion (50 acres per Mi'kmaw family) as reserve lands (McGee 1974: 58–62; Upton 1979: as quoted in Prins 102–108).

The pattern of deprivation that beset the Mi'kmaq in the early stages of colonization persisted throughout the first half of the 19th century, as noted by historian Jennifer Reid:

> In 1831, the Mi'kmaq at Rawden, Nova Scotia, possessed ten blankets for fifty people, and in 1834, those of Windsor were naked and without shelter. Between 1846 and 1856, the Mi'kmaq at Digby were said to be "dying for want of food and sustenance," those in Cape Breton and at New Glasgow were "ready to drop from hunger," and those at Pictou were "actually starving [and] crying for food."

(Reid 1995: 42)

Moderate attempts by the provincial government to address the problem of poverty were altogether inadequate and ineffective. Although the terms and conditions of settlement laid out in the treaties signed between the Mi'kmaq and the British Crown were legally and morally binding, under British rule these treaties were openly violated. Difficulties were to continue for the Mi'kmaq after the founding of the country of Canada in 1867, when they were faced with a different series of problems.

Social and Political Organization

After the formation of Canada in 1867, Aboriginal peoples were no longer under the direct control of the British Crown. However, life for the Mi'kmaq did not change for the better under the new system of government. The Government of Canada assumed jurisdiction over Aboriginal affairs. In 1876, it passed the Indian Act, which consolidated all rules and regulations pertaining to Aboriginal peoples. The act was implemented with a view to alleviating "Indians" of their state of dependency. The term applied to this process of establishing Aboriginal independence was *enfranchisement*. For Aboriginal peoples throughout Canada, however, the term became synonymous with assimilation. With the inception of the Indian Act, the federal government claimed authority over all affairs pertaining to Indian reserves and resources and also claimed the right to define and determine Aboriginal status. The institution of this act was nothing short of ethnocide. The freedoms promised under the new governmental policies were in actuality restrictions that deprived Aboriginal peoples of the right to maintain their social, cultural, and political traditions. In the Mi'kmaw case, the Grand Council was stripped of its authority. A system of governance through the establishment of elected local band councils was put in place. As was the case with all other Aboriginals in Canada, Mi'kmaw status was subject to the formal guidelines and definitions set down in the Act. The Mi'kmaq could no longer decide for themselves who was or was not "an Indian." And, like all Aboriginal groups, they were no longer given freedom of movement on and off the reserves. For instance, no Aboriginal could travel from province to province without first gaining permission from the Indian Agent. However, if you became enfranchised, that is, gave up your status, then you were granted the full rights and privileges provided to Canadians. This included the right to travel freely and to vote in federal and provincial elections.

From 1930 to the late 1960s, the assimilationist policies entrenched in the Indian Act were augmented by another series of programs that had devastating results for the Mi'kmaq. In

Nova Scotia, resource management programs, the centralization project, and the residential school system were set in motion.

Resource management programs instituted in the 1940s were aimed at alleviating stress on natural resources. While both Aboriginals and non-Aboriginals once enjoyed open access to forest harvesting and hunting and fishing rights, the commercialization of local game, fish, and forestry resources precipitated the start of licensing programs. For the Mi'kmaq, purchasing licences was practically impossible, primarily because very few Aboriginals had the necessary financial means. Prior to the institution of these programs, the Mi'kmaq were issued fishing and hunting permits in accordance with treaty agreements. These permits were rescinded. It became illegal to engage in traditional subsistence strategies without a proper licence.

In the early 1940s the centralization project was implemented. Centralization was a cooperative venture on the part of the federal government of Canada and the provincial government of Nova Scotia. It was designed to facilitate government assistance by moving Aboriginals off smaller reserves into larger, more manageable communities. In Nova Scotia, Shubenacadie (also the site of the regional residential school) and Eskasoni were the reserves selected for "development." By 1949, centralization was deemed a failure both by government officials and by those who were subject to its policies (Paul 1996).

Lured by the promise of increased governmental assistance aimed at fostering an overall improvement in living, many Mi'kmaq moved from smaller communities to the designated relocation sites. The government encouraged resettlement by promising improved housing, better education, acreage for farming, and supplies of livestock. The vision for this new life under the centralization program was so impressive that local Aboriginals jokingly called Eskasoni "The Big Rock Candy Mountain" in reference to an idyllic setting described in a popular song of the time. However, most of the promises made by the government to encourage resettlement were never realized. Instead of receiving improved housing, those who resettled were supplied with a barrel of nails and some lumber to construct their own homes. The livestock provided came in the form of a herd of goats, housed in a communal barn, to be shared by the entire community. The promised farmland was not supplied. Furthermore, many of those who owned productive farms at previous locations were reduced to living on smaller tracts of land where farming was next to impossible. Disillusioned by the centralization process, many families attempted to return to their former communities. There they found that their properties had been either sold or destroyed.

In coalition with the Catholic Church, the government did make good on the promise of support for education, which came in the form of the residential school system. The Shubenacadie residential school was located in the town of Shubenacadie, Nova Scotia, approximately 370 kilometres southwest of Eskasoni. The school, called "Shubie" by many Mi'kmaq, opened in 1930 and operated for 37 years. Government and religious representatives led parents to believe that the quality of life at residential schools was far superior to the life of poverty and deprivation that existed in their communities. Parents were assured by church leaders and government officials that their children would be well clothed, well fed, and well educated—assurances that they did not have if children remained on the reserve. While many Mi'kmaw parents agreed to enroll their children at "Shubie" for these very reasons, the reality of life at the school was quite different. Children were frequently forced to work long hours at laborious tasks. They were often hungry and were severely punished for such minor transgressions as speaking their native language. The "Shubie" school closed in 1967 in the midst of much controversy relating to charges of physical, emotional, and sexual abuse of Aboriginal children by the nuns and priests who ran the institution.

During the postcolonial era, the Mi'kmaq were subjected to a series of governmental policies, programs, and regulations that did little to improve their condition. It could be argued, in fact, that the situation progressively worsened. Children were taken away from their families and subjected to harsh treatment. Aboriginals were practically denied access to natural resources by being forced to participate in a licensing system that they could not afford. Under the centralization project, reserve lands diminished and the ability of Aboriginals to engage in subsistence farming was seriously compromised. Many of the social, cultural, and economic repercussions from this period are still felt today. Overall, it seems that the government plan to "free" the Aboriginals from dependency had the opposite effect.

Religion: Being and Becoming Christian

In New France, the introduction of Christianity precipitated the near elimination of precontact beliefs and rituals. In their attempt to Christianize the inhabitants of the New World, Christian clergy essentially outlawed precontact traditions. However, the degree to which precontact beliefs and expressions were supplanted has been and continues to be a topic of much debate. For instance, does Father Jessé Fléché's baptizing of Sagamaw Membertou (and 21 family members) into the Catholic faith in 1610 mean that conversion actually took place? The suggestion that conversion to Roman Catholicism began in the early 18th century is challenged by Mi'kmaw oral tradition and by an increasing number of scholars. While visiting New France in 1611, Father Pierre Biard complained that, despite baptism, the Natives "keep up the same manners and traditions and mode of life, the same dances and rites and songs and sorcery; in fact all their previous customs" (Thwaites, *JR* 2: 89).

Conversion of the Mi'kmaq to Catholicism was not immediate because the conversion process posed logistical and ideological difficulties for the missionaries. First, there was a significant language barrier between the Mi'kmaq and European clergy. It is questionable whether Father Fléché and Chief Membertou had sufficient knowledge of each other's religious and social systems to make this first conversion anything more than a symbolic political gesture. Fléché acknowledges that he had "not been able to instruct them as he would have wished, because he did not know the language . . . " and that the Mi'kmaq were essentially unaware of the ceremony's religious significance (Thwaites, *JR* 1: 161–63). Second, historically the Mi'kmaq-European encounter has been understood from a Western perspective, which tends to interpret the conversion process within Christian contexts. Accordingly, ethnohistorian Kenneth Morrison argues that since scholars often "fail to understand Algonkian religious life in its own terms," a reassessment of interpretive strategies is in order (Morrison 2002: 171). Morrison's proposed alternative interpretations encourage a shift in perspective. For instance, it is now commonly accepted that the Mi'kmaq viewed conversion and baptism differently than their European counterparts did. For the Mi'kmaq, ritual baptism was essentially a political alliance. Father Biard noted that "they accepted baptism as a sort of sacred pledge of friendship and alliance with the French" (Thwaites, *JR* 2: 89).

Mi'kmaw conversion to Christianity does not appear to have occurred until after the arrival of Father Chrétien Le Clerq in the latter part of the 16th century. Le Clerq's success as a missionary is due to his adoption of a Mi'kmaw hieroglyphic system that he expanded to include Christian concepts. However, even with the means of a more effective system of communication, the adoption of Catholicism among the Mi'kmaq cannot be considered strictly a product of Christian instruction. Evidence shows that the Mi'kmaq actually revised Catholicism to accommodate their beliefs and values. This process of adaptation was not only possible but perhaps necessary because the Mi'kmaq had limited access to the services of a priest until the middle of the 20th century. The alliance between the Mi'kmaq and the French was solidified during the colonial period. Many of the priests who ministered to the Mi'kmaq from the early to late 18th century are frequently referred to as the "warrior-priests." Prominent among these was Father Maillard, who worked among the Mi'kmaq during the politically volatile period of the mid-1700s. Maillard is believed to be responsible for initiating Se'tta'newimk, or St. Anne's Mission, and for revitalizing and expanding the hieroglyphic system used by Le Clerq.

The mid- to late 18th century proved to be a turbulent time for the Mi'kmaq. Along with their French allies, the Mi'kmaq fought to preserve their presence in New France. By 1750, the British had firmly established themselves in the region and by 1759 succeeded in expelling the French from the area. With the removal of the French, the Mi'kmaq lost not only valuable political allies but also their religious leadership. Under British rule Catholicism was marginally tolerated but was not financially supported by the Crown. For the greater part of the 18th and 19th centuries, the religious leadership of the Mi'kmaq was provided primarily by the Sante' Mawio'mi, or Grand Council, and annual visits from the mission priest. This is one of the reasons behind the popularity of Se'tta'newimk. It was one of the few times during the year that the Mi'kmaq had the benefit of a priest's services.

In Nova Scotia, the mission system persisted well into the 20th century, until parishes were established throughout the region. However, Holy Family Parish (established in 1944) remains the only Mi'kmaw parish in Cape Breton. From the 1940s to the present, the majority of Mi'kmaq have been receiving regular services from priests in neighbouring parishes. Prior to this time, the Mi'kmaq had carried out religious services as they had for generations. Most Mi'kmaw communities had mission churches where members of the Sante' Mawio'mi met with the people each Sunday to say prayers and sing hymns. They received the services of a priest only on special occasions, such as Easter and Christmas.

The majority of present-day Mi'kmaq still claim affiliation with the Catholic Church. However, since the 1970s there has been a slow but steady resurgence of Aboriginal Traditional religion, which emerged in response to a period of cultural renaissance among Aboriginal North Americans (Barker 1998; Churchill 2000; Goulet 1982; Grim 2000; Kidwell 2000). In the past three decades, increasing numbers of Mi'kmaq have become involved in powwows, sweats, and sacred circles as part of a general revival of Aboriginal cultural, spiritual, and religious expression. In some cases, Catholicism has been entirely rejected, while in others, aspects of Aboriginal religious expression are practised alongside traditional Catholicism.

CONCLUSION AND DISCUSSION

MI'KMAQ IN THE 21ST CENTURY: CANADIAN APARTHEID?

The notion of apartheid resonates in the minds of most North Americans as a political reality belonging to a different time and a different place. Historically, however, the past and present experiences of Aboriginal peoples in Canada can be interpreted as a form of domestic apartheid. Like most Aboriginal Canadians, the Mi'kmaq are "a people set apart" in the sense that they continue to be socially, culturally, politically, and economically marginalized. For 21st-century Mi'kmaq, the influences of the past weigh heavily on present-day realities. The rampant unemployment, inadequate housing, poor health, and political impotency that exist today are part of a historical pattern that began in the early contact period. Mi'kmaq attempts to establish political autonomy and to improve their overall social and economic situation often meet with general resistance from government officials and mainstream society. For instance, the struggle for recognition of their fishing, hunting, and harvesting rights has been one of the greatest challenges for present-day Mi'kmaq. This struggle has met with some success in recent rulings by the Supreme Court of Canada (Marshall Decision, 1999) and the New Brunswick Court of Appeal (Bernard Decision, 2003), which found in favour of Mi'kmaw fishing and logging rights, respectively. While the majority of Mi'kmaq are united in their views concerning specific rights and freedoms, many aspects of Mi'kmaw social and cultural identity are subject to internal and external debate.

This present work focuses on the "politics of identity" that affects the interrelationships between religion, spirituality, and identity in present-day Mi'kmaq society.

CONTENT QUESTIONS

1. What are the most significant changes in Mi'kmaw socio-economic patterns in the post-contact period?

2. What effects did the centralization program have on Mi'kmaw society?

3. What are the roles of the Saqamaw and Kji-saqamaw?

4. Identify the most pressing issues faced by the Mi'kmaq in the 21st century.

ENDNOTES

1. There is some debate among scholars as to whether the seven-district model of Mi'kmaw political territoriality is a postcontact or a precontact phenomenon. The position taken here is that it is precontact.

chapter three

Ta'n ninen telo'ltiek ("The Way We Are"): Mi'kmaw Lifeworlds

Our father taught us to respect all life,
the life that we have been given,
the beauty of the sun, star and sky,
the animals that walk with us,
one must die, so one may live.
Ahay, it is good to give.

Helen Sylliboy, from "Life and Death"

LEARNING OBJECTIVES

After reading this chapter, students should be able to:

- Distinguish between the concepts of lifeworld and world view.
- Recognize the key cosmological and ideological differences between Western and Mi'kmaw understandings of the world.
- Understand the relationship between Mi'kmaw language and lifeworld.
- Outline the ways in which the Mi'kmaq have responded creatively to Western influences.
- Identify the diverse uses of the term *tradition* among the Mi'kmaq.

INTRODUCTION

While working on the original title for this chapter, "T'an ninen telo'ltiek: Mi'kmaw World Views and Ethos," I found it difficult to "fit" Mi'kmaw systems of thought and belief into the category of world view. However, after reading Michael Jackson's "Introduction" in *Things As They Are: New Directions in Phenomenological Anthropology*, I began to understand that I had taken the wrong tack in my approach. Despite my efforts to rid myself of any preconceived biases, I was applying the term *world view* inappropriately. Instead of explaining my findings on Mi'kmaw systems of thought and belief in their own terms, I was confining those findings to Western categories, which, of course, they did not fit into. Part of the problem is that Mi'kmaw views of the world and of their existence in it are not derived from one specific orientation. Currently, Mi'kmaw culture and patterns of socialization are drawn from both Western and non-Western perspectives.

Jackson states that as "an attempt to describe human consciousness in its lived immediacy, before it is subject to theoretical elaboration or conceptual systematizing" (Jackson 1996: 2) phenomenological anthropology avoids many of the problems encountered in the process of translating, analyzing, and constructing ethnographic texts. Jackson argues that it is "presumptuous and unedifying" to give "intellectual viability" to any non-Western system of thought simply by assimilating it to the categories of Western philosophical and scientific discourse (Jackson 1996: 6). He suggests that philosophies and theories should be regarded as part of the world in which we live, "rather than transcendent views that somehow escape the impress of our social interests, cultural habits, and personal persuasions" (Jackson 1996: 1). **Phenomenology** is a way of revealing "things by bringing them into the daylight of ordinary understanding" and by refusing to invoke cultural privilege as a basis for "evaluating world views or examining the complex and enigmatic character of the human condition" (Jackson 1996: 1). To this end, Jackson suggests that "when we make cross-cultural comparisons between various 'systems of thought,' we would do well to construe these not as worldviews ... but as lifeworlds" (Jackson 1996: 6):

> [Lifeworld is] that domain of everyday, immediate existence and practical activity, with all its habituality, its crises, its vernacular and idiomatic character, its biographical particularities, its decisive events and indecisive strategies, which theoretical knowledge addresses but does not determine, from which conceptual understanding arises but on which it does not primarily depend.
>
> *(Jackson 1996: 7–8)*

Decontextualization/recontextualization is one of a number of problems that may be encountered in the process of transposing the lifeworlds of non-Westerners into texts to be received by Western readers. *Lifeworlds*, as the term is used throughout this book, refers to the process whereby the Mi'kmaw people construct and apprehend the world in which they live. This term involves sociological contexts and also includes collective and individual systems of belief and the symbolic representations of those beliefs.

Recently, critiques of anthropology have unveiled several tendencies that lead to inaccurate, or at least inadequate, representations of the "Other." First, there is the tendency to stress the distinctiveness of non-Western cultures to the point that they become radically "other" (Fabian 1983, Appadurai 1988). Arjan Appadurai maintains that anthropologists have tended to deny non-Western peoples the same capacity of movement and interaction that Westerners have. In other words, the fluidity of group languages, practices, and boundaries has been sacrificed to establish untouched or enduring cultures (Abu-Lughod 1993a: 11). Second, there is the notion that non-Western cultures have "blindly and spontaneously" reacted to external domination (Jackson 1996:37; Blanchard 1982; Delâge and Hornbeck-Tanner 1994; Guha 1983; Morrison 1981). Third, in constructing portraits of the "other," many scholars lend primacy to the power of politics over existential concerns in influencing the ways in which the lifeworlds of persons and groups are constructed (Jackson 1996: 22). Fourth, in the process of depicting the "other," scholars have often subjugated the creative and idiosyncratic features of personal identities while giving preference to normative cultural traits and distinctions (Jackson 1996: 25–29). Finally, debates about "the invention of tradition" are also pre-empted, or are at least seriously called into question, by the phenomenological approach. Phenomenological anthropology is, at base, ahistorical and apolitical. This does not mean that the political and historical aspects of any given tradition are ignored but, rather, that they do not take precedence over the *existence* of a specific tradition. Therefore, political and historical considerations should be addressed, not to establish the "authenticity" of a specific rite, belief, or ritual, but to elucidate the significance of a tradition in the various contexts in which it appears. As Jackson suggests, the existence of specific traditions within a culture should be considered more important than the verification of their historical precedence or validity. "Phenomenology is less concerned with establishing what happened in the past than exploring the past as a mode of present experience" (Jackson 1996: 38).

Critiques of ethnography have emerged that question the very nature of the work of anthropologists; in fact, anthropologists are asked to seriously consider the ways in which we translate encounters with "others" into accurate accounts of the living subjects that we study. A number of anthropologists suggest that the most effective means of constructing adequate ethnographic accounts is by paying particular attention to the personal lives of individuals (Jackson 1996; Abu-Lughod 1993a; Drewal 1992). For instance, Abu-Lughod argues that by drawing on the complex personal narratives of Bedouin women, she offers a challenge to "the capacity of anthropological generalizations to render lives, theirs or others', adequately" (Abu-Lughod 1993a: xvi). Abu-Lughod proposes that rather than attempting to explain cultural differences in terms of collective identities we need to focus on the ways that "individuals and the particularities of their lives" uncover similarities and differences between "a world set up to produce the effect of structures, institutions, or other abstractions (as T. Mitchell [1988] argues the modern West has been) versus worlds that have not" (Abu-Lughod 1993a: 27).

Similarly, in writing on the *Yoruba* of southwestern Nigeria, Margaret Drewal observes that there are key cosmological differences between Yoruba and Western perceptions of the world. In describing Yoruba beliefs and rituals, Drewal notes that *ase* is a "generative force or potential present in all things," including hills, rocks, streams, mountains, animals, plants, deities and ancestors as well as "in utterances—prayers, songs, curses and even everyday speech . . . *Ase* has no "moral connotation: it is neither good nor bad" (Drewal 1992: 27). Humans also possess this generative force and "through education, initiation and experience learn to manipulate it to enhance their own lives and the lives of those around them" (Drewal 1992: 27). What Drewal identifies as *ase* resembles the Mi'kmaw understanding of active "spirit,"[1] or life force, from which spirituality arises. However, among the Mi'kmaq, spirituality is variously understood and interpreted. Giving voice to the particular through personal narratives allows for diversity of meaning and provides a depth of expression that helps to illuminate the multidimensionality of Mi'kmaw belief systems.

After numerous conversations, interviews, and formal and informal meetings, the familiar and deceptively simple phrase "The Mi'kmaq are a spiritual people" took on unanticipated complexities of meaning. For many Mi'kmaq, spirituality extends beyond the strictures of what Westerners perceive to be religious and finds expression in the day-to-day life of the community. For many, spirituality is often associated with Mi'kmaw culture. Still, for others spirituality may be part of religious orientation or, conversely, separate from religion altogether. Although spirituality is variously interpreted, for many Mi'kmaq it is at the core of Mi'kmaw personal and social identity. That which is spiritual or sacred in Mi'kmaw terms cannot be confined to specific religious observances. A "power," or a spiritual outlook on life, unites Mi'kmaw peoples, collectively and individually. Spirituality may be expressed in such profane events as birthday parties, family or clan gatherings, and anniversaries, or in such rites as weddings, funerals, salites, and christenings. The Mi'kmaq band together in times of plenty and scarcity, in times of sorrow and happiness. These gatherings provide the Mi'kmaq with the opportunity to support each other in a fellowship that encompasses physical, emotional, and spiritual needs. However, the heterogeneity of Mi'kmaw religion and spirituality cannot be contained by any single homogenized view. Each individual experiences and expresses his or her own understanding of what it means to be religious or spiritual in Mi'kmaw society.

In order to render an accurate account of the ways that the Mi'kmaq perceive their lifeworlds, I have adopted the phenomenological approach described by Jackson and followed by Drewal and Abu-Lughod. My intention in this chapter is to relate the ways in which current philosophical, ideological, and cosmological understandings inform present-day religious practices—not to extract some romantic or stereotypical rendition of Mi'kmaw reality. The Mi'kmaw voices that appear here demonstrate that Mi'kmaw belief systems are variously interpreted.

MI'KMAW VOICES

Dr. Bern Francis: Mi'kmaw Language As the Key

The interrelatedness of Mi'kmaw spirituality, culture, and language was explained to me in great detail by the Mi'kmaw linguist, Dr. Bern Francis. Bern, now in his early 50s, grew up on the Membertou (Sydney) reserve and was raised a Roman Catholic. As a young boy Bern participated fully in the Catholic faith and for a period of time served as an altar boy. However, he left the Church in his early teens and has not returned to it.

As a linguist and as a Mi'kmaw, Bern maintains that for himself and for most Mi'kmaq Mi'kmaw beliefs and values are firmly embedded in the language. He suggests that a close look at the structure of the language can bring to light key cosmological and philosophical concepts that influence present-day Mi'kmaw culture. Bern explains that the reason for this close relationship between language and cosmology is straightforward. He contends that the process of translating ideas and concepts from Mi'kmaq into English is difficult, principally because the Mi'kmaw language is verb-oriented whereas the English language is noun-oriented (Francis, personal communication).

Box 3.1	Verb-Oriented Versus Noun-Oriented Language

It is a linguistic fact that Mi'kmaq (as with other Algonquian languages) contains far more verbs than nouns, while the opposite is true of English (as with other European languages). Typical Aboriginal dictionaries contain far more verbs than nouns, while the reverse is true for English. In addition, many of the Mi'kmaw words that do appear as nouns can also be declined as verbs. Try this exercise. Take one page of an English or French dictionary and count the nouns and then count the verbs. The nouns will dominate.

According to Bern, the implications of identifying the Mi'kmaw language as verb-oriented are difficult to discern, especially in terms of their effect on culture and, ultimately, spirituality:

> For one thing, it would be very, very tough to establish a dogma in the Mi'kmaw spiritual aspect of the culture simply because of the structure of the language . . . [which] tells me that it [the language] is very capable of changing very fast . . . as compared to English . . . The second thing, of course . . . is that the language is not capable of seeing the world and the universe as any other way except as being in constant flux. It's not capable of doing so. So, it would be difficult to pin down any particular dogma and expect people, Mi'kmaw people, to follow it to the letter a thousand years from now . . . A concept of "god" in Mi'kmaw culture and Mi'kmaw language is also not stationary. In fact, the words, or many of them, that we have for "god" are all verbs. They conjugate like any other verb in the Mi'kmaw language, and that's an indicator that "god" is not someone who is sitting up in the sky who oversees all things. It is difficult for a *true* Mi'kmaw mind to conceptualize something [god] like that.
>
> *(Francis to Robinson, taped interview)*[2]

For Bern, then, Christian dogma or doctrine cannot be adequately translated into a system of belief compatible with the Mi'kmaw way of thinking. For instance, the notion that God oversees the universe from afar is inimical to the "true Mi'kmaw mind," which perceives the process of creation as unfolding and as something in which the Creator continues to participate fully.[3]

According to Bern, Mi'kmaw speakers do not refer to the Creator using a noun, thereby expressing the concept as an abstract entity who is altogether remote and transcendent, but rather, using a verb, thereby expressing it as an active presence in the world (Fieldnotes, Book I: 8). Bern suggests that this perspective is evident in devotional expression as well. He comments that in making the sign of the cross the Mi'kmaq do not say, "In the name of *the* Father and *the* Son." Rather, they say, "In the name of a father who has a son and a son who has a father" (Fieldnotes, Book I: 6). In the Mi'kmaw language personal relationships are understood in terms of possessive reciprocity: "You cannot be a son unless you have a father, and you cannot be a father unless you have a son or daughter" (Fieldnotes, Book I: 6).

This perspective implies that there is no Creator without creation, and there is no creation without a Creator. Bern understands the view of creation as expressed in the Mi'kmaw language to be in direct contrast to the predominant Western or Christian view that God exists as a transcendent being whose existence is independent of creation.[4]

Bern is critical of the Church but not because he fundamentally disagrees with the philosophies contained in Jesus Christ's teachings. Rather, he objects to the ways in which Catholic teachings subvert the Mi'kmaw way of thinking. Bern suggests that the Catholic Church has been instrumental in replacing Mi'kmaw systems of belief with Westernized concepts of the relationship between God, man, and the rest of creation. Since Mi'kmaw communities are losing many of the elders who retain what Bern defines as "the Mi'kmaw way of thinking," he fears that their knowledge and understandings will die with them (personal communication). Therefore, he insists that the next generations of Mi'kmaq must understand the basic distinctions between Mi'kmaw and Western/Christian conceptions of the world. For instance, Bern feels that one of the most important Mi'kmaw teachings is respect for the self and for others, but the Church does not reinforce this teaching:

> The Church is negligent in this regard. It teaches about the sinfulness of persons and how we are insignificant and too human. We are not taught respect of the self, but that we are sinful creatures. Also, that we are masters of the earth, that all living creatures are beneath us. This is wrong! We should teach respect for all living things, ourselves, others and all other living matter on the planet. The Church is much more concerned with souls than the welfare of the Mi'kmaw people. We were granted souls in 1610, before that we didn't have any. The Mi'kmaw people have been in servitude to the Church ever since. Many [Mi'kmaw] people do not go to Church out of love and respect for God, but out of fear. Fear is not a solid spiritual base.

(Fieldnotes, Book I: 4–5)

Bern suggests that Catholic teachings, which, in his view, are based on fear and sinfulness, serve to undermine the very beliefs and values that define Mi'kmaw society and culture:

> The missionaries told the Mi'kmaq that you must believe this [the Catholic] way otherwise you will be damned and you will go to hell ... You must believe in Jesus as being the absolute and only begotten son of God and you must believe that Jesus is the only way—that's more conditioning, and that's more based on fear than any reality in the mind of the Mi'kmaw person. In other words, because of that fear, they will ascribe to that kind of belief, at least on the surface. But really, a reality check will tell us that many of the elders, when you begin to speak with them in the Mi'kmaw language, you will say "Gee, I know they go to church, but just listen to them! Look at what they're saying!" They speak very differently than the way any Christian would speak ... I consider myself fortunate in that I was able to look at Native spirituality, specifically Mi'kmaw spirituality, not Mohawk, not any other, but Mi'kmaw spirituality and I was able to speak with elders who spoke to me without being threatened and without being pressured and without having fear ... they have taught me so much over the years.

(Bern to Robinson, taped interview)

Bern claims that beneath the surface, God, religion, and spiritual beliefs can only be conceived by Mi'kmaw speakers within a specifically Mi'kmaw context. Despite extensive conditioning, Mi'kmaw elders continue to comprehend the world in the way their language allows. In Bern's view, the basic spiritual understandings to which many elders subscribe are in keeping with a Mi'kmaw way of thinking rather than a Catholic, or Western, way of comprehending faith, belief, and the sacred.

Bern's description of the way the Mi'kmaw language operates suggests a way of looking at the world that is conceptually different from the teachings espoused and disseminated by the Catholic Church. Catholic cosmology and philosophy promote exclusivist claims of Roman Catholicism as the authority on all things. Can the adaptable and inclusive beliefs and values linked with the Mi'kmaw language be reconciled with the more inflexible and exclusionary principles of Catholicism?

Dr. Marie Battiste: A Mi'kmaw Catholic

Some Mi'kmaw Catholics manage to reconcile these two positions. For certain people there is no public recognition, at least, that tension exists between the two perspectives. Marie Battiste is one Mi'kmaw spokesperson for whom the primacy of language in determining and maintaining Mi'kmaw culture cannot be too strongly emphasized. As a devout Catholic, Marie does not consider Catholic teachings to be a threat to Mi'kmaw tradition. Born in Chapel Island, she was raised in Maine and now works extensively in the areas of Aboriginal language and education. Prior to her appointment to the University of Saskatchewan's College of Education, Marie Battiste worked as an educational adviser in Eskasoni. Because of her extensive education and her involvement in the community, many residents of Eskasoni recognize her as an authority figure. However, others consider her an "outsider," because she is not a fluent speaker of the language and is not a permanent resident of the community (Fieldnotes, January 2000; March 2000).

Marie suggests that Mi'kmaw lifeworlds and the philosophies that inform them can be understood through their oral tradition:

> In the beginning when the Mi'kmaq people awoke naked and lost, we asked our Creator how we should live. Our Creator taught us how to hunt and fish and how to cure what we took, how to make clothes from the skins, to cure ourselves from the plants of the earth. Our Creator taught us about the constellations, to make our way through the darkest of nights, and about the Milky Way which was the path of our spirits into the other world. Our Creator taught us how to pray, to sleep, and to dream and told us to listen to the animals that would speak to us in the night bringing us guidance and support. Our Creator taught us all that was wise and good and then gave us language, a language in which we might be able to pass on this knowledge to our children so that they could survive and flourish. Our Creator also taught us about the two worlds that were divided by a cloudlike wall that opened and fell at various intervals and the firm and believing of heart could be able to move between those worlds unscathed but the weak and unbelieving would be crushed to atoms.
>
> *(Battiste 1997b: 147)*

In reference to the concepts of Creator and creation described by Bern Francis, the description of the Creator and the act of creation provided by Marie Battiste is more in keeping with the Christian view of God as noun than with the Mi'kmaw view of a Creator who is an "active presence in the world." Teachings about "our Creator" as the overseer of creation, as one who provided teachings and instruction, are dogmatic in nature and are more in line with what Francis perceives to be a Western concept of God and God's works. For some Mi'kmaq this hybridization of Mi'kmaw and Western concepts poses a problem.

There are, however, a number of obvious similarities between Marie Battiste's description of precontact Mi'kmaw lifeworlds and Bern Francis's observations on the ways the Mi'kmaw language articulates the world. For instance, Marie's reference to "our Creator" as opposed to "*the* Creator" acknowledges the relational concept of God implicit in the Mi'kmaw language. She also suggests that the Mi'kmaq understood the significance of a Creator prior to European contact. Interestingly, Marie does not include a description of the act of creation. This omission may result, in part, from precontact Mi'kmaq belief that they emerged from the earth. As Ruth Holmes Whitehead states, "The People [Mi'kmaq] were born from the body of the earth . . . In the eighteenth century, prayers to the sun and the moon . . . acknowledged the role of both in the creation of the world" (Whitehead 1988: 8). In addition, Marie does not see the incongruities between Christian and Mi'kmaw conceptions of the world that Francis sees. In the following passage Marie claims that "[t]he formal and ceremonial rituals of spirituality have been imbedded in Christianity." This suggests that Mi'kmaw spirituality has been incorporated into Mi'kmaw Catholicism without unduly affecting the belief system that existed prior to European contact:

> The Mi'kmaq are deeply spiritual people who throughout their daily life demonstrate their spiritual consciousness. Spirituality is a very strong part of a child's growth and development and is very evident in all aspects of Mi'kmaq life. The formal and ceremonial rituals of spirituality have been imbedded in Christian traditions, although there have been changes occurring as Mi'kmaq search their identity through pan-Indian spirituality and traditions. But Mi'kmaq history holds a rare relationship with the Catholic church. In 1610 the Mi'kmaq people entered into a compact with the Holy Roman Empire when our Chief Membertou and 140 others were first baptized. While our alliance with the Church was more political than spiritual, it was solidified in daily rituals when the French priest Father Antoine Maillard learned Mi'kmaq and began addressing the spiritual questions of the people . . . Following the expulsion of the French priests . . . [the] Mi'kmaq people held to their strong spiritual rituals in the Catholic church by conducting their own adopted Catholic rituals. They had prayer leaders who led Sunday prayers, baptized children, accepted promises of marriage, and provided last rites for the dying . . . These Catholic rituals continue today in many communities, and elders play still an important role in them, although a priest in the community offers the primary services.

> *(Battiste 1997b: 157–158)*

In Marie's view, then, the relationship between the Mi'kmaq and the Roman Catholic Church was at first a political alliance. That initial acceptance of Catholicism by the Mi'kmaw was based on political rather than existential concerns. Accordingly, Marie appears to be receptive to Catholicism principally because the alliance formed between the Catholic Church and the Mi'kmaq provided an opportunity for autonomy, leadership, and religious self-expression. However, she does not explain the far-reaching effects of Catholicism on Mi'kmaw culture and society, nor does she explain how Catholicism has, or has not, gained religious acceptance among the Mi'kmaq.

For Marie Battiste, it would seem that Catholicism does not threaten the integrity of Mi'kmaw culture but, rather, is a feature of it. Although she does not explain how Catholicism became incorporated into Mi'kmaw tradition, Marie does state that the Mi'kmaq conducted "their own adopted Catholic rituals." This phrase suggests that the Mi'kmaq actively participated in, and exercised some degree of control over, the ways in which Catholicism was incorporated into Mi'kmaw culture. For Marie, Mi'kmaw lifeworlds remain intact through Mi'kmaw oral tradition and socialization, of which Catholicism is only one part:

> The Mi'kmaq language exists as the essential base of knowledge and survival. More than just a knowledge base, Mi'kmaq language reflects a philosophy, a philosophy of how we shall live with one another, a philosophy that reflects how we treat each other, and how all things in the world fit together ... Mi'kmaq people believe that because all things are connected, all of us must depend on each other and help each other as a way of life, for that is what it means to be in balance and harmony with the earth. If we do not care about each other and about the animals, about the plants and their survival, about the trees and their survival, then we will not survive ourselves for very long ... Mi'kmaq language embodies the verb and relationships to each other; how we are kin to each other ... How we are with one another, how we treat one another and our life together in community is more important than the degree of education, the wealth, or the kind of job we have. So, within the philosophy of language is a notion of how we should relate to one another and how we should retain that relationship. The verb-based language provides the consciousness of what it is to be Mi'kmaq and the interdependence of all things.

> *(Battiste 1997b: 147–48)*

There are noticeable incongruities between Mi'kmaw lifeworlds and related philosophies, as they are described by Marie Battiste, and the world view that informs Christian teachings. Again, Marie's understandings of Mi'kmaw lifeworlds as they are related through language are consistent with those explanations offered by Bern Francis. However, while Bern views Catholicism as assimilationist, Marie suggests that only specific aspects of Mi'kmaw spirituality have been assimilated into Christian contexts, while others are syncretic or exist alongside Catholicism without being unduly affected by it. For Marie, the most immediate challenge confronting present-day Mi'kmaw people is not directly related to religion and religious identity per se. It centres on the need for Mi'kmaw people to "unleash" themselves "from colonial doubt, inferiority complex, and confusion created by public and federal schooling and Eurocentric assumptions and fallacies" (1993: 160). Marie does not associate Catholicism with Eurocentrism but views Catholicism as a religious tradition that Mi'kmaw culture and society have adopted.

Eva: Spiritual Duality

Another Mi'kmaw woman, Eva, agrees with Marie Battiste. Eva, in her mid- to late -50s, is also an educator and is a lifelong resident of Eskasoni, where she currently lives with her husband. Her children, grandchildren, and many members of her extended family also reside in the community. Eva has a strong sense of what it means to be Mi'kmaq and considers her Catholic faith to be very much a part of her Mi'kmaw identity:

> One of the main reasons why the Mi'kmaq became followers of Christianity is because of the vision of the three crosses. We were already a nation of cross-bearers

before the missionaries arrived. It is a symbol that was not alien to them [the Mi'k-maq]. The shaman knew that the third cross was going to appear, so when the missionaries arrived with the cross, then the vision was fulfilled. I believe that Jesus was not alien to the Mi'kmaq either—that many of the teachings about Jesus were similar to what the Mi'kmaq already believed. The Mi'kmaq are a communal people—they have a strong sense of what is good for the group. To our people, someone who was willing to die for the good of all had to be good, and in this way Jesus appealed to the Mi'kmaw sense of community. At first, the Natives did not understand the rituals and the sacraments of the RC church. They were mysterious to the Mi'kmaw people. They did not understand the wholeness of the faith, but the generosity, kindness and forgiveness taught resembled traditional Mi'kmaw beliefs. The Christian faith is something that is always unfolding. The Mi'kmaq have something to teach the Church and the Church has not caught up with the Native way of thinking. Religion unfolds like the seasons. The seasons happen four times a year, there is constant changing, but nature is also constant. It is hard not to make things hierarchical but in the interconnectedness of things it is easy to see God in nature. You just have to look … For the Mi'kmaq there is a spiritual duality. The Mi'kmaq respect nature and in doing so have respect for the Creator. How can you respect nature if you do not respect the Creator? One follows from the other, but I do not see any problem between thinking this way and being a Catholic as well.

(Fieldnotes, Book I: 17–19)

Although Eva locates Mi'kmaw Catholicism in the past, she does so with the claim that the Mi'kmaw people knew Christianity prior to European contact. For her, the introduction and acceptance of Catholicism into Mi'kmaw culture and society was a logical extension of existing Mi'kmaw faith and belief. It is significant that Eva's understanding of religion and spirituality is contextualized within a Christian framework. Eva's insistence that the Mi'k-maw were "a nation of cross-bearers" before the arrival of the missionaries suggests that the Mi'kmaq were not only a religious people in their own right but that they had an awareness of Jesus and the Christian God. For Eva, little has changed in this regard. The arrival of the Christian cross was simply the fulfillment of a pre-existing prophecy. The basic teachings of the Church were "not alien" to her people. The Christian sense of community and the concepts of "generosity, kindness and forgiveness," which are cornerstones of the Christian faith, existed among the Mi'kmaq prior to European contact. Catholicism merely offered a different religious context for the expression of such beliefs.

The Mi'kmaw "spiritual duality" of which Eva speaks implies that Mi'kmaw cosmology does not coincide with Christianity cosmology. Eva suggests that for the Mi'kmaw people life is a continuous process, and nature is constantly "unfolding." "[I]n the interconnectedness of things," God/the Creator is very much a part of this process. For Eva, respect for nature and respect for the Creator follow logically from each other, but she is also aware that the Church does not share this view. In effect, the view that the "Christian faith is something that is always unfolding" is a reinterpretation of Christianity within the Mi'kmaw understanding that nature, life, and all of existence is a continuous process. Eva suggests that the Church fails to recognize faith as a process and in this regard has not "caught up with the Native way of thinking." So, while Eva defends Mi'kmaw Catholicism, she has reservations about the role of the Church in her community.

Jonal: Catholicism and Mi'kmaw Lifeworlds

Another of my respondents, Jonal, attends church regularly but expresses a certain degree of dissatisfaction with the role of the Church in Mi'kmaw society. Jonal, a man in his late 50s, has lived in Eskasoni for over 50 years. He is married, the father of five children, and the grandfather of nine. Jonal has little formal education, but he is an intelligent, articulate man who has given considerable thought to Mi'kmaw religion and spirituality. Jonal is a moderate Catholic. While he acknowledges that the Church fulfills a specific function in the community, Jonal is critical of the Catholic Church as an institution. He is reluctant to cede spiritual authority to it:

> I do not have much use for the Catholic authorities, but I still go to church. I spent a lot of time thinking about the definition of religion and of spirituality. Spirituality is how you live your life and religion is just one way of making contact [with] or praying to the Creator. You can be spiritual without being religious. You really don't need religion, but spirituality is a completely different matter. You must be able to strike a balance between mind, spirit, and body and too much of any one is no good ... I am a victim of the residential school. I have nothing but contempt for the nuns, priests, lawyers, and politicians who always treated us as subservient. I go to church not because of the priest, but because it is part of my upbringing and there are good points to the church.
>
> *(Fieldnotes, Book I: 199)*

For Jonal, attending church is a religious matter but not necessarily a spiritual one. In his estimation, the Church provides some essential services, but it has been remiss in its responsibilities to the Mi'kmaw people. From his experiences at residential school,[5] Jonal has learned to mistrust the Roman Catholic Church as an institution. Still, he remains faithful to it. This is not because of belief but for more pragmatic reasons, namely family tradition and services to the community. In some respects, Jonal sees the Church as being inimical to Mi'kmaw lifeworlds:

> It [the Church] does provide us with some things that are good, but I don't buy into certain dogmas. For instance, I don't buy into the way in which the hierarchy of God-man-nature is divided up. I've done a lot of thinking about this and when you think about such things there is a logic that defies Church teachings. First, there is water—our life-blood—then plants and animals. If you think logically about the structure of how things are then Christian dogma doesn't make any sense. Everything on the planet needs water, and animals need plants and water, but man needs animals, plants and water. The last three can exist without man, but man can't exist without those three things. This should tell us something, how dependent we are and where we really are in the order of things.
>
> *(Fieldnotes, Book I: 199–200).*

Jonal views Christian teachings as illogical and misleading, especially in respect to this way of thinking. The notions of dependency and interrelatedness expressed by Bern Francis, Marie Battiste, and Eva resonate with Jonal's understanding of how we as humans must rely on the rest of creation for subsistence. For Jonal, the Christian world view is not logically coherent. He considers other aspects of Christianity unacceptable as well:

> When the missionaries came they gave us a White God who spoke English.[6] What does a White God who speaks English have to do with us? For us, God is not a noun. God is a spirit—an active spirit. The White God is inactive in the spirit of the people. You [White people] pay allegiance to a noun and do not act on your own beliefs. The God that we knew before colonization is as valid as the Christian God. What about all the other nations and the gods they had before Christianity? How old is Christianity? Two thousand years old. What happened before that? What about the other nations of the world and their beliefs, didn't they exist? ... Another thing, God is genderless. There's no gender in the Mi'kmaw language, there's equality for all ... We have lost our place in the cosmos, but how do we get it back? I would say, not in the Church.
>
> *(Fieldnotes, Book I: 199, 213)*

While Jonal acknowledges the social function of the Catholic Church in Mi'kmaw society, he also understands that many of its tenets and beliefs are not consonant with Mi'kmaw lifeworlds. Jonal points to linguistic and racial and ideological differences as specific areas of divergence between non-Aboriginal and Mi'kmaw cosmologies. Jonal's understanding of God as a verb is consistent with what Bern Francis says about the way in which God is conceived and understood within the Mi'kmaw language. Jonal also recognizes that Christianity has displaced the Mi'kmaw cosmos. While this point is not explicitly stated, Jonal does comment that the Mi'kmaw people do not think in terms of hierarchies but believe in "equality for all," even that "God is genderless."[7] Such beliefs indicate that the Christian/ Western world view violates Mi'kmaw cosmology at a fundamental level.

Jonal also told me of the spiritual teachings of the Mi'kmaq. He said that humility, charity, equality, respect, honesty, and love are among the most important teachings passed on to children by their parents and grandparents. When I asked about the origins of these teachings Jonal told me that "we [Mi'kmaq] do not look for origins. For instance, I asked to be born. It's also possible that I asked to marry [my wife]. What does that tell you about origins?" (Fieldnotes, Book I: 201).

Tanas: A Non-Western Perspective

Tanas, another respondent, offered a very different perspective on Mi'kmaw origins. Tanas (pronounced Danas) is a man in his late 40s who was born and raised in Eskasoni, where he currently lives with his wife, children, and grandchildren. Tanas's opinions on Western concepts of the world are similar to those held by Jonal. Like most Mi'kmaq, Tanas was born and raised Catholic. However, Tanas has abandoned the Church and focuses his energies on reclaiming his Mi'kmaw roots. Many people in Eskasoni refer to Tanas as a Traditionalist, but he does not claim this identity himself. Like Bern Francis, Tanas considers the Mi'kmaw language to be the key to reclaiming precontact understandings and teachings. He also views the Church as hindering the understanding of Mi'kmaw lifeworlds:

> I don't think the Church is for spirit conditioning ... Cultracide is what Catholicism has done ... We don't have anything like God. No such thing. No such thing as angels,

that's bullshit ... That's something that people believe, what they were taught to believe. If you believe in Santa Claus, then you will surely ask for toys ... I can't even claim that anything I do is mine ... [It's] Lnu, the people's ... [Lnu] believed in life force. Everything that has life has a life force ... life force of water ... It's very nice to have people go back to their culture and identify their culture. What is, what's there, but another thing ... you don't confuse it with somethin' else ... We have to go back into the origin of the words. My family grew up with old Mi'kmaw [language] ... We have to go back to our language ... What is it that we're deciphering? We have a descriptive language. We don't have a labelistic language ... No such thing as a woman. How do you describe a woman? No such thing as a man. No aunt, uncle, girlfriend, boyfriend ... These are very violent, violent labels on people ... I know my language. [We must] use what we have today. People change the descriptions of words. We might as well not teach ... I could say "this is wrong, that is wrong" and everybody's doing it.

(Tanas to Robinson, taped interview)

For Tanas, much of what was known and understood by Lnu has been lost to the past. However, he does not rule out the possibility that much can be regained. Like Bern Francis and Jonal, Tanas feels that there are profound differences between the God of Christianity and the Mi'kmaw conception of God. Tanas also agrees with Bern's assessment that Christian and Western influences have obscured the "true meanings and understandings of Mi'kmaw language and culture." Tanas claims that as the language changed, people's ideas and understandings changed with it. In effect, Western concepts have infiltrated Mi'kmaw language and thinking to the extent that what was once held sacred has now been demonized. Tanas also feels that the former conceptions of social and familial relationships have been radically transformed. They are now "labelistic" and foreign to the Mi'kmaw way of thinking:

The thing is we're sort of adapted to cults—to all that stuff, and Traditionalism ... The people here in Eskasoni are very racist about ... stereotyping. There's people that might label themselves as Traditionalists ... [There are] different kinds of Traditionalists ... Traditionalism is a very bad way to describe a person, [it's] not very polite because it's labelistic ... How do you get away from that? That's your environment and that's conditioning. That's conditioned violence ... I think that the role of devil lingers in the mind. Some people say, "Oh, this guy is working for a devil," but if we take the word *mn'tu* (what we know today as "devil") means life force—we will call it life force—and *kji* means "great." Kji-mn'tu is great life force ... Today you say Kji-mn'tu, devil! But, yesteryear it was great life force ... Of course, if you're looking at something like *niskam*, *Kji-niskam*, which is the same thing as Kji-mn'tu ... *Niskam* today we know as God, but *niskam* means what it means ... we got to get away from this God thing ... God! What is God? God must be busy, huh? ... But they don't know what God is first of all. How can you believe in something that you don't know? Gee, this is how stupid the whole thing is. It's stupid.

(Tanas to Robinson, taped interview)

Tanas suggests that, through conditioning, the original Mi'kmaw understanding of Kji-mn'tu/Kji-niskam as great life force has now been replaced by alien ideas of God or devil. He suggests that the only way to reverse this process and reclaim original Mi'kmaw understandings and teachings is through etymological analysis of the language. He feels that people no longer understand the true meanings of Mi'kmaw words and their usage, that "cultracide" and the Westernization of the Mi'kmaw language have taken hold. However, Tanas is insistent that, despite the intrusion of Western ideology into Mi'kmaw culture and society, past practices can be revitalized, on both individual and collective levels. Tanas also asserts that it is through "looking *in*" (or knowledge of the self) "rather than looking up" toward the Christian God that the process of reclaiming Mi'kmaw origins is to be realized:

> If you're smart enough ∙∙∙ you can step out [of] your conditioning, or whatever you grew up with, and step back, then you can look *in* rather than looking up. You know the difference then. Some people make it outside. Some have a better understanding of what life force is. Once you understand that then you're into what we call visions, or vision centres ∙∙∙ Subconsciously and mentally you start using these [visions]. When you see something important ∙∙∙ you are aware of what it is that you are receiving. What is real and what is a dream ∙∙∙ we need to recondition ourselves—to accept the other [Mi'kmaw] way of teaching. We cannot use something that has been a constant of the Europeans ∙∙∙ That's all silly. Very silly how they kept control here ∙∙∙ They're still doing it.

> *(Tanas to Robinson, taped interview)*

Tanas recognizes language as the most powerful medium in the transmission of fundamental ideological and pedagogical principles. At the very heart of Tanas's analysis of Western influence on Mi'kmaw culture and society is the recognition that the failure to preserve the language has resulted in a ceding of power to the West. Like Bern Francis, Tanas fears that if attenuation of the language is allowed to persist Mi'kmaw lifeworlds will become increasingly susceptible to the destructive powers of Western discourse. However, one could argue that (phenomenologically) the language is always changing and that, as it accommodates Western concepts, something new is emerging—different from the past, but still Mi'kmaw. In other words, trying to regain the pure Mi'kmaw culture through a return to the language, unadulterated by Western concepts, may be impossible: phenomenologically what exists now *is* Mi'kmaw.

CONCLUSION AND DISCUSSION

The five people whose words we have read in this chapter are a small but representative sample of the various ways in which Mi'kmaw personal and social identities are constructed. I encountered a number of Mi'kmaw people who, like Bern Francis and Tanas, consider analysis of the Mi'kmaw language to be the key to cultural survival. However, I did not meet anyone who expressed as much passion for the Mi'kmaw language as Bern Francis and Tanas. I have, however, met a substantial number of people like Eva and Marie Battiste, who share the Catholic faith and who recognize it as part of what it means to be Mi'kmaq. I also met others, like Jonal, for whom the abuses experienced in residential school have resulted in feelings of resentment toward and distrust of the Catholic Church.

While all five of these people are unique individuals with their own personal views on the subject of religion and spirituality, their voices also relate experiences, ideas, and opinions similar to those held by many other Mi'kmaw people. Throughout this book, I explore most of the ideas and opinions expressed in the communications of this chapter and attend to their various points of convergence and divergence. However, some of the motifs merit attention at this point, both to summarize some of the central issues that have been raised and to provide context for subsequent chapters.

I have also found that the role of institutionalized and noninstitutionalized religion in forming individual and collective identities is significant for most Mi'kmaw people. In the discourses presented in this chapter, the role of religion as it pertains to Mi'kmaw lifeworlds is emphasized. This is primarily because religious and spiritual views help shape the way in which the world is perceived in relation to the self and others. While Catholicism remains the predominant form of institutionalized religion in Eskasoni, its ideologies and teachings do not entirely eclipse Mi'kmaw lifeworlds.

One apparent feature of Mi'kmaw religion is the tension between Traditional and what is perceived to be nontraditional religious expression. For some Mi'kmaw speakers, the culture and society in which they live is firmly embedded within the Mi'kmaw language, in the sense that the language retains and conveys a particular cosmology along with the philosophies that emerge from such a view. They feel that because it is verb-based the Mi'kmaw language exhibits a flexibility that can readily accommodate change and thereby reflects the Mi'kmaw understanding that the universe is active and ever-changing. Such notions of fluidity and adaptability are also evident in Mi'kmaw spirituality and culture.

For Bern Francis and Tanas, etymological analysis of the language provides a privileged source for reclaiming, retaining, and reconstructing original Mi'kmaw ideas and beliefs. Both Bern and Tanas are critical of the Catholic Church. They claim that it has had, and continues to have, an adverse effect on Mi'kmaw culture and society. Conversely, the other three participants' views on the role of the Church in Mi'kmaw society counter this claim. Their interpretations of Mi'kmaw society and culture are not so much concerned with origins as with what the speakers perceive to be valid religious beliefs and expressions. These individuals suggest that the Church plays a vital role in the religious lives of the Mi'kmaw people. However, while the Church is accorded some degree of status and authority in the community, its position is not accepted naively or without qualification. Although Jonal and Eva both attend church, they articulate some misgivings about the institution. The participants' dynamic and ambivalent views on the Church reveal the importance of Mi'kmaw autonomy and self-expression as they pertain to religion and spirituality generally. In addition, the divergence among these views may also reflect the difficulty with which Mi'kmaw personal and social identities are currently constructed and maintained.

Of equal importance to understanding Mi'kmaw lifeworlds and culture is the Mi'kmaw perception of humanity's place in the cosmos. During the 1990s, scholars writing on Mi'kmaw culture and society dealt almost exclusively with the significance of attachment to place, or "rootedness in the land," in the formation of Mi'kmaw social and cultural identities (Parkhill 1997 Reid 1995). However, it is important to note that the Mi'kmaw metaphysical sense of place, which informs locality, also holds significant philosophical and teleological (arguments using cosmic order as proof of the existence of God/Creator) orientations that impact on existing Mi'kmaw culture. In general, Mi'kmaw understandings of the cosmic order have a direct bearing on the beliefs and values that underlie present-day Mi'kmaw culture and social organization. More specifically, Mi'kmaw perceptions of the cosmological order influence the diverse ways in which the sacred is understood and venerated by the Mi'kmaq on both personal and collective levels.

We see, then, that the diverse cosmological perspectives held by the Mi'kmaq are not confined to the Western or Christian view that God/the Creator stands in a hierarchical relationship to the rest of creation. Many Mi'kmaq claim that all aspects of creation are interdependent. Attendant to this belief is a Mi'kmaw concept of spirit that may or may not be identified with institutionalized religion and that is markedly different from the notion of spirit located within Christian discourse. For some Mi'kmaq, the idea of life force or spirit is very much an active part of the physical world. In this perspective, all aspects of creation hold a spiritual element that binds us all together. The nature of the spirit gives each aspect of creation its purpose and its unique character.

This book draws upon the crucial themes identified above. It is primarily concerned with the past and its uses, the multiplicity of religious or spiritual frameworks that individuals may either invoke or subvert, the ambiguous role of religion, and the ambivalent process of constructing positive Mi'kmaw identities. In an effort to address these concerns in a holistic fashion, the following chapter deals with the historical and social aspects of the Catholic Church in Eskasoni.

CONTENT QUESTIONS

1. What are the various ways in which tradition is understood among the Mi'kmaq?
2. According to some Mi'kmaw speakers, what are the main differences between Mi'kmaq and English?
3. How does the Mi'kmaw language influence the ways that key cosmological and ideological concepts are understood?
4. What are the main features of the two cosmologies discussed in this chapter?
5. Explain the complex relationship between religion, spirituality, and tradition within Mi'kmaw society.

ENDNOTES

1. The Mi'kmaw understanding of spirit must be distinguished from the Christian concept of soul. *Spirit*, like *ase*, is a generative force existing in all things, whereas within Christianity the *soul* is attributed only to humans, and owing to human failings is often corrupted through sinfulness.

2. Bern Francis cautions that although the language conceptualizes God as an active entity, "many [Mi'kmaw] people think that God is overseeing everything and anytime you want something you can simply pray to God . . . [but] there's a very thin veneer, especially with many of the elders, that separates them from Christian Catholicism and Mi'kmaw spirituality. You don't have to scratch too deeply through the surface to see that a lot of the elders understand spirituality in the way that our ancestors understood it because they have no other recourse. They speak only the Mi'kmaw language" (Francis to Robinson, taped interview). Francis also provided me with the following list of Mi'kmaw verbs used to refer to the Creator: *ankweyulkw*, or "she/he/ it who is looking over us"; *kisu'lkw*, or "she/he/it who creates us"; *tekweyulkw*, or "she/he/it who is with us"; *jikeyulkw*, or "she/he/it who is watching over us" *(Francis to Robinson).*

3. Writing about Mi'kmaw myths and stories, Ruth Holmes Whitehead expresses ideas similar to Bern Francis's views. She observes that for the Mi'kmaq "Creation itself was fluid, in a continuous state of transformation. Reality was not rigid, set forever in form . . . This Creation is clearly depicted in Micmac stories: not only through their content, interestingly, but through their basic structure and the language in which they were told" *(Whitehead 1988: 2).*

4. For instance, Genesis 1:1, 20, which states, "In the beginning God created the heaven and the earth . . . And God said, Let the waters bring forth abundantly the moving creatures that hath life, and the fowl that may fly above the earth in the open firmament of heaven," suggests that God exists independent of earthly life.

5. The former students of "Shubie" with whom I spoke often refer to themselves as victims. Current research on the topic of residential schools in Canada reveals widespread physical sexual and emotional abuse. For further reading on the treatment of Aboriginal children in residential schools, refer to Elizabeth Furniss's *Victims of Benevolence: The Dark Legacy of the William's Lake Residential School* and Isabelle Knockwood's *Out of the Depths: The Experiences of Mi'Kmaw Children At the Indian Residential School At Shubenacadie, Nova Scotia.*

6. Jonal's reference to a "White God who spoke English" is quite obviously a mistake. The first missionaries to the Mi'kmaq were French, which Jonal is very much aware of. It appears that Jonal is superimposing present-day power structures and discourse on early contact history. The main point made by Jonal is that the "White God" introduced into Mi'kmaw society spoke a non-Aboriginal language and was from a different cultural milieu.

7. As is the case with other Algonquian languages (e.g., Ojibwe, Cree, Innu, and Blackfoot), there is no distinction made between *he* and *she* prefixes and suffixes in Mi'kmaq nouns and verbs (e.g., *kisu'lkw*—"she/he/it who creates us"). Further, *negm*, the independent pronoun for the third person singular, refers to either *he*, *she*, or *it* (Fieldnotes, October 12, 1999).

chapter four

Alasutmuo'kuomk ("At the Wigwam Where We Pray"): The Church

Bored, uniformed, knowing the ghostly silt
Dispersed, yet tending to this cross of ground
Through suburb scrub because it held unspilt
So long and equably what since is found
Only in separation—marriage, and birth,
And death, and thoughts of these—for which was built
This special shell? For, though I've no idea
What this accoutred frowsty barn is worth,
It pleases me to stand in silence here.

Philip Larkin, from "Church Going"

LEARNING OBJECTIVES

After reading this chapter, students should be able to:

- Distinguish between prescribed and practised religion.
- Describe the role of the Catholic Church in Eskasoni.
- Outline the changes occurring within Mi'kmaw Catholicism in the last half of the 20th century.
- Identify the significance of the Sante' Mawio'mi ("Grand Council") for the Mi'kmaq.
- Identify the significance of Catholic writings in the Mi'kmaw language.

INTRODUCTION

Anthropologist Ruth Behar suggests that when writing about "popular"[1] religion and "official" church religion we must be "cautious about attributing too much power to the Church" (Behar 1990: 78). Behar tells us that religious practitioners have always been selective and creative in their interpretations of religious belief (1990: 78). This creativity is particularly evident among the Mi'kmaq of Eskasoni. It is generally acknowledged that the Mi'kmaq have been followers of the Catholic faith since the early 17th century, but this claim alone tells us little about the actual practice of Catholicism in Mi'kmaw communities. In general, this chapter is concerned with the ways in which Catholicism remains socially, culturally, and historically relevant, and religiously meaningful for many Mi'kmaq at the turn of the 21st century. More specifically, this chapter addresses two particular issues relevant to Catholicism in Eskasoni. First, the chapter looks at the ways that Catholicism became accepted as a traditional practice, ways that continue to define *religion* in the community today. Second, this chapter draws attention to the different perceptions—of both the parishioners and the priests who have ministered to them—of the role of the Church.

THE CHURCH IN ESKASONI

When you enter Eskasoni from the East Bay Road, the most prominent building you see is Holy Family Catholic Church. This church is somewhat of an anomaly in Unama'ki, or Cape Breton. It is the only Mi'kmaw parish church in the area. All other reserves are served through the Catholic mission church system. Holy Family Church was erected in 1910, replacing a previously existing mission church.[2] However, Eskasoni did not achieve parish status until 1944, during the period of centralization.

The Catholic faith and Holy Family Church as an embodiment of this faith are meaningful for many residents of Eskasoni in a number of ways. As an institution, the Church offers local residents a formal religious structure in which to raise their children, to observe rites of passage, and to express themselves religiously. Many people in Eskasoni also view the Church as socially, culturally, and historically significant. The historical and cultural relevance of Catholicism derives from the early contact period when alliances between the Mi'kmaq and the Church were established. For instance, one respondent told me that this alliance is actually a treaty that has been orally transmitted, "and like all treaties it has to be honoured.... We honour what has been passed on to us by our elders" (Fieldnotes, Book IV: 730). Many Mi'kmaq believe that the Church was a repository for Mi'kmaw culture during the periods when the demise of Mi'kmaw lifeways and beliefs appeared imminent.

The Church also remains one of the most important religious and social institutions in Eskasoni. For many Mi'kmaq, the Church provides the religious direction necessary for personal and social well-being. To a certain degree, Catholic pedagogy is reflected in Mi'kmaw understanding of what constitutes moral or immoral behaviour and is also evident in the way certain social distinctions are made. For instance, Father Martin,[3] a former priest of Eskasoni, told me that the Mi'kmaq are "good churchgoers":

> Church is very important to them. I think probably they might look down on someone that didn't go. This is a thing that you do, you don't miss Church. You're expected to go. They laugh at you if you go once at Christmastime. They'll say to them, "Well, you're here!"

(Fieldnotes, Book I: 43)

Pictured above is the tabernacle (where Communion wafers are kept) in Holy Family Church in Eskasoni. This particular tabernacle was made by local craftspeople.
Photo: Angela Robinson, 2000

Although Martin contends that church attendance is important to the Mi'kmaq, he is actually speaking of a particular group of people in the parish. There is a core group of families who go to church regularly, while the majority of the population attends periodically (Fieldnotes, personal observations). Another priest stated that "missing Mass is not a big deal with them [the Mi'kmaq] . . . It's a place for rites of passage" (taped interview).

It is not exactly true that the Mi'kmaq "might look down on someone that didn't go." Rather, regular church attendees are looked up to as leaders or role models within the community. Broadly speaking, the Mi'kmaq are nonconfrontational. While often critical of one other, they consider an individual's involvement in community matters to be just as important as his or her reputation for attending church regularly. Those who voice opposition to the Church are often openly criticized, principally because such outright dissension is often perceived as a threat to, or at the very least an infringement on, personal religious convictions.

History and Tradition

In general, Catholicism is significant for Mi'kmaw Catholics and Catholic Traditionalists alike. As mentioned in chapter one, those who subscribe to the Catholic faith consider it to be equal, or perhaps superior to, many Native religious traditions found in present-day Mi'kmaw culture. For some, loyalty to the Church is commensurate with respect for one's forebears. To be Catholic means to participate in the religious traditions embraced and upheld

Box 4.1	Chief Henri Membertou

Chief Henri Membertou is one of the most well known Mi'kmaw leaders in history. It is reported that Membertou recalled Jacques Cartier and his visits to the North American continent from 1534 to 1542. He was considered to be an aged but vigorous man when the de Monts' expedition arrived in 1604. Membertou apparently embraced his new French friends and could certainly have made their acquaintance when de Monts, Champlain, and 79 others first wintered over on St. Croix during the winter of 1604/05. In 1607, Lescarbot wrote of Membertou that the chief, or Saqamaw, was "already more than 100 years old." Membertou led a following of Mi'kmaq who hunted and fished in the area of Port Royal, which is known today as Annapolis Basin. Membertou was reputed to be an upright and honourable man, who respected the Mi'kmaw way of life and was instrumental in protecting his people. He was among those who greeted the French upon their return to Port Royal in June of 1610. At that time he expressed his faithfulness to the French by converting to Catholicism. Jesuit Father Antoine Biard wrote the following of Membertou:

This was the greatest, most renowned and most formidable savage within the memory of man; of splendid physique, taller and larger-limbed than is usual among them; bearded like a Frenchman although scarcely any of the others have hair upon the chin; grave and reserved; feeling a proper sense of dignity for his position as commander.

(Thwaites, JR 2: 23)

by Mi'kmaw ancestors. One respondent told me that he supports the Church because it "connects to our past," and a denial of that past is an admission that "our ancestors were wrong." There exists "an agreement between the Mi'kmaq and the Vatican. If we [the Mi'k-maq] deny that, then we deny our ancestors...They [the Catholic Church and the Mi'kmaq] were in trouble and there was a mutual agreement between them to protect each other. We have to uphold this agreement" (Fieldnotes, Book IV: 729).

The Mi'kmaq trace their affiliation with Catholicism to the conversion of Chief Membertou in 1610. The historical development of Mi'kmaw Catholicism during the 18th and 19th centuries is marked by contestation and general adversity. Missionary activity in what is now Cape Breton was reasonably consistent from the early 17th until the mid-18th century when the area was under French control. However, once New France was entirely ceded to Britain in 1763, British authorities instituted penal statutes that outlawed the practice of Catholicism and forbade the presence of Catholic priests and missionaries in the region. Despite attempts by the British to eliminate the Catholic faith, Catholicism persisted among the Mi'kmaq. This is due, for the most part, to the efforts of Father Pierre Maillard and the tenacity of the Mi'kmaw people. Maillard, who was missionary to the Mi'kmaq from 1735 to 1762, appointed lay catechists and leaders of Mi'kmaw bands to oversee religious matters in the absence of a priest (Johnston 1958: 72, 86). The practices introduced by Maillard were born of necessity—itinerant priests could manage to visit their mission posts only once or twice a year. The lay involvement in Catholic ritual resulting from Maillard's instructions was intended only as a short-term solution. However, in the long term it became the basic means by which the Catholic faith was sustained among the Mi'kmaq of Cape Breton and throughout Mi'kma'ki.

In addition, Maillard supplied the Mi'kmaq with religious writings based on the Mi'k-maw hieroglyphic writing system. The use of hieroglyphics for religious instruction was first introduced by Father Chrétien Le Clercq. Most Mi'kmaq insist that the writing system formalized by Le Clercq and expanded by Maillard was based on an existing writing system:

[S]ome children were making marks with charcoal upon birch-bark, and were counting these with the finger very accurately at each word of prayers which they pronounced. This made me believe that by giving them some formulary, which would aid their memory by definite characters, I should advance much more quickly than by teaching them through the method of making repeat a number of times what I said to them. I was charmed to find that I was not mistaken, and that these characters that I had formed upon paper produced all the effect I could wish.

(Le Clercq 1968 [1691]: 131)

Maillard improved on Le Clercq's system, developing a prayer book that the Mi'kmaq used in the absence of a priest:

Each Sunday, in the absence of a priest, the chief of the place gathered the Indians about him in the church, took the book in his hands with profound reverence, deciphered the hieroglyphics, and then, with great earnestness, impressed upon the minds of his hearers its most important truths. And when the Catholic Indian was laid to rest, the chief read the burial ritual from this book. Again, when Catholic couples were united in the bonds of matrimony, the chief read the prayers of the Church from the Micmac book. And in the homes of the lowly Indians, the head of the family opened the Micmac book each Sunday morning and on other occasions, to read the instructions and prayers for the edification of his wife and children. In this way the Micmac book had taken the place of the missionary for nearly a hundred and seventy years.

(Lenhart 1932: 22)

The method of devotion developed by Maillard and aided by the hieroglyphic prayer books was instrumental in the performance of rites of passage and congregational services and provided guidelines for general religious instruction. Aside from their practical function, Maillard's prayer books held cultural, religious, and historical significance for the Mi'kmaw people. The Mi'kmaw poet, Rita Joe, recounts how import the prayer book was to her father:

One of my most memorable experiences as a child was a trip to Halifax with my father. I will never forget how happy father was to get a hieroglyphic prayer book. My father could read the hieroglyphics and had a prayer book that had gone missing. My father was overjoyed and read the prayer book over and over from cover to cover. He would read some part out loud and taught me some of the symbols that I now forget.

(Fieldnotes, Book III: 424)

Box 4.2	Rita Joe

Rita Joe was born in Wycocomagh, Nova Scotia, in 1932. Rita has received the Order of Canada and an Honorary Doctor of Laws from Dalhousie University in recognition of her work as a Mi'kmaw poet and spokesperson. Rita's publications include *Poems of Rita Joe* (Abenaki Press); *L'nu* *and Indians We're Called, Song of Eskasoni: More Poems by Rita Joe,* and *Song of Rita Joe: Autobiography of a Mi'kmaq Poet* (all by Ragweed Press); and with Leslie Choice is co-editor of *The Mi'kmaq Anthology* (Pottersfield Press). Rita currently lives in Eskasoni, Nova Scotia.

Rita also told me that her father was not exceptional in this practice. She remembers as a young child hearing her father and some of the older men in the community talking: "They were always talking and after a while I realized that they were talking about the hieroglyphics" (Fieldnotes, Book III: 424).

The Mi'kmaq appeared to have a great attachment to the prayer books, but this attachment was not based solely on religious conviction. In many cases, family prayer books were handed down from generation to generation and treated as sacred. They were treasured for other reasons as well. For one thing, the mere existence of the texts proved that the Mi'kmaq were an intellectually sophisticated people, thereby negating the non-Aboriginal perception of the Mi'kmaq as illiterate and incompetent.

The current *Kji-keptin,* or "Grand Captain," of the Sante' Mawio'mi, Alec Denny, told me that the Mi'kmaq were always, and still are, a highly intelligent and learned society:

We were not stupid. [My father] used to write letters … He knew French, Gaelic, and Mi'kmaq—the language and the hieroglyphs. There were educated people, some did writing, others spoke. In the 60s and 70s some people appeared to come out of the woodwork. We are persistent! ... My father told me that the Mi'kmaq used different systems to communicate with each other. They would write letters in the Pacifique system, then they would change [them] to hieroglyphics to encrypt letters.

(Fieldnotes, Book V: 983)

Although Catholic parishes were firmly established in Nova Scotia by the turn of the 20th century (Johnston 1958[II]: 112–15), many Mi'kmaq continued to rely on the system established by Maillard. Although one of Maillard's works was republished as late as 1917, in the early 20th century the works of Father R. P. Pacifique largely replaced Maillard's writing system and prayer books. Pacifique developed the first Mi'kmaw orthography based on French language usage. It was not until the early 1980s that his orthography was replaced by the English-based Smith-Francis system (composed by Bernard Francis and Douglas Smith in 1980), which is now in general use throughout Nova Scotia. However, the Mi'kmaq of New Brunswick retain the Pacifique system of writing (personal communication).

The most commonly used prayer books during this period were Pacifique's two-volume set, entitled *Alasotmamgeoel Le Paroissien Micmac* (loosely translated as "prayer book"), which includes hymns, prayers, and liturgies written in the Mi'kmaw language. The first volume was published in 1912, and the second, and final, volume was published in 1926.

In Eskasoni, Pacifique's *Paroissien* and the Maillard system remained in use until the mid-1940s, and were dispensed with only upon the arrival of the first resident priest, Father A. A. Ross. Prior to Ross's arrival in 1944, the Mi'kmaq of Eskasoni depended on members of the Sante' Mawio'mi and priests from neighbouring parishes to preside over religious services. If no priests were available, members of the Sante' Mawio'mi, especially the Kji-saqamaw, the Keptins, and the *nujialasutma'jik*, or "those who pray,"[4] served as catechists who oversaw religious matters. One respondent, Dora, now in her 60s, remembers Grand Council leaders officiating at religious services:

Although we had a church we did not have a priest. Sometimes the priest from Christmas Island would come for Mass, but only on special occasions like Easter and Christmas. Sunday Mass was held once a month and was led by Grand Chief Gabriel Sylliboy. If he could not do it for some reason, then the Grand Captain or one of the members of the Grand Council would. Even though we didn't have a priest we always had a choir. I remember a wake ritual, which is now dying out, where the choir, or certain members of the choir, would come to the wake and sing all night for two nights in a row.[5]

(Fieldnotes, Book III: 381–82)

In a conversation with two prominent Mi'kmaw elders in Eskasoni, Wilfred Prosper and Dr. Margaret Johnson, I learned that, in addition to special services like wakes, the Mi'kmaq gathered on holy days, especially during Lent, to conduct prayer services. Wilfred recalls that the readings for these meetings were mostly taken from the hieroglyphic prayer books. He also remembers participating in many of these types of services and vividly recollects how they were conducted:

During Lent prayer leaders and the elders would gather in someone's house and say prayers and sing. They would do this all through the night. Whenever an elder came they would start up praying and singing until everyone was exhausted, sleeping where they sat or on the floor ... At wakes they used to do pretty much the same thing, but this is no longer done.

(Fieldnotes, Book III: 435–36)

From Wilfred's account of community religious practices it is clear that devotional services were not restricted to those held at the Church. The fact that the Mi'kmaq gathered on their own to recite prayers and to sing hymns suggests that the lay persons who congregated with prayer leaders in informal gatherings also contributed to maintaining the Catholic faith among the Mi'kmaq.

Another Mi'kmaw elder, Mrs. Suzie Denny, recalls that before Kji-saqamaw Gabriel Sylliboy moved to Eskasoni, church services were conducted by Grand Council members and laypersons:

There were six or seven men along with Peter Denny who said prayers every Sunday in the church. They did not give Holy Communion, but they could bury people and baptize children if it was an emergency. The priest would come over once a month from Christmas Island to hear confession and serve Mass. Peter Denny and the choir would say prayers and sing at wakes. They would bury people and when the priest came he would bless the grave. Fr. Ross was the first priest to live in Eskasoni. Before we had a priest First Communion would be done in the community. It was the children from Malagawatch, Potlotek[6] and Barra Head who had First Communion at Potlotek. If you wanted to get married, you went to Christmas Island. People also got married at Potlotek, but not too many, just sometimes. I got married in 1945. Fr. Ross married me and my husband ... Steven Simon used to say prayers and read at the mission and also did things in the church here. He used to say prayers from the prayer books and light candles. He was an altar boy and did the Stations of the Cross during Lent.

(Fieldnotes, Book V: 828)

In the late 1990s, many Mi'kmaq could remember back to pre-1944 days, when the church at Eskasoni was still very much a church of the Mi'kmaq. With the arrival of resident priest Fr. Ross in 1944, however, local religious services changed—promptly and dramatically. Many of the old Mi'kmaw traditions were quickly set aside and were replaced with official Church policies and practices administered by the local parish priest.

Speaking of the changes that occurred after the arrival of Father Ross, Dora remarks that the *pa'tlia's,* or "priest," had a decided effect on the way the Church functioned in the community. Before a priest was stationed in Eskasoni, the Mi'kmaq had control of their own church and were accustomed to conducting prayers, rituals, and devotional services in their own way. They were not used to the intervention of Church representatives in regular devotional services. As mentioned, most religious events were overseen by various members of the Sante' Mawio'mi, both inside and outside the church. Dora, who witnessed the transfer of power and authority from a primarily community-based system to one that was an official Church system, recalls that many of the changes were not fully accepted by the Mi'kmaq, especially because they were imposed by an outsider who knew little about the community and its people:

Once Fr. Ross came ... many practices stopped. I guess you have to take the good with the bad. Fr. Ross was very authoritative and controlled everything that went on in the parish. He stopped the Mi'kmaw prayers, the choir and changed everything to Latin. He picked his own people for the choir and stopped a lot of the things that people used to do. I thought this was a direct challenge to Mi'kmaw culture because once they stopped using the language they started to lose their culture. Fr. Ross insisted that Mi'kmaq not be spoken in the schools and you were punished when you did.

(Fieldnotes, Book III: 383–85)

Dora points out that the patriarchal authority assumed by the parish priest extended beyond strictly religious matters and was perceived as a formidable threat to Mi'kmaw culture. She makes it clear that the people did not acquiesce to the priest's prohibition on the use of the Mi'kmaw language but, in fact, actively protested this restriction:

I was personally delivered home by Fr. Ross one day. He insisted that I be punished for saying a Mi'kmaw word. But, my father refused to punish me and he told the priest "if we lose our language, we lose our culture." He [my father] knew what would happen. I know that the Church itself is authoritative and that the priest was only doing his job, but it's awful the way that priests come into communities and take over.

(Fieldnotes, Book III: 384–85)

Box 4.3	Priests and the Mi'kmaw Language

Dora adds that an incident at Conne River, Newfoundland, is a good example of how priests asserted control:

My grandfather was the Grand Chief in Conne River. Fr. Croix ordered that no Mi'kmaq be spoken. If you went to confession and confessed to speaking Mi'kmaq there would be no absolution. My grandfather argued against the priest and as a result two camps developed in the community: those who supported my grandfather and those who supported the priest. From what I've been told, grandfather was chased out of Conne River. A group of men who supported the priest came to my grandfather's house in the middle of the night armed with guns, sticks and weapons and threatened his life. This was enough for my grandfather, so he took his family and moved here to Cape Breton, which was another country at the time. It must have been a terrible time for him ... When my grandfather left he took his Grand Chiefs medal and placed it on the statue of St. Anne. I remember seeing it there on trips to Conne River.

(Fieldnotes, Book III: 385–86)

While in conversation with a group of Catholic women in Eskasoni, I also learned that in addition to the reforms noted earlier, Fr. Ross took it upon himself to change the name of the parish from Holy Family to St. Anne's. The people were not consulted about this change, and they voiced their opposition to it. However, their objections went unnoticed. The church retained the name of St. Anne's for the duration of Father Ross's stay in Eskasoni.

However, when Fr. Ross left the parish in 1954, the people insisted that it revert back to Holy Family, the name by which it is known today (Fieldnotes, Book III: 379).

Indeed, the appointment of a priest to Holy Family parish appears to have been a mixed blessing. At last, the Mi'kmaq had their very own priest. However, judging from the information provided by Dora and Mrs. Suzie Denny, the formal Church structure imposed by Fr. Ross in the mid-1940s involved the reconfiguration of local Catholic practices. From what Dora tells us, the arrival of a resident priest changed the balance of the existing power structure. Essentially, the parish priest ushered in dramatic changes to the liturgy and limited the involvement and control of the Sante' Mawio'mi and lay persons in the church. Although such innovations were consistent with mainstream Catholic practice, the residents of Eskasoni were faced with sudden imposed changes in "local" religious practice and expression. While modifications to devotional procedures were somewhat disconcerting to the Mi'kmaq, they were not perceived to be as intrusive as the unwarranted censure of the Mi'kmaw language and culture enforced by the parish priest. Even in the late 1990s tensions existed between perceptions of the Church held by Mi'kmaw Catholics and the views and policies embraced by Church officials.

THE PRIEST, THE CHURCH, AND THE PEOPLE

Many Mi'kmaq claim that Mi'kmaw Catholicism is distinctive from mainstream Catholic practice. The differences in the character of Mi'kmaw Catholicism can be attributed to centuries of historical development and interactions, or lack thereof, between clerical authorities and local parishioners. As noted, the formalization of church services in Mi'kmaw communities like Eskasoni is a fairly recent phenomenon, essentially developed in the early half of the 20th century. Prior to that, participation in Catholicism among the Mi'kmaw people was essentially guided by local religious specialists (members of the Sante' Mawio'mi) and lay leadership. However, once Eskasoni officially became a parish and the authority of the priest was established, the privileging of Church policies and procedures by Catholic officials over and above local devotional practices generated conflict between official and unofficial religion in the community.

Anthropologists studying the interaction between popular and official religion suggest that ongoing conflict between the religious experiences of ordinary people and the religious practices sanctioned by church officials are relatively common (Abu-Lughod 1993a, 1993b; Badone 1990; Behar 1990; Brettell 1990; Christian 1992, 1996; Freeman 1978). For instance, in her study of a Bedouin community, Abu-Lughod observes the following:

> [S]cholars often artificially separate localized practices ... from the official religion, and then devalue them. Distinctions are drawn between popular and orthodox religion, local and universal belief and practice ... or, in the worst case, between ignorance and the knowledge of true religion ... Practices disapproved of by learned religious authorities may be dismissed as superstitious vestiges of the past or corruptions. In more socially grounded analyses, the orthodox and "universal" versions of religion might be recognized as the ideology of certain social groups or the world religions themselves as the imposition of dominant outsiders.

(Abu-Lughod 1993b: 189)

Abu-Lughod states further that anthropologists are aware of such distinctions and normative claims and now examine "without judgement the interaction of the complex of practices" that make up religious contexts (Abu-Lughod 1993b: 189). Likewise, in her study of Roman Catholicism in Portugal, Caroline Brettell contends that conflict between local and official traditions is a notable feature of "popular" religion. In general, Brettell focuses on "the contractual relationship between the doctrinal definition adhered to by the parish priest and other church officials and the ideas about religion and community behaviour that are the will of the people" (Brettell 1990: 55). Brettell also recognizes that the rootedness of local Catholic practice is "such that manifestations of religious practice (embodying both belief and behaviour) are neither of the orthodox institution (represented by its priests) nor totally of the people. They are, more often than not, an accommodation between the two" (Brettell 1990: 55–56). More specifically, Brettell identifies "four structural oppositions" within Portuguese Catholicism, two of which can be applied to Catholic practice in Eskasoni.

The first structural opposition relevant to the Mi'kmaw case "is rooted in the notion of anticlericalism as religious belief. The parish priest must carry out his orthodox functions in cooperation with his people and in the face of censure and criticism" (Brettell 1990: 56). In other words, there is conflict between priest and local parishioners. For instance, in Eskasoni, adherence to Mi'kmaw cultural and social conventions is often (but not always) perceived by the Catholic clergy to be in contravention of orthodox Catholic teachings. In some cases, the attitudes of the priest toward popular religious beliefs and practices among the Mi'kmaq are paternalistic and perpetuate the notion that the priest as a figure of authority knows what is best for the Mi'kmaw people. Specific devotional practices—such as the veneration of St. Anne, the incorporation of non-Christian religious traditions into Catholic practices, and the insistence on Mi'kmaw autonomy regarding religious matters—are all features of Mi'kmaw Catholicism that have been, and to some extent still are, sources of conflict between parishioners and the priest.

The second of Brettell's structural oppositions that applies here is "the uneasy balance between the sacred and the profane" (Brettell 1990: 56). Brettell states that the sacred and profane "are not separate realms but instead complexly intertwined aspects of Portuguese Catholicism" (Brettell 1990: 56). As stated in chapter 1, for many Mi'kmaq the realm of the sacred is very much a part of everyday life. The "spiritual duality" of which Eva speaks in chapter 3 is a particular religious orientation that is not perceived by many Mi'kmaq as inimical to Catholicism but rather as a logical extension of belief in God/Creator.

William A. Christian maintains that "popular religion," or "religion as practiced," is "rooted in particular historical communities and geographical localities and that is often conservative, resisting changes imposed by nonlocal authorities" (as quoted in Badone 1990: 6). Such is the case at Eskasoni. During my fieldwork I interviewed a number of priests who ministered to the Mi'kmaq in Cape Breton, most of whom were former parish priests at Eskasoni. Father Ryan described his time with the Mi'kmaw people as an experience that he thoroughly enjoyed but sometimes found frustrating and demanding. Prior to his arrival in Eskasoni, Father Ryan had never ministered to an Aboriginal community. His previous assignments were carried out in primarily English-speaking orthodox Catholic parishes. Although Father Ryan received some special training before being assigned to Eskasoni, he told me that on his arrival he experienced a certain degree of culture shock. Holy Family parish was an unusual ministry for him and required a period of adjustment both for the priest and for his parishioners. He was particularly struck by the fact that many liturgical prayers and devotional practices at Eskasoni were distinctively different from those in most Catholic parishes:

> It's all old church prayers. Even like they do the Stations of the Cross in Mi'kmaq and they're all old, old prayers that we used to say in church that they still have. They translated all these old prayers and that's what they keep saying. It's not very good really ... Like, from the point of view of our Church, and since Vatican II with the changes and all that ... I'd like that they learn the new rites of the Church. But some of these old hymns that they sing ... I guess they're nice, but they're boring. I find them boring ... The new choir ... they're hip and hype ... joyous, but some of them when you get the older ones singing the old Native hymns, they're just like Gregorian chant. Not that Gregorian chant is bad, it's nice if you were in a monastery. If you just wanted to sit back and listen, but when you're having liturgy with the group it's too slow. The atmosphere doesn't provide for it ... I'm pretty sure the hymns are old hymns from the Church that were put into Mi'kmaq. When [they] say the Creed in Mi'kmaq on Sunday, it's the oldest Creed going[7] ... the Nicene Creed is older than the Apostle's Creed and even before the Nicene Creed there's still another Creed and I think that's the one they translated and that's the one they say ...

> *(Fieldnotes, Book I: 141)*

The "old hymns" of which Father Ryan speaks are no longer in use except on special occasions, such as funerals and St. Anne's Mission. The hymns that are now commonly used in many Catholic parishes have been translated into Mi'kmaq by the Holy Family Church choir and are typically sung each Sunday at Mass in Eskasoni. Local historian and elder Wilfred Prosper suggests that the old hymns were not hymns at all, but were actually biblical passages set to metre in Mi'kmaq. He suggests that this was the way the early missionaries taught the Bible to the Mi'kmaw people because many Mi'kmaw ancestors spoke primarily Mi'kmaq and had a limited grasp of English:

> [T]he genealogy in Matthew is sung in Mi'kmaq—that's quite a feat!—really something difficult to do to get all those names to rhyme and to be able to put them to music. I always wondered why these hymns were so long and draggy. I think it's because that's the way the gospel was taught. The missionaries knew that the Mi'kmaq liked music and loved to sing, so they put the gospels to music. There's another prayer, Hail Holy Queen, usually said at the end of the rosary, but the Mi'kmaq did not use it that way, they sung it.

> *(Fieldnotes, Book V: 994–95)*

Father Ryan's statement provides a suitable starting point for an analysis of the relationship between the institutional church and popular religion in Eskasoni. The discrepancies between the views held by priests and those held by the parishioners indicate that there are different understandings about the role of the local community church. Father Ryan's comments suggest that most practising Mi'kmaw Catholics in the parish wish to retain the traditions held by their ancestors. The "old church prayers" that "[t]hey translated" are actually taken from Pacifique's *Paroissien*, and are very much a part of what is considered by the Mi'kmaq to be ancestral Catholic tradition. Therefore, in addition to being part of a valued religious tradition, these prayers preserve important aspects of Mi'kmaw history. The changes that Father Ryan would "like to see," while moving closer to the contemporary liturgy of the official Church, detract from traditional Mi'kmaw Catholicism as it is currently known and practised in the community. While Fr. Ryan is somewhat critical of Mi'kmaw devotional practices, he appears to be unaware that resistance to change is essentially an attempt to retain Mi'kmaw Catholic tradition and identity. However, Fr. Ryan did tell me that shortly after his arrival in the community he realized that the people of Eskasoni valued their Mi'kmaw heritage. He said that this fact was impressed upon him by a Mi'kmaw elder, who offered him some unsolicited but very useful advice:

> Many of the people in Eskasoni are proud of their Mi'kmaw heritage. When I first arrived there, a male elder said, "Do you want to be happy here Father?" I said, "I've never been happy, why start now?" The elder said, "Well Father, if you want to be happy you have to change. Eskasoni has four thousand people who will not change, and it's easier for you to change than everyone else." That was one of the soundest pieces of advice I ever received.

(Fieldnotes, Book I: 141)

In effect, the elder was letting the priest know that the Mi'kmaq claim ownership of their religion and that interference from any outsider, even a priest, is an unwelcome intrusion. For instance, one prominent Church leader intimated that "we're [the Mi'kmaq] having a hard time getting the Church to see things our way . . . He [the priest] could make things easier," suggesting that ordained Catholic officials do not always comply with the wishes of the people (Fieldnotes, Book V: 871). Several other people also mentioned that when priests are first assigned to Holy Family parish they are unfamiliar with the Mi'kmaw way of doing things and must be "trained" (Fieldnotes, Book III: 449). Sometimes this period of training lasts for years and the Mi'kmaq never become content with the priest who has been assigned to their parish. It is generally understood that conformity to local ways on the part of the priest usually ensures the happiness of both priest and people.

Box 4.4	Training the Missionaries

Laura, a resident of Eskasoni, related an incident that illustrates how people in the community keep the actions of the priest in check. Her anecdote recalls a newly appointed priest's reaction to the noise level in the church during Mass. Laura told me that one Sunday the priest announced that there was no point in showing up for Mass if children were allowed to disrupt the service. The following week the church was unusually quiet as many people had not bothered to bring their children or grandchildren to church, nor had they taken the trouble to attend themselves.

Fr. Connor, another priest who ministered to the Mi'kmaq in Eskasoni, observes that the Mi'kmaq "take a great deal of pride in . . . and have taken a real ownership of the Catholic faith, certainly in Eskasoni more than in any of the other reserves" (Fieldnotes, Book I: 77). Fr. Connor's claim that Catholicism is the "dominant force" or "the power structure . . . [that]

binds the community together" (Fieldnotes, Book I: 77) suggests that he does not consider the influence of Mi'kmaw ancestral tradition to be significant. He does stipulate, however, that Catholicism as it is practised and understood in Eskasoni is distinguishable from mainstream Catholicism in a number of ways:

> The Mi'kmaq give Catholicism a beautiful flavour ... The faith concepts taught by the Church are unlike the more tactile or natural types of beliefs with Mi'kmaw traditions . . . The Mi'kmaq are truly a spiritual people. They look upon nature as very important. It is one and the same as themselves. They are a part of the cycle of nature . . . They still have a large number of children and this is part of the natural progression of nature. They take on the responsibility of creating as part of their role [in life] ... The Mi'kmaq make a close connection between nature and spirituality. For instance, the seasons, the spring emphasizes new life which arises from the darkness of winter. It is not hard to make connections between Mi'kmaw traditional beliefs and the Liturgical seasons ... The Mi'kmaq taught me more than I taught them. For instance, Pentecost Sunday is supposed to be one of the most sacred days in the liturgical calendar, but we hardly commemorate it at all. For the Mi'kmaq, this day is a very special one ... I believe this developed from an early teaching. The symbols and motifs associated with Pentecost—the descent of the Holy Spirit, the dove and the circle of fire, all had meaning for the Mi'kmaq and they identified and understood these symbols. These things fit into their culture. Of course, the dove becomes an eagle in the Mi'kmaw interpretation, but this is not such a stretch, really.
>
> *(Fieldnotes, Book I: 26–30)*

In Fr. Connor's view, the "tactile or natural types" of traditions upheld by the Mi'kmaq depart from the "faith concepts" taught by the Catholic Church. From his comments, it is clear that Fr. Connor does not see the non-Christian features of Mi'kmaw tradition as a negative influence on Catholicism but rather as an enhancement of it. Even though Fr. Connor articulates a positive view of the Mi'kmaq, his terms of reference suggest that he does not fully appreciate, or perhaps recognize, the interdependent relationship between Mi'kmaw lifeways and cultural expression. For example, his depiction of the Mi'kmaq is consistent with stereotypical portrayals of the "Indian" in Western culture (see Francis 1992; Gill 1987; Jansen 1995; Krech 1999). Fr. Connor's observations that the Mi'kmaq "make a close connection between nature and spirituality," that nature is "one and the same as themselves," resemble attributes often applied to Aboriginal culture at large. Essentially, such descriptive terms serve only to establish the Mi'kmaq as "typically" Aboriginal, indicating a rather cursory or naive understanding of Mi'kmaw culture. While Fr. Connor does not suggest that Mi'kmaw expressions of faith are in any way inferior or misdirected, overtones of inherent colonialism are apparent in his assessment of Mi'kmaw religious beliefs and practice. However, Fr. Connor does express a great deal of admiration for the Mi'kmaq and also credits them as primarily responsible for maintaining the Catholic faith in Cape Breton:

> I believe the survival of Catholicism in Cape Breton is because of the efforts of the Mi'kmaq. The Mi'kmaq protected priests. They hid Bibles and hid priests when the British were at war with the French ... [The Mi'kmaw] Roman Catholic community is oriented as a community of faith. They can still teach us many things ... The Natives

[Mi'kmaq] have a different type of spirituality that I wish non-Natives had. Non-Natives compartmentalize their faith—it fits into a category. For Natives, spirituality pervades being and is an important part of everyday life.

(Fieldnotes, Book I: 30)

Clearly, Fr. Connor recognizes the influence of a "different type of spirituality" on Mi'kmaw expressions of faith and on aspects of daily life, but he does not adequately explain how this "spirituality" reflects a specifically Mi'kmaw religious orientation. He does, however, point out that Mi'kmaw spirituality is non-compartmentalized. This means that religious beliefs and expression are not restricted to specific times and places, like Sunday Mass. They are a part of daily life. The spiritual aspect of Mi'kmaw religious belief identified by Fr. Connor is also recognized by the Mi'kmaq themselves and to some degree is why they feel priests are in need of "training." One Mi'kmaw woman told me that, in her opinion, "some priests . . . are not truly Christian . . . I'm more pagan than Christian, but I feel more Christian than some of those priests act." This means, of course, that priests from non-Aboriginal cultures have a more formal or institutionalized approach to the Catholic faith. Interestingly, several priests also made similar remarks to me. One priest told me that the Mi'kmaq were "holier" than he was. Another priest said that he wished non-Aboriginals had the same spiritual appreciation for the Catholic Church as the Mi'kmaq have (Fieldnotes, Book I: 30; Book III: 445).

Fr. Ryan, Fr. Connor, and several other priests with whom I spoke generally agree that Mi'kmaw Catholicism is distinctive from orthodox Catholic beliefs and practices. However, there *are* contrasting views, such as those offered by Fr. Greene. Fr. Greene has never been assigned to an Aboriginal parish but has worked as a mission priest to the Mi'kmaq for more than seven years. Fr. Greene believes that Mi'kmaw culture is quite simply a "rural culture." In his opinion, a Mi'kmaw cultural orientation, that is, an appeal to "Indian ways," is actually a counterfeit technique used by Aboriginal peoples to advance social, cultural, or political causes:

I have real problems with this whole business "it's Indian ways" . . . all this business about love for the environment and all this stuff. I think it's all BS . . . They're going to do what they want . . . They have also exploited their position and they know they're on the winning side and I see such a change in them. Their leadership is so different, so articulate, and they are just so clever, naturally clever. They have a very brilliant streak in them and they are exploiting it every inch of the way and so they get what they want . . . There's no culture. It's a rural culture, but there's a nomadic streak and there's I think a strong spirit of superstition that . . . must be part of their culture, and their beginnings, and the Great White Spirit and that kind of thing . . . it seems to me that they're hiding behind the culture thing and I don't think that it will get them anywhere, because that's not it! You have to have basic things, values, discipline or else the whole thing is gonna fall apart . . . You see they're growing up without religion because the adults, their parents, are not practising . . .

(Greene to Robinson,
taped interview)

In Fr. Greene's view, the Mi'kmaw reliance on ancestral tradition is essentially a ruse. Not only are the Mi'kmaq lacking in "authentic" culture, they do not have such "basic things" as "values and "discipline." Obviously, Fr. Greene regards Western values and codes of behaviour as preferable to those of the Mi'kmaq. During the interview, Fr. Greene also remarked that "some of the better ones [Mi'kmaq] could pass as white people quite easily in their behaviour, in their customs—the way they live and so forth . . . they could be integrated into white customs" (Greene to Robinson, taped interview). This type of discrimination is also apparent in his claim that the Mi'kmaw predisposition toward "superstition" and their reverence for a "Great White Spirit" are vestiges of a pre-Christian past. It is also evident from Fr. Greene's apparent disapproval of Mi'kmaw devotionalism that tension exists between "prescribed religion" and "religion as it is practised." He states that it is for this principal reason that his mission to the Mi'kmaq proved frustrating, and that his attempts to introduce faith concepts more in line with appropriate Church teachings were futile:

> I used to get so frustrated that I tried to introduce them to Kateri Tekakwitha[8] . . . to someone you can touch, someone real in our era . . . They don't come [to church] . . . See, missing Mass is not a big deal with them. It's interesting because I think the white people have picked up the habits of the Indians very quickly. So, we've become a Church that is very much Mi'kmaq really. It's a place for rites of passage. It's a place where a lot of people can identify with superstition and a whole lot of stuff. It's not very healthy. They cling to crazy things. This is happening more and more with people who are vulnerable to superstition. We have tons of people that are as tied up with Mary as this crowd is tied up with St. Anne. You can hardly identify them as Catholics because you know to me it's an extreme. So, you know they're not any different than we are except that we're not into St. Anne . . . They can tell us what it's like because I think all they've had is what I look upon as the superstitious side of faith and that doesn't tell you very much about how to live. It really doesn't tell you what the value system is. So, you make your own rules and in their case they tell us that it's Indian rules. In our case, we say it's poverty because people are deprived and haven't integrated their faith with life . . . We don't preach that stuff, so where does it all come from? We may have in the past, but for the past 25 years we've been preaching homilies that are reflecting the Gospel and that has nothing to do with devotional life . . . So, where did all this come from? . . . I think it's becoming increasingly a problem for the Church because Catholic religion for a lot of people is simply a place to go for rites of passage. The Catholic Church is, and so it becomes associated with a lot of peripheral things and you know Jesus, as the Saviour, that way of life, the Son of God, can enrich your lifestyle, I think, goes by the wayside . . . It's a very frustrating ministry and if I went back into it I would be better equipped because I knew nothing, absolutely nothing.
>
> *(Greene to Robinson, taped interview)*

In Fr. Greene's estimation, the Mi'kmaq are only nominally Catholic and have a utilitarian attitude toward the Church. His suggestion that "missing Mass is not a big deal" for the Mi'kmaq shows that Fr. Greene's standard of religious obligations includes compulsory attendance at Mass. However, as one Keptin of the Grand Council points out, the Mi'kmaq do not necessarily share this view:

> They [the Mi'kmaq] still believe, but you won't see them in church. Look at Ash Wednesday, the church is full to the rafters. They will go when they feel like it. They will tell God that they will do everything for the next forty days. Another day is Good Friday . . . everyone goes, it's a tradition.
>
> *(Fieldnotes, Book V: 979)*

It appears, then, that the understanding of religious obligations defined by Fr. Greene and those held by the Mi'kmaq are divergent. The Keptin suggests that a failure to attend Mass does not necessarily mean that the Mi'kmaq do not believe but indicates that the Mi'kmaq have their own ideas of how to practise their faith. By downplaying the importance of Mass attendance, the Keptin emphasizes that while the Catholic faith is meaningful to his people, Mi'kmaw Catholicism is not necessarily Church-dependent. Some Mi'kmaw Catholics find spiritual refuge in the Church, but others do not.

In addition, Fr. Greene denies the Church's role in the introduction and promotion of the "extreme," "superstitious side of faith," or the "crazy things," such as the veneration of St. Anne among the Mi'kmaq. Instead, he attributes this type of devotionalism to the influences of pre-Christian Aboriginal traditions. Although the Church does not currently "preach this stuff," it is ultimately responsible for establishing St. Anne as the patron saint of the Mi'kmaw people.

William A. Christian establishes that, historically, the Catholic Church has tended to use aspects of local culture to communicate its message. For instance, there were two levels of Catholicism that developed in rural Spain during the late 16th century: "that of the Church Universal, based on sacraments, the Roman liturgy, and the Roman calendar; and a local one based on particular sacred places, images, and relics, locally chosen patron saints, idiosyncratic ceremonies, and a unique calendar built up from the settlement's own sacred history" (Christian 1981a: 3). However, Christian also points out that local communities have always adopted and domesticated "the symbols and discourses of the Universal Church for local votive use" (Christian 1981a: 181). This two-way system of adoption and adaptation is the case with the veneration of St. Anne among the Mi'kmaq. It is commonly believed that in the early 18th century, Catholic missionaries to the region understood the significance of the grandmother figure in Mi'kmaw society and chose St. Anne, the grandmother of Jesus, as the patron saint of the Mi'kmaq. At the turn of the 21st century, St. Anne is still a religiously meaningful and culturally relevant symbol for many Mi'kmaw people. The significance of St. Anne for the Mi'kmaq will be discussed at length in chapter five.

Ruth Behar points out that in the post–Vatican II era the Catholic Church, both in Europe and in other areas, has "fought battles against forms of popular religion that it defines as 'idolatry'" (Behar 1990: 80):

> The concern to separate religion from what is viewed as a magical view of the world in order to purify the faith is evident in the various changes introduced by the Second Vatican Council . . . [R]ationalizing reforms were, from the point of view of the Vatican, an effort to "divest Catholicism of much of its mystery and mysticism."
>
> *(Brandes 1976: 25; Behar 1990: 80)*

As a priest schooled in the post–Vatican II Church, Fr. Greene maintains that non-prescribed traditions, such as the veneration of St. Anne and other "superstitions," should be suppressed and replaced with more appropriate devotions. His view both overlooks and undermines the significance of St. Anne for the Mi'kmaq and the degree to which her patronage is considered to be an integral part of Mi'kmaw culture and tradition. In effect, for Fr. Greene Catholicism as it is believed and practised among the Mi'kmaq is palatable only if it is transformed into a system of belief that coincides with current Church teachings.

One of the most popular priests to serve at Holy Family parish was Fr. Martin. Fr. Martin considers his time with the Mi'kmaq to be the most enjoyable and rewarding period of his career: "I think I loved every day I was with them [the Mi'kmaq]. I enjoy them. They are never of a nature to get ruffled, never get bored or tired. I've gotten along great in the parishes" (Fieldnotes, Book I: 43). Fr. Martin's approach to his ministry in Eskasoni involved participating in every aspect of Mi'kmaw Catholicism. He accompanied his parishioners on trips to the shrine of Sainte-Anne-de-Beaupré,[9] regularly attended the Chapel Island Mission, and even travelled to the blueberry barrens in Maine to serve Mass. The Mi'kmaq have migrated to Maine for generations to help with the harvest. In many cases, the labour-intensive work of picking blueberries and harvesting potatoes is the only lucrative employment for the entire year (personal observations/communication).

Fr. Martin took his ministry seriously, but his considerable attention to the Mi'kmaq was also born out of genuine respect and affection. However, Fr. Greene believes that Fr. Martin "patronized" the Mi'kmaq:

> I think he [Fr. Martin] patronized them [the Mi'kmaq]. I think he had some wisdom in his approach and I had to deal with that and come to terms with it . . . But, I don't feel he allowed them to grow and I don't think he challenged them [religiously]. I don't think he wanted them to grow . . . he affirmed them in their superstitions. I know a case one time . . . someone died at the hospital . . . He got the call. The person was already dead and he came in the middle of the night and anointed the person! . . . I think that says a lot and I think he patronized them terribly.

> *(Greene to Robinson, taped interview)*

Fr. Greene's claim that Fr. Martin did not challenge the Mi'kmaq religiously implies that the latter did not interfere with existing traditions, or at least was unwilling to impose innovative religious teachings on his parishioners. In contrast, Fr. Greene's assessment of Mi'kmaw Catholicism is informed by a vision of the contemporary Church in line with post–Vatican II reforms, reforms that pose a direct challenge to key features of Mi'kmaw Catholicism. By adopting the official Church position, Fr. Greene is unable to perceive Mi'kmaw Catholicism as a unique and valid expression of the Catholic faith. For him, "true faith" demands both conformity to orthodox beliefs and practices and an outright rejection of what is perceived to be anachronistic "popular" Catholicism. Fr. Martin, on the other hand, does not view Mi'kmaw Catholicism as an inadequate or misguided religious orientation. Rather, he sees it as a particular expression of the Catholic faith that has depth and breadth of meaning for the Mi'kmaq. He comments that "when you experience their [the Mi'kmaq] love for St. Anne and for religious things . . . it's really something" (Fieldnotes, Book I: 40–41).

CONCLUSION AND DISCUSSION

The main points considered in this chapter deal with Mi'kmaw perceptions of the Catholic Church and the role of the Church within Mi'kmaw society. This chapter establishes that Mi'kmaw Catholicism is very much a religion of the people. It also illustrates that, at the turn of the 21st century, in addition to being religiously meaningful, the Catholic Church is historically, socially, and culturally relevant for Mi'kmaw Catholics.

For many Mi'kmaq, Catholicism is as important a tradition as it is a religious orientation. When British incursions into Nova Scotia threatened to eliminate both the Catholic Church and the Mi'kmaq, it was to their mutual benefit to form an alliance. The strength of this alliance figures prominently in Mi'kmaw Catholic society today. Many Mi'kmaq, especially Mi'kmaw Catholics, consider the Catholic Church to be one of the first institutions to acknowledge the Mi'kmaq as a sovereign nation. Among the Mi'kmaq, it is generally believed that Catholicism was embraced by Mi'kmaw ancestors not merely for spiritual reasons, but because it also provided leadership roles and the opportunity for self-expression in the face of persistent racism and severe social and cultural marginalization. The importance of the historical alliance between the Catholic Church and Mi'kmaw ancestors is sometimes referred to as "a treaty like any other," which must be honoured and protected (Fieldnotes, Book IV: 730).

For the most part, the Mi'kmaq resist changes to the existing liturgy and the traditional features of Mi'kmaw Catholicism, such as devotion to St. Anne, essentially because such changes involve a departure from ancestral tradition. One key aspect of claiming "ownership" of the Catholic faith is the retention of Mi'kmaw traditions passed down to them from the past. Many Mi'kmaw Catholics continue to read Pacifique's *Paroissien* and continue to follow the lead of their parents and grandparents in their devotion to the Catholic faith. The Mi'kmaw people experience Catholicism in culturally specific ways that may appear to be anachronistic or superstitious to outsiders. However, among Mi'kmaw Catholics "old prayers," specific hymns, and ancestral devotional practices are historical and cultural patterns of significance that are continually and repeatedly reinforced.

While the Mi'kmaq uphold ancestral traditions, Mi'kmaw resistance to liturgical and devotional changes should not be overstated. Mi'kmaw Catholicism has undergone a number of changes in routine devotional practices during the 20th century. For instance, the Eskasoni choir has translated modern hymns into Mi'kmaq, and the parish has introduced innovations to the Mass service consistent with Vatican II reforms. However, Mi'kmaw Catholicism remains very much a religion of the people despite attempts by Church officials to initiate faith concepts consistent with contemporary orthodox Catholicism. While some Church officials may point to Mi'kmaw Catholicism as a discursive tradition, for many Mi'kmaq a move toward a contemporary Church necessitates a move away from the ancestral traditions that are an integral part of Mi'kmaw culture and society. Reluctance on the part of ordained Catholic clergy to accept local expressions of faith can be viewed as a challenge to Mi'kmaw autonomy and self-identity. There are a number of specific practices associated with Catholicism that are unique to the Mi'kmaq. Of these, the tradition of pilgrimage in general and the annual St. Anne's Day celebrations in particular are prominent features of Mi'kmaw religious tradition. The following chapter looks at pilgrimage as a specific feature of Mi'kmaw tradition with an emphasis on St. Anne's Day celebrations.

CONTENT QUESTIONS

1. What are the main arguments for Catholicism as a Mi'kmaw tradition?
2. What is the primary role of the Catholic Church within Mi'kmaw society?
3. What specific changes in liturgical celebrations occurred with the formation of Holy Family parish?
4. How was Mi'kmaw Catholicism practised prior to the 1940s?

ENDNOTES

1. References to "popular" religion as it is used in this context follow from William A. Christian's understanding of the term. Christian refers to "popular" religion as "religion as practised" rather than "religion as prescribed" (Christian 1981a: 178).

2. Most of the information concerning the history of Holy Family Church was provided by the Sisters of Martha and the current priest of Eskasoni, Fr. Robert MacNeil. The Sisters of Martha also own early photographs of the interior and exterior of the church.

3. Owing to the sensitive nature of much of the material presented here, biographical information and the actual names of priests are withheld unless otherwise noted.

4. Schmidt and Marshall state, "Prayer leaders were trained by the missionary [Maillard] to provide religious instruction, administer baptisms and marriages, and officiate at funerals. Many nujialasut-ma'jik were local and regional chiefs who, in the absence of a priest, gathered their people on holy days to recite from hieroglyphic books" (1995: 11). More recently, in each Mi'kmaw community there are prayer leaders (usually, but not exclusively, female) assigned by the Sante' Mawio'mi to oversee various types of prayer services in the community.

5. Mi'kmaw elders, Dr. Margaret Johnson and Wilfred Prosper, recall participating in local religious services from the early 1930s until the 1980s.

6. Here, Mrs. Denny is referring to the community of Potlotek (Chapel Island) and not the island where the annual St. Anne's Mission is held.

7. The *Nujjinen*, or "The Lord's Prayer," recited in the late 1990s is also an older form of the prayer. The Mi'kmaw version omits the section "for thine is the kingdom, the power and the glory, for ever and ever," which was added as part of Vatican II reforms. This final section is recited in English immediately after the Nujjinen and the priest's invocation.

8. Kateri Tekakwitha is a Mohawk who lived from 1656 to 1680. After her death a variety of miracles were attributed to her spiritual intercession. In 1980 she was declared beatified, making her the only Aboriginal American to be named a blessed. Kateri is a symbol of virtue and holiness for many Aboriginal Catholics in North America. There is a statue of Kateri in the church at Eskasoni, and there is a chapel dedicated to her in the nearby Mi'kmaw community of Chapel Island. (See also Weiser 1972.)

9. Each year hundreds of Catholic Mi'kmaq, especially elders, carry out the long-standing tradition of attending the shrine of Sainte-Anne-de-Beaupré in Quebec. During the months of May and June bus-loads of Mi'kmaq from different communities throughout Mi'kma'ki travel to the site (personal observations/communication).

chapter five

Se'tta'newimk[1]: The Mi'kmaw Annual Pilgrimage to Potlotek

And thus it was: I, writing of the way
And race of saints in their own gospel day,
Fell suddenly into an allegory
About their journey and the way to glory,
In more than twenty things, which I set down:
This done, I twenty more had in my crown,
And they began to multiply,
Like sparks that from the coals of fire do fly.

John Bunyan, from *The Pilgrim's Progress*

LEARNING OBJECTIVES

After reading this chapter, students should be able to:

- Discuss the theoretical literature relating to pilgrimage.
- Outline the importance of pilgrimages to the Mi'kmaq.
- Explain the importance of St. Anne to the Mi'kmaq.
- Identify the various reasons the Se'tta'newimk gathering is important for the Mi'kmaq.
- Discuss the significance of Potlotek to the Mi'kmaq.

INTRODUCTION

On the eve of St. Anne's Day in late July, a large group of women were gathered at the mission church at Potlotek. I watched as the women at the front of the church gently washed the statue of St. Anne with soft white cloths. After the ritual washing, the women divided the washing cloths into long, thin strips and passed them around to those in attendance, who then tied the cloth ceremonially around their ankles or wrists. Some women took extra pieces of cloth, which they carefully folded and placed in pockets or purses for safekeeping. They would later be given to the sick and elderly who were unable to attend this event. Many women came forward with bottles and vials to fill with the water in which St. Anne had been bathed. Many Mi'kmaq consider both the water and the cloth strips to be sacred items that serve to help protect or cure the user.

This ritual is carried out each year in preparation for the St. Anne's Day procession. St. Anne is adored and revered by many Mi'kmaq. The act of bathing and decorating St. Anne's statue is very much an expression of love and devotion. The origin of this ritual event is uncertain, but the event is considered to have always been a feature of St. Anne's Mission. Women members of the Grand Council usually wash the statue, while those in attendance are invited to "dress" St. Anne and to decorate the *wkutputim* (a carrier or covered litter designed to seat one passenger). St. Anne and the child Mary are provided with capes handcrafted by Mi'kmaw women. On my first visit to Potlotek in 1997, the capes were made of blue and purple satin trimmed with gold tassels. However, these adornments have since been replaced with deerskin capes embroidered with beadwork. The canopy covering for the wkutputim has also been replaced. At one time the canopy was decorated with gold satin and tassels similar to those on St. Anne's cape. Like the capes for the statue, the satin canopy cover has been replaced with one made of deerskin adorned with beadwork (personal observations).

ST. ANNE: PATRONESS AND KI'JU ("GRANDMOTHER") OF THE MI'KMAQ

The veneration of St. Anne as the patron saint of the Mi'kmaq predates the mission at Chapel Island by approximately 125 years. Extant documentary evidence suggests that St. Anne was introduced to the Mi'kmaq as early as 1629 when Jesuit Father Barthélmey Vimont dedicated the first chapel at Fort St. Anne in Cape Breton to St. Anne d'Apt (Chute 1992: 51; Johnston 1960: 8–9; MacPherson 1910: 59). Historian A. A. Johnston claims that it was "Father Vimont who first planted in the heart of the Micmac Indians the tender love they have for Mary and her mother, and this devotion led them to dedicate most of their later chapels in honour of St. Anne" (Johnston 1960: 9).

As anthropologist/ethnohistorian Janet Elizabeth Chute notes, by the 1730s when Fr. Maillard arrived in Cape Breton, St. Anne had taken on additional symbolic meanings associated with the Mi'kmaw mythic character of "Grandmother Bear" or "Bearwoman." Chute suggests that "[b]earwoman's capabilities, which underline the need to respect the potential for healing and renewal in even the old and incapacitated, bear close associations with the revitalizing powers ascribed by the Micmac to St. Anne, who aids infants, the elderly and mothers in child-birth" (Chute 1992: 52–53). However, in the late 1990s within Mi'kmaw society there was no longer any close connection made between the role of the bear (*muin*)[2] figure and that of St. Anne. Currently St. Anne is viewed as *ki'ju,* to whom the Mi'kmaq pray for protection and healing.

This photo, taken at Potlotek in 1997, shows the statue of St. Anne carried in the annual procession. Note the handcrafted adornments for the *wkutputin* (carrier) and the capes worn by St. Anne and the child Mary. *Photo: Angela Robinson*

For the Mi'kmaq, that St. Anne is the mother of Mary is less significant than her relationship to Jesus. The fact that St. Anne is *ki'ju*, or a grandmother, resonates within Mi'kmaw culture because of the elevated familial role extended to ki'ju within Mi'kmaw society. As progenitor of the family, ki'ju is given special status as the protector and giver of life. She is also looked upon as a provider of spiritual and physical nourishment and as a source of wisdom and knowledge. The attributes ascribed to ki'ju within the family unit are also ascribed to St. Anne. As patron saint and ki'ju to the Mi'kmaq she is appealed to for guidance and for thaumaturgic (healing through miraculous acts) aid in matters of emotional, spiritual, and physical healing.

Pilgrimage to St. Anne for the purpose of healing or appealing for special favours has a long history among the Mi'kmaq:

> They [the Mi'kmaq] make often pilgrimages in honour of St. Anne. When they are in great danger on the sea in their canoe, or in the winter hunting in the woods, or to obtain the grace of baptism for a child not yet born, or to be restored to health, or to obtain some other favours from heaven through the intercession of St. Anne, they make a vow to visit one of the places where she is honoured, and to offer some presents in that place. I saw an Indian who was very sick and given up by all. He made a vow to St. Anne in Canada, if God would restore him to health. His petition was granted, and he walked all the way to Canada and back. In general, they make the vow to go to the Indian Island, C. B., [Cape Breton] and to other chapels, and also to places where crosses are erected.
>
> *([Kauder ?] 1868: 239)*[3]

The sacredness attached to the bread, water, and cloth received at Se'tta'newimk is an affirmation of the healing powers the Mi'kmaq attribute to St. Anne. These religious items are usually stored and are only used when someone is in need of healing. The following testimonials and personal narratives provided by Mi'kmaw pilgrimage participants attest to the efficacy of prayer to St. Anne. One woman said that she has attended the mission "for as long as I can remember" and places great faith in St. Anne's ability to help the sick. She has first-hand knowledge of this ability, as she firmly believes St. Anne cured her son:

> My son was born in July ten days before St. Anne's. It was the oddest thing, the boy didn't cry. I had someone stay up with him all the time. He mewled, but couldn't cry. I was afraid he would choke . . . My son didn't cry for a long time, so I took him to Chapel Island. I took him to St. Anne on Saturday evening and washed him with the cloth that the statue was washed in. The next day I took him to the St. Anne's Day mass and prayed for him. On Monday he began to cry. It's too bad in a way because he hasn't shut up since.
>
> *(Fieldnotes, Book I: 35–36)*

A young man in his early 40s also told me that he has "never missed a mission" since he was cured by St. Anne more than 30 years ago:

> When I was a young boy I used to have seizures, or fits, you know. I had them for a long time until I was seven or eight years old. My mother took me to the doctors but

they could not stop them. One time she took me to St. Anne's, I was about eight then. She prayed for me and asked St. Anne for a cure. I had one more seizure when I was on the island and I never had one after. I believe St. Anne cured me.

(Fieldnotes, 1997)

An elder from Eskasoni, now in her mid-80s, also told me about the healing powers of St. Anne:

St. Anne is good to the Indian people. She is special to us and she helps us ... I remember one time at Chapel Island when I was much younger, the men brought over a man for the Mission. There were no wheelchairs at the time so the men put two pieces of two by four under a wood chair and carried him that way. The man was very sick and couldn't walk. They carried the man to the church and put him in front of St. Anne. The man was carried into the church, but he walked out. No one could believe it ... I was there. I saw it!

(Fieldnotes, Book IV: 567–68)

One Mi'kmaw woman describes St. Anne in the following manner: "St. Anne is an elder. Elders give us knowledge, wisdom and care ... She is also a grandmother. The grandmother holds the family together" (Fieldnotes, Book I: 19, 21). While the grandmother "holds the family together," there is a real sense in which, as ki'ju, St. Anne is a symbol of Mi'kmaw group solidarity for Catholics. However, among non-Catholic Mi'kmaq, the significance of St. Anne is open to dispute.

SE'TTA'NEWIMK (ST. ANNE'S MISSION): TRAVEL TO POTLOTEK

The spring and summer seasons are, for many Mi'kmaq, a time of travel. Throughout Mi'kma'ki, groups of Mi'kmaq congregate at formal and informal gatherings to participate in feasts, powwows, clan gatherings, and, especially, pilgrimages. Each year, hundreds of Mi'kmaq make pilgrimages to various shrines, including Sainte-Anne-de-Beaupré[4] in Quebec, the Virgin of Guadalupe in Mexico, and Medjugorje in Bosnia-Herzegovina. In addition to these well-known locations, there is a local Mi'kmaw pilgrimage every Good Friday at Eskasoni. One of the most notable features of the Eskasoni landscape is the prominent 15-foot cross situated at the top of Holy Mountain, sometimes referred to as Poulette's Mountain (Schmidt and Marshall 1995: 1). The original cross was erected by Fr. Placide, a Capuchin priest who was missionary to the Mi'kmaq from 1915 to 1941. Fr. Placide began the pilgrimages "up the mountain" and in 1922, on the feast day of the Holy Cross, erected a cross at the top ([Kauder ?] 1868). The climb up the mountain is primarily a Catholic devotion. Beginning at sunrise, residents of Eskasoni and Mi'kmaq from nearby communities begin the trek up the mountain, stopping periodically to pray at the Stations of the Cross (*Glotjeioie Aogtigtog*) located along the way. The climb up the mountain is intended to replicate Jesus' journey to Calvary.

However, the most important and popular pilgrimage undertaken by the Mi'kmaq of Cape Breton is to the local site of Se'tta'newimk, or St. Anne's Mission, at Potlotek (Chapel Island). In late July between 3500 to 4500 Mi'kmaq travel to Potlotek to attend the annual

Se'tta'newimk, which is held on July 26, the feast day of St. Anne, or on the following Sunday.

For most Mi'kmaq Se'tta'newimk, also referred to as "the mission," is the focal point of Mi'kmaw summer gatherings. With the possible exception of Treaty Day, Se'tta'newimk is by far the most important and well-attended event on the Mi'kmaw calendar. St. Anne's Mission, rather than being a strictly religious celebration as the name implies, is significant in a number of ways for Mi'kmaw Catholics, Catholic-Traditionalists, and non-Catholics alike.

Box 5.1	Treaty Day

Treaty Day began in 1986 and is an event of political, social, and cultural significance for most Mi'kmaq. Each year on October 1, regional Band Chiefs and Grand Council leaders meet with government representatives in the Nova Scotia legislature to renew treaty agreements and to discuss the significant events of the past year. There are numerous social and cultural activities associated with Treaty Day, such as concerts featuring Mi'kmaw musicians, special museum exhibits, and an annual dinner ("feast"), with venues provided for the exhibition and sale of Mi'kmaw arts and crafts at most events.

The official St. Anne's Mission at Potlotek runs each year for approximately one week, usually at the end of July and the beginning of August. The Potlotek mission is not the only St. Anne's celebration within Mi'kma'ki. There are similar but smaller and much less elaborate celebrations held in other Mi'kmaw communities. For instance, the community of Membertou commemorates St. Anne's Day on the Sunday prior to the Potlotek celebration. The communities of Conne River (Newfoundland), Restigouche (Quebec), Big Cove (New Brunswick), Shubenacadie (Nova Scotia), and Lennox Island (PEI) also hold St. Anne's festivals. However, the mission at Chapel Island is the largest celebration and is considered the oldest. It is the one that all members of the Grand Council are expected to attend. Since Se'tta'newimk attracts about half of the Aboriginal population of Cape Breton (3500–4500 people out of approximately 8000 resident Mi'kmaq), it is identifiably one of the most significant events for the Mi'kmaw people. Although the Se'tta'newimk celebration is attended primarily by the Mi'kmaq of Cape Breton, many Mi'kmaq who no longer reside in the area return each year for the gathering. In addition, Mi'kmaq from other provinces also attend, especially members of the Sante' Mawio'mi, which comprises representative members from Mi'kmaw communities throughout Mi'kma'ki. This chapter explores the meanings of Se'tta'newimk for the Mi'kmaq.

THEORETICAL PERSPECTIVES ON PILGRIMAGE AND SE'TTA'NEWIMK AT POTLOTEK

The Mi'kmaw practice of pilgrimage is considered here in the framework of two distinct, yet related, sets of theoretical literature. The first set, applicable to the distinctiveness of Mi'kmaw Catholicism in general, serves to identify this particular form of religious expression as an example of "vernacular," "local," "popular," or "folk" religion (Badone 1990; Barker 1998; Christian 1987, 1981; Freeman 1978; Riegelhaupt 1973).

Research on the role of popular forms of Aboriginal–Christian religious expression has been limited, essentially because such work usually demands interdisciplinary skills and because these forms of religious expression are not contained under the rubric of mainstream ritual practice. Canadian anthropologist John Barker suggests that, in North America, contemporary forms of "vernacular" Christian expression may be obscured by an overemphasis on "standard mission histories and biographies and occasional anthropological studies of acculturation" (Barker 1998: 433). However, the theoretical frameworks developed by anthropologists working on popular, local, and grass roots forms of Catholicism in Central America, rural Europe, and Asia can usefully be applied to the Mi'kmaw case (Badone 1990; Behar 1990; Brandes 1976; Christian 1996, 1992, 1991, 1987, 1984, 1981a; Davis 1974; Freeman 1978). Researchers dealing with such expressions of local Catholicism have established a clear distinction between "religion as practised" and "religion as prescribed" (formal church dogma) in order to understand the complexities of contemporary Catholic practice (Christian 1981a; see also Badone 1990; Behar 1990; Brandes 1976; Freeman 1978; Davis 1974; Miller 1997). This distinction is pertinent to Se'tta'newimk, because Mi'kmaw Catholicism is understood both by participants and nonparticipants to be a local form of Catholic expression (Henderson 1997: 102; Battiste 1997a: 17; Marshall 1995: 109; Milliea 1989: 263).

The second set of theoretical literature relevant to Se'tta'newimk includes anthropological studies relating to the function and meaning of pilgrimage. The particular theoretical approaches considered are those of Victor and Edith Turner 1978; John Eade and Michael Sallnow 1991; Simon Coleman and John Elsner 1995; Jill Dubisch 1995; and Alan Morinis 1992.

Victor Turner suggests that the pilgrimage process exhibits identifiable characteristics of **liminality** and **communitas.** According to this perspective, participants symbolically leave behind ordinary social structure and are caught between two different social worlds (1995 [1969]: 107). This movement from structure to antistructure brings with it a dismissal of the stasis that usually accompanies "normal" existence and includes a re-evaluation of the social constructs and norms associated with the usual day-to-day aspects of life (Turner and Turner 1978: 2,13).

Simon Coleman and John Elsner recognize that commonly held definitions of pilgrimage impose limitations on the meaning and significance of ritual travel. They maintain that pilgrimage is a cultural and social phenomenon that cannot necessarily be restricted to sacred/religious categories (1995: 214). Coleman and Elsner suggest that any form of visit that contains elements of spatial and temporal dislocation (i.e., travelling across physical space and across time) shares structural similarities with pilgrimage. Therefore, a visit to a museum or to an exotic destination may "serve as a licence for experiment and self-discovery" and may offer similar experiences to those found on more traditional pilgrimages (1995: 214). Essentially, Coleman and Elsner expand on former definitions of pilgrimage by suggesting that the types of travel associated with trade, vacations, and social gatherings may represent forms of pilgrimage.

The pilgrimage site determines the diverse motives behind pilgrimage participation. As several anthropologists have suggested, there can be multiple, overlapping, sacred, and secular motivations for participation in such ritual gatherings (Coleman and Elsner 1995; Dusenberry 1962; Eade and Sallnow 1991; Morinis 1992; Turner and Turner 1978).

These theories of pilgrimage represent two approaches. The first is the Turnerian model, which emphasizes liminality and communitas as the essence of pilgrimage. The second approach allows for broader contextual considerations. It is one in which differences in the meaning and significance of ritual journeys can be uncovered and assessed (Coleman and Elsner 1995; Dubisch 1995; Eade and Sallnow 1991; Morinis 1992). The theoretical position assumed in this chapter accommodates both perspectives. Following Dubisch, the notions of liminality and communitas are considered dimensions of pilgrimage rather than central features (Dubisch 1995: 45). My analysis of Se'tta'newimk also takes into account the specific cultural, political, and historical contexts in which the pilgrimage events at Potlotek are set. This analysis also highlights a number of competing views surrounding these events. In addition, I will consider the possibility that for some (if not all) participants the annual visit to Potlotek has more than a single meaning or purpose. Se'tta'newimk participants represent a broad cross-section of Mi'kmaw society. Participants range from newborn infants to the elderly, from the poor to the wealthy, from the less-educated to the well-educated, and from those who hold significant political and social positions in the Mi'kmaw community to those who have no officially recognized social or political status. Accordingly, it is assumed here that there are multiple discourses about Se'tta'newimk, rather than one dominant and deterministic (specifically directed) discourse. And they each contribute to the meaning and significance of St. Anne's Mission at various interpretative levels.

POTLOTEK: SACRED LAND

Most Mi'kmaq attach historical, social, and cultural significance to the island of Potlotek. Potlotek, located on Bras D'Or Lake, is a short ferry ride from the main part of Cape Breton. Pilgrims arrive singly and in groups during the week prior to St. Anne's Day, as well as on the day itself, to participate in a variety of activities. Religiously oriented activities include the veneration of St. Anne, through the preparation of her statue and participation in the St. Anne's Day procession, novenas, rosaries, confessions, and special masses. Socially oriented events include playing cards and bingo, sharing meals, and socializing with family and friends.

According to Mi'kmaw oral historians, prior to becoming the official venue for Se'tta'newimk in 1742, Potlotek was the site of premissionary Mi'kmaw gatherings[5] (Battiste 1997a: 17; Chute 1992: 53). Mi'kmaq Will Basque maintains that, before Catholicism, the annual gathering at Potlotek "was already a spiritual gathering, so it was an ideal opportunity for the Church. Both sides were able to integrate the faith with traditional Micmac faith" (1995: 276). One respondent told me that "the missionaries took advantage of the [Mi'kmaw] sense of community and introduced St. Anne's Day into an already existing event" (Fieldnotes, Book I: 12).

When Maillard began his mission to the Mi'kmaq in 1735, he resided alternatively at Malagawatch (currently uninhabited) during the spring and summer seasons and at the Fortress of Louisburg during the fall and winter. Oral tradition suggests that at the time of Maillard's residency Malagawatch was recognized as the centre, or "capital," of Mi'kma'ki (personal communication). Around the year 1742, in the midst of British-French hostilities, Maillard relocated the "capital" of Mi'kma'ki territory (Hoffman 1946) from Malagawatch to Potlotek and established St. Anne's Mission on the island. One possible incentive for the relocation may have been for reasons of security. Malagawatch is located on a small, low-lying peninsula that juts into the Bras D'Or Lakes with no elevated land for use as sentinel points. An approaching enemy could easily take advantage of this location by cutting off the single entrance to the site. However, the island of Potlotek has several advantageous features. As an island it can only be approached by water. It has several elevations that can be used for lookout points. One woman told me that the church at Potlotek was built on a hill so that "we [the Mi'kmaq] could see the enemy approaching" (personal communication). It is unclear whether or not St. Anne's Day celebrations took place at Malagawatch. However, several people suggested that historically Malagawatch was the official burial site for the Mi'kmaq and was also the centre where Catholic Mi'kmaq congregated during the spring and summer. This would in part explain why Maillard took up residence at the Malagawatch location.

During the 1980s a resident of Eskasoni, Noel Denny, sought to preserve the Malagawatch site. Through the personal efforts of the Denny family and several other members of the Eskasoni community, a stone cross and a stone tepee-style altar were erected at Malagawatch. At the end of the summer, usually in late August, Mi'kmaw Catholics gather at Malagawatch to attend Mass and to share in a communal meal hosted by the Denny family. The Mass is held in the graveyard where the cross and altar have been erected. The fact that many Mi'kmaq have ancestors buried at Malagawatch gives added significance to the location. However, interments are no longer carried out at this site (personal observations).

Potlotek is regarded as sacred by Catholic and non-Catholic Mi'kmaq alike, who separate it, physically and conceptually, from the everyday world. However, for members of each of these two groups, the sacredness of Potlotek derives from different sets of criteria. And it is a contested site. That the site is now the location for specifically Catholic religious functions represents a point of contention for some non-Catholic Mi'kmaq. On my first trip to Potlotek, I learned that a particular group of Mi'kmaq had requested permission to hold a powwow on the island during the mission. The Grand Council considered this proposal but refused the group access to the site (Fieldnotes, 1997).

Non-Catholic Mi'kmaq assert their claim to Potlotek on the basis that it was always a sacred site. Among the Mi'kmaq, it is generally believed that prior to and after European contact both Potlotek and Malagawatch were preferred areas for annual assembly. Political, economic, and social matters were said to have been discussed, and ritual celebrations and religious ceremonies such as weddings and burials took place. One non-Catholic man told me that he was certain that there were multiple burial sites on Potlotek and that "before the French, it [Potlotek] was always a sacred site. Could be a thousand years old, could be more than that. Actually, could be more than ten thousand years old" (taped interview). Another non-Catholic man agreed:

> I go to Potlotek every year and usually a few heads turn, ha! ... I go, but not for St. Anne's. I go because it's part of family tradition and it's social. The island belongs to my people—has always belonged to my people long before the Catholics came. So, that's why I go, because of my ancestors.
>
> *(Fieldnotes, Book IV: 741)*

Some Mi'kmaq believe that the spirits of the ancestors remain at Potlotek. One pilgrimage participant, a Catholic woman from Eskasoni, told me that the "old ones" (ancestors) sometimes appear on the island: "When [my husband] and some other men were working on the church, they heard the 'old ones'...paddling. I heard of this before but I was not sure of it until [my husband] told me about it" (Fieldnotes, Book II: 327).

While partisan sectors of Mi'kmaw society are unified in accepting the site as sacred, fundamental disagreements exist about the reasons for its sacredness. It is sacred to Mi'k-maw Catholics because it is the site of St. Anne's Mission, but it is also sacred to many Mi'kmaq who believe that the island was important to their ancestors. Since the mid-18th century the island of Potlotek has emerged, on one level, as a sacred space central to Mi'k-maw spiritual revitalization and social solidarity. On another level, it serves as a locus of dispute, since many non-Catholic Mi'kmaq reject Catholicism as a legitimate form of Mi'kmaw religious expression. In line with those theoretical approaches to pilgrimage that emphasize multiple discourses, Potlotek may be understood as both a centre of unity and of conflict within the Mi'kmaw community (cf. Coleman and Elsner 1995; Eade and Sallnow 1991).

SE'TTA 'NEWIMK: THE FESTIVITIES

With the possible exception of the Grand Council assembly[6] on St. Anne's Day and the speeches immediately following St. Anne's procession, formal activities at Potlotek are primarily devoted to religious observances. The schedule of events distributed to mission participants outlines the date and time of the various devotional events to take place on the island. The schedule also refers to specific amusements—such as games of *waltes* (a traditional game involving a bowl, six dice, and 55 counting sticks), bingo, horseshoes, and karaoke competitions—that are held during the mission, but these diversions are not promoted as central features of St. Anne's Mission.

On St. Anne's eve, the mood on the island is one of excitement. Exchanges of greetings, the sharing of food, and the renewal of old friendships and the forging of new ones add to the festivity of the occasion. There are large numbers of people on the island by Saturday evening, but not nearly as many as there will be on St. Anne's Day. It is common to see friends and family embracing each other, talking and laughing. People congregate in groups and catch up on the past year's news. Many more work together to prepare for the Sunday gathering. Every family provides more food than they can eat, and whatever is available is freely given. Some of the visitors to the island come from distant towns, cities, provinces, and countries. Many have made the trip home to coincide with the mission.

Like all social events held by the Mi'kmaq, people of all ages attend the mission. Parents encourage their children to attend. One woman told me the following:

> The [Catholic] faith is important to me and my family . . . I don't make too many demands on my children, but I insist they come to St. Anne's . . . It is very important for the Mi'kmaq to come to the mission. It revives your religion. Potlotek is heaven on earth for many Mi'kmaw people. We come here and if at all possible, try not to move off the island. Some people can't do that because they do not have the ability. They have to go for water, showers and food, but some of us have everything we need.

> *(Fieldnotes, Book II: 323)*

As "heaven on earth," Potlotek implies a dichotomy between inclusive and exclusive domains of the sacred. While Potlotek is considered "sacred" ground, the mainland side of the camping area, or "the other side," is very much a part of the ordinary world. In the nearby mainland community of Chapel Island, a number of tepees mark the site for non-religious activities, such as a children's pageant and other sorts of amusement. According to

Tord Larsen, they were once part of St. Anne's celebrations on the island (Larsen 1983: 113–14). Most older adults and the elders do not participate in the festivities off the island. They restrict their entertainment to social activities, such as sharing company with friends and family at Potlotek and playing cards and bingo. On "the other side" there are numerous recreational vehicles and campers with amenities such as showers and baths. Some of those who own RVs also have cabins on the island and choose to stay on Potlotek, making periodic visits to "the other side." For health reasons, some people find it difficult to move on and off the island, so those who wish to be a part of the mission choose to stay in the more comfortable accommodations available on the mainland. However, many people do not stay on the mainland side because teenagers and young adults tend to "party" during the mission. Most parents and elders do not approve of such behaviour and the island remains "dry" at all times. Alcohol and recreational drugs are strictly forbidden.

During the mission, the church at Potlotek is rarely empty. Throughout the day and long into the night, Mi'kmaw people go to the church for personal prayer or to attend the various services such as evening Mass, the rosary, or special services provided during the mission. Special services associated with Se'tta'newimk begin on the eve of St. Anne's Day with the preparation of her statue. They end on the Monday following "Procession Day" with the Stations of the Cross and special Prayers for the Living and the Dead. Once St. Anne's statue is prepared for the Sunday procession, visits to the church increase. On Saturday night, people go to pay their respects to St. Anne. Many stop to say prayers. Each person who visits the church kneels at the statue with head bowed, often touching or kissing the statue after prayers are said. These are inaudible personal prayers, invocations to St. Anne requesting personal favours for family members and loved ones, especially those who are ill or who have passed away.

The afternoon of St. Anne's eve is a special time for women attending the mission. In the early afternoon the priest offers a special blessing for women who have given birth. The church is usually full at this time, since all mothers, old and new, come to receive blessings

---

Box 5.2	The Churching of Women

The "churching of women" is the "name of the rite that invokes God's blessing on a woman after childbirth, probably having its origin in Jewish purification rites (cf: Lv 12:1 and Lk 2:22–24)" (*Catholic Encyclopaedia* 1991: 218). This was common practice in the Catholic Church until the latter part of the 20th century. At that time, "churching" was replaced with a new rite found in the Catholic *Book of Blessings* emphasizing "the dignity of women, who, like Our Lady, give new life, so great a gift to the world" (*Catholic Encyclopaedia* 1991: 218). The blessing of women rite held annu-ally at Potlotek probably goes back to the time when the mission was the only time that women could be properly "churched" by an officiating priest. An 1868 author (possibly Christian Kauder) notes that Mi'kmaw women were careful to partake in the Catholic ritual for postpartum benediction: "the hieroglyphical book of rites which they possess tells the woman that [after giving birth] they have to receive the churching before confession," otherwise if a woman dies without having received this special benediction "she cannot enter heaven" ([Kauder ?]1868: 244–45).

for themselves and their children. After the blessing of the women the priest leaves, and the women are given possession of the church while St. Anne's statue is being prepared. At this time no men are allowed on the church premises. Members of St. Anne's security are posted just outside the doors to ensure that the women are not interrupted in their duties.

Confessions are held throughout the week of the mission. Each evening before Mass, there is a recitation of the rosary. However, on St. Anne's eve liturgical celebrations have the added elements of invocations for the sick and the benediction of the Blessed Sacrament, which is exposed for an hour after Mass. The Benediction of the Blessed Sacrament and the Stations of the Cross are liturgical practices typically associated with Easter within mainstream Catholicism. The inclusion of these two rituals as regularly scheduled features of St. Anne's Mission probably originated during the period the Mi'kmaq relied on itinerant missionaries to perform "official" religious services, and Easter duty was included as part of the mission.

On St. Anne's Day, Potlotek is bustling with activity. Although many family "feasts" have been prepared in advance, there is much to be done. St. Anne's Day is considered a formal occasion for many Mi'kmaq. Most make an effort to look their best on this special day. Children are washed and groomed, and many people have purchased new outfits. Some are dressed in traditional Mi'kmaw dress, or "regalia." The wearing of Mi'kmaw regalia has regained popularity in recent years. Some of the men wear ribbon shirts and the women wear ribbon skirts with beaded accessories, such as the traditional pointed cap, **wijipoti**, and various types of jewellery and hair adornments. Besides the obvious Aboriginal attire, personal religious jewellery, such as medals and crosses, are also quite common.

Box 5.3	Wearing the Regalia

Wilson D. Wallis points out that the regalia once worn by the Mi'kmaq at Se'tta'newimk went out of style in the decades following World War II. Mi'kmaq youth no longer took pride in wearing the beaded frock coat and sashes, men and women discarded the peaked beaded caps, ceremonial skirts, and beaded bodices in favour of more fashionable attire (Wallis and Wallis 1955). Similarly, anthropologist Harald E. Prins notes that although the Mi'kmaq continue to observe this annual celebration, "by the early 1960s ... the gathering had lost much of its ceremonial character. Even at Chapel Island, a Cape Breton bastion of Mi'kmaq conservatism," participants no longer wore traditional dress or carried out many of the rituals that were once central to the event (1996: 204). However, anthropologist Elsie Clews Parsons notes that the wearing of regalia was not common in the 1920s. Parsons observes the following:

> [The Mi'kmaq at Potlotek] greatly admired the oldtime coat from Prince Edward Island, likewise the oldtime pointed cap and dress worn by the chief's wife, the only complete costuming from antiquity on the Island. Two or three women at different times wore the full skirt and the jacket with "braces" down the front, and at the war dance one woman wore her hair in braids, but the braids, instead of falling either side in front, were fastened behind, a fashion started about forty years ago.

(1926: 467)

Church services begin early on St. Anne's Day. At 11:00 in the morning there is a General Absolution Service for the Sacrament of Penance followed by a short break before the official procession begins. The church is decorated specifically for St. Anne's Day. Alongside the regular statuary and liturgical decorations, the altar is embellished with arrangements of cut and potted flowers. To the left and right of the altar are two large baskets of bread. The blessing of the bread begins the main event of the St. Anne's Day procession. People congregate in the church and outside while the blessing is taking place. The church is far too small to accommodate all those present, so it is usually reserved for elders, the sick, and those who are to participate in the procession. Most members of the Grand Council are in attendance along with representatives from the Knights of Columbus, a Catholic fraternal benefit society (a recent addition beginning in 1997). The Catholic Church is also well represented at the mission. The diocesan bishop normally attends this function as do a number of parish priests, who serve the different Mi'kmaw communities throughout Mi'kma'ki.

With the exception of the bearers of St. Anne's statue and the chief of security, all members participating in the procession make their way to the outdoor altar just outside the church. St. Anne's statue remains inside the church until Mass is over and the formal procession begins. The clergy, key members of the Grand Council, and the choir are seated on the outdoor altar. All remaining mission participants congregate on the grounds in front of the altar to hear Mass.

The choir is central to St. Anne's Day celebrations, because singing many of the hymns in Mi'kmaq is considered part of traditional practice. The St. Anne's Day Mass is *Mesgig Alames* ("High Mass"), overseen by the officiating priest and visiting Catholic clergy. Before the close of the Mass, officials of the Grand Council announce the appointment of new members to the council.[7] Once announcements have been made, communion has been dispensed, and the closing prayers have been said, the blessed bread is distributed among the congregation. People who are ill may consume their portion, while most others reserve the bread for future use.

Immediately after Mass the church bell tolls to announce the beginning of the main procession. The members of the procession take their respective positions and move toward the church. The order of the procession is as follows: flower bearer (who strews wild rose petals in front of the procession); cross bearer; flag carriers; St. Anne and her bearers; First Communion girls; church representatives (priests and bishop); Kji-saqamaw, Kji-keptin, and *Putus ("wampum keeper")*[8]; Keptins; choir; and pilgrimage participants. The Knights of Columbus flank the procession.

On St. Anne's Day, attending members of the Grand Council are easily recognized by their attire. Each member wears a coloured sash that designates his or her specific position within the council: Kji-saqamaw (Grand Chief) in royal blue/white; Kji-keptin (Grand Captain) in deep yellow/white; Putus (Wampum Keeper) in pale yellow/white; secondary Keptins in pale blue/white; St. Anne's bearers in dark green/white; chief of security in red/white; cross bearer, St. Anne's security, bread servers in red; flag carriers in pink; and choir members in pale yellow. In addition, the Kji-saqamaw wears a special medallion that was presented to him upon taking up this special office within the Grand Council. Girls who have recently received their First Holy Communion also participate in the procession. Many wear white lace and satin dresses, while others wear white deerskin dresses embroidered with Mi'kmaw double curve motifs and beadwork. The flag bearers and members of the choir are also variously dressed. Some choose to wear handcrafted Mi'kmaw attire, while others wear common dress. In addition, members of the procession as well as many pilgrimage participants accessorize their outfits with jewellery and adornments of Mi'kmaw or other Aboriginal designs.

After the members of the procession leave the main outdoor altar, St. Anne's statue is carried out of the church to join with the procession. The procession moves in a counter-clockwise direction around the church and then slowly moves along "St. Anne's Way," which is a grassy incline bordered on both left and right with flags bearing the symbol of a red cross upon a white background. "St. Anne's Way" is considered to be sacred ground and is an area that is kept clean and well manicured at all times. As the procession moves up the hill, people are careful not to cross in front of the procession. To do so is considered disrespectful to St. Anne.

At the top of the incline, the procession passes through an arch fashioned from bowed saplings, green boughs, and flowers. The procession then pauses near a rock and a cement basin at the site where Maillard reportedly offered the first Mass on the island. Some local Mi'kmaw historians note that at Potlotek the location of the rock where the first Mass was said was once the site of Mi'kmaw council fires (personal communication). The water in the basin is blessed, and a short prayer is said. Then the clergy, Kji-saqamaw, and Kji-keptin advance to a small outdoor stage, overlooking St. Anne's Way, to address pilgrimage participants.

The clergy typically pray for the deceased and offer special prayers for those who are ill. However, the content of the greetings and messages given by Grand Council members is not restricted to specifically religious matters. Public addresses made by members of the Grand Council at Se'tta'newimk are in keeping with longstanding Mi'kmaw tradition. It is believed

The rock and crucifix mark the site where Fr. Maillard is believed to have said the first Catholic Mass at Potlotek. The white concrete basin in the foreground is where water is blessed and dispensed on St. Anne's Day. *Photo: Angela Robinson, 1999*

that Mi'kmaw biannual assemblies of district and local chiefs served to address "matters of treaties and alliances, trade, births, deaths, marriages and the general welfare of the people . . . " (McMillan 1996: 40). Jesuit missionary Father Biard wrote the following:

> It is principally in summer that they [Mi'kmaq] pay visits and hold their State Councils; I mean that several Sagamores [chiefs] come together and consult among themselves about peace and war, treaties of friendship and treaties for the common good. It is only these Sagamores who have a voice in the discussion and who make the speeches.

> *(Thwaites, JR 3: 93)*

Traditionally, during Mi'kmaw summer gatherings band leaders and elders made important social, political, and economic decisions. Parsons notes that Grand Council assemblies once made up a significant portion of the mission period and a special day, separate from the St. Anne's Day celebrations, was allocated for the council's special assembly (Parsons 1926).

The commentaries made by the Kji-saqamaw and Kji-keptin may address any number of topics of social, cultural, or political relevance to the Mi'kmaq. For instance, the address given by Kji-saqamaw Sylliboy in 1999 emphasized the need for parents to take special care of their children. Kji-keptin Denny's remarks were directed at combatting the continued social, cultural, and political inequalities with which the Mi'kmaw people are continually confronted. The current Kji-keptin, Alex Denny, is well aware of the traditional role of the Kji-keptin, who in former times was responsible for the social and political welfare of his people.

After the public address, the procession moves back down the hill. After the procession makes a clockwise circle of the church, the members of the procession enter the church and St. Anne is restored to her position to the right of the altar. The Kji-saqamaw and the officiating priest then take up positions in front of the altar and wait to receive the large number of pilgrimage participants who have formed a line outside the church. The priest holds a relic of St. Anne and the Kji-saqamaw holds a Grand Council medal received upon his initiation into the office of Kji-saqamaw. People now enter the church in double file. Upon approaching the altar, they kiss both the relic and the Kji-saqamaw's medal. This is a significant gesture as it marks equally the importance of St. Anne as the patron saint of the Mi'kmaq and the Kji-saqamaw as a spiritual leader. After the religious observations of St. Anne's Day are completed, Grand Council members assemble at the church to hold their main meeting of the year. The end of the council meeting signals the closing of the St. Anne's Day celebrations.

By the official close of the mission on the Monday after the St. Anne's procession, many people have left Potlotek. For those who have full-time employment, Monday is the beginning of the workweek. In addition, a significant number of young and middle-aged adults leave directly from Potlotek to travel to the potato and blueberry farms in Maine, where many will work as field-hands for the harvest season. As previously mentioned, the work supplied to Mi'kmaw labourers in Maine is often the most meaningful employment that many Mi'kmaq will manage to obtain for the entire year. Some families who work as a group are able to earn several hundred dollars a day. Each day away from the fields means lost wages. Some of those who stay behind at Potlotek will travel to Maine after the official close of the mission.

On Monday, the closing day of the mission, Mass begins at 11:00 a.m. One woman attending the morning Mass explained Monday's sequence of events to me:

> After the Stations of the Cross we come back to the church. A man has to enter first and the Chief of Security makes sure there is no one in the church. Then money is paid and prayers are requested for families, the sick and those who have just died. After the money is collected and the list is made out the list is read, then we enter the church on our knees. You don't have to go on your knees until you reach the knave.

> *(Fieldnotes, Book II: 370)*

Directly after the morning Mass, the Stations of the Cross begin, led by the cross bearer, the officiating priest of the mission, and several members of the choir. The steps along "St. Anne's Way" are retraced for the Stations of the Cross. Upon approaching each of the 12 stations, the priest announces the station and says a short prayer, after which a hymn "*O Sapeoin Ana*" ("Good St. Anne") is sung in Mi'kmaq. After the Stations of the Cross are completed, most participants gather at the front of the church where a Grand Council representative collects money for the special prayer service dedicated to the Living and the Dead. As mentioned, prayers are requested in honour of family members, deceased and living, with special mention given to those who are ill. Those offering pledges usually donate a small amount of money (from $2.00 to $20.00), which is subsequently used for expenses associated with the mission. After the list is prepared and read, those in attendance line up outside the church. Upon entering the door of the church, they fall to their knees. People continue two abreast on their knees to the altar, where they kiss St. Anne's statue. This act of supplication is believed to add to the effectiveness of the prayers being offered. Parsons stated that the Mi'kmaq believed that if you had "'a strong heart, a pure heart, any sickness you have is sure to be cured 'by going to see St. Anne on your knees'" (1926: 468) After prayers are said to St. Anne for the benefit of the ill and recently deceased, the annual Se'tta'newimk gathering is officially finished.

Today, there are fewer people (300 to 400, which is approximately 10 percent of the number of people attending the St. Anne's Day procession) participating in the Monday ritual. However, the low attendance rate does not detract from the significance of this particular religious service. Many of those present are family representatives entrusted with the responsibility of carrying out a family duty, to ensure that deceased, ill, or dying family members and loved ones receive the benefit of healing prayer.

Historically, St. Anne's celebrations provided a number of religious services that are no longer central features of the mission. Prior to the installation of priests in local parishes, Potlotek was perhaps the only time that many Mi'kmaq saw a priest for the entire year. It was during the mission that certain sacraments or rituals such as marriage, first communion, confirmation, baptism, and the churching of new mothers were carried out. However, since all Mi'kmaw communities now have the regular services of an ordained priest, the performance of such rituals at Potlotek is no longer necessary. By the latter part of the 20th century, marriages were no longer performed on the island, and first communion and confirmation services were made available within local parishes. On rare occasions baptisms are still performed.

At the turn of the 21st century, the religious services and devotional practices observed at Potlotek are less concerned with rites of passage and the receiving of sacraments and are more focused on the figure of St. Anne as benefactress of the Mi'kmaq. Since most religious observances are directly related to sickness, death, and healing, the religious context for the

Potlotek mission can be accurately described as *doulia*, a Greek word referring to devotion in honour of a saint.

THE SIGNIFICANCE OF SE'TTA'NEWIMK

Se'tta'newimk is promoted as a time of reflection, friendship, and prayer. Although many people view St. Anne's as religiously meaningful, travel to Potlotek is multipurpose. For most Catholics and Catholic Traditionalists, in addition to being religiously significant, the mission has a number of important social, cultural, and historical dimensions. Potlotek also has the liminal aspect of being set apart from the rigours and routine of everyday life. Quite a number of the families who own large, comfortable cabins on the island move to Potlotek well in advance of the mission, staying as long as three weeks to a month. One resident of Eskasoni told me that she preferred the time leading up to the mission week because "there's less noise and [it's]more relaxing" (Fieldnotes Book II: 238). For many Mi'kmaq, Potlotek is associated with vacation and rest. For those Mi'kmaq who work or live some distance away from Cape Breton, vacation times are often arranged to coincide with the mission. For many local residents, Potlotek is considered a retreat away from home.

Since St. Anne's attracts a large number of people from different demographic groups, the social matrix at Potlotek is complex. Although the religious aspects of the mission are often promoted as a central feature of Se'tta'newimk, this gathering also offers a number of social opportunities for those who attend. For some elders and for others who are unable to travel extensively, Potlotek provides an opportunity to meet friends and acquaintances from around the province or from different provinces and countries. In addition, the younger generation sees Potlotek as an opportunity to spend time with cousins and friends and in some cases even to begin a romance. For others, it is an opportunity to catch up on the past year's news, to welcome the newly born into the community, and to pass condolences along to families who have experienced the loss of a loved one.

To a large degree, the social aspects of St. Anne's contribute to the Mi'kmaw sense of community, which is a principle feature of Mi'kmaw collective identity, inclusive of both Catholics and non-Catholics. One mission participant, Jim, told me the following:

> [O]utside the religious aspect of St. Anne's there are many other things happening. There's sharing of meals, games played (cards, waltes, bingo) and many young people go to find a partner . . . I have no official role at St. Anne's, I'm just part of the rabble, but I've never missed one . . . St Anne's Day is so popular . . . due to the fact that the Mi'kmaw people are given an opportunity to meet. The Mi'kmaq have a great sense of community and the Mission provides a way for this to be expressed.

(Fieldnotes, Book I: 12)

As Jim suggests, St. Anne's Mission provides an ideal context for socializing, where the sharing of food and friendship is central. Most people provide more food than is personally needed in anticipation of the many occasions when refreshments and meals will be shared with visitors. Throughout the mission it is common to see people moving from cabin to cabin visiting one other. Among the Mi'kmaq, it is considered impolite to fail to offer food and refreshments to guests, and it is also considered inappropriate to refuse such offers. During the mission special foods are served, such as family favourites or speciality items that are not eaten on a regular basis. Many people prepare traditional Mi'kmaw dishes, such as baked salmon, stewed eel, and moose roasts, all of which are shared. Baked goods are also plentiful. Homemade cakes, cookies, pies, and *luskinikin* (a local bread) frequently accompany the offer of tea. In many respects, the spirit of giving and sharing associated with the Christmas season within mainstream Christian culture is comparable to the social atmosphere surrounding Se'tta'newimk. In effect, the gathering offers the Mi'kmaq as a group an ideal opportunity to extend generosity and goodwill to one another. Like most Mi'kmaw social events, Potlotek is an arena in which spiritual, emotional, and physical nourishment is in abundance.

Another social aspect of Se'tta'newimk, especially among young Mi'kmaw adults, is that of courtship and marriage. Although marriages are no longer performed on the island, younger people attend the mission to seek out a long-term partner. Historically, the mission was considered the best time to find and secure a mate. Parsons relates that "in one of the exhortations by the Grand Chief at the close of church service he urged parents not to oppose their girls getting married, here was a good chance, with the priest coming: it was 'safest' to let them marry, not to have them around at nights" (Parsons 1926: 460). One woman, now middle-aged, told me that she prayed to St. Anne to "send me a man who loved me for myself—for who I am . . . I continued to pray and finally I met [my husband]. I met [him] at Potlotek and we eloped a few months later . . . This was over twenty years ago and we have been together ever since . . . I thank St. Anne for the man I asked for" (Fieldnotes, Book I: 35). St. Anne's, then, has a special appeal for young marriageable men and women who wish to establish meaningful personal relationships.

CONCLUSION AND DISCUSSION

In many respects, identifying Se'tta'newimk as a strictly religious celebration overlooks the multiplicity of reasons that encourage participation in the event. Essentially, the annual gathering at Potlotek has a dual traditional aspect from which different meanings of sacredness are derived. First, since Potlotek is viewed by Catholic and non-Catholic Mi'kmaq as a sacred precontact gathering site, pilgrimage to the island retains meaning as a continuation of precontact ancestral tradition and patterns of social interaction. Furthermore, the Se't-ta'newimk gathering holds significance as a communal gathering where the sharing of food and friendship is facilitated. The second aspect of pilgrimage, the annual St. Anne's Day procession, holds specifically religious meaning for devotees of St. Anne and for those who accept Catholicism as a meaningful and legitimate traditional religious orientation.

Pilgrimage to Potlotek as an enactment of and a respect for long-standing Mi'kmaw traditions bears similarities to the Lac Ste. Anne pilgrimage of Métis and Cree in Northern Alberta as described by the anthropologist Alan Morinis.[9] Morinis argues that pilgrimages persist through cultural change because the ritual form itself can accommodate new cultural content, and that people continue to seek out the "salving ideal" that stands beyond time and space in sacred places (Morinis 1992: 102). This perspective suggests that although what is believed to constitute the sacred and the ideal may change, these values continue to be perceived as being accessible in special locations "situated beyond the sphere of everyday life" (Morinis 1992: 103).

In Morinis's view the Lac Ste. Anne pilgrimage performed and continues to perform many of the cultural and social functions of the Plains Indians' premissionary summer assemblies (e.g., the Sun Dance). Morinis argues that pilgrimage to Lac Ste. Anne is an extension of premissionary gatherings and that rather than being an exclusively Catholic ceremony, it serves multiple purposes. He sees the Lac Ste. Anne pilgrimage as an occasion in which social interaction, trade, information exchange, and vacationing are facilitated and anticipated (Morinis 1992: 109). Morinis's observations on Lac Ste. Anne can also be applied to the Mi'kmaw case. For non-Catholic as well as for many Catholic Mi'kmaq, Potlotek is viewed as a sacred site because it retains historical and cultural meanings separate from the Christian context in which it is now embedded.

From an ethnographic viewpoint, annual pilgrimage to Potlotek is a complex mosaic of devotionalism, socialization, group solidarity, and conflict. On one hand, Se'tta'newimk can be viewed as a continuation of historically earlier Mi'kmaw summer gatherings in which matters of social, political, economic, and religious significance were addressed. On the other hand, however, the structured and more formal aspects of the mission currently focus on the veneration of St. Anne as ki'ju—the spiritual overseer, patroness, protector, and healer of the Mi'kmaw people.

CONTENT QUESTIONS

1. What are the key theoretical approaches to the study of pilgrimage?

2. Discuss the importance of St. Anne for the Mi'kmaq.

3. Identify and explain the various reasons that attendance at Se'tta'newimk is important.

4. Discuss the significance of Potlotek for the Mi'kmaq.

ENDNOTES

1. The terms *Se'tta'newimk* and *Se'tta'newey* are frequently used as references to St. Anne's Mission. Both of these forms appear in Mi'kmaw spoken and written expression, but *Se'tta'newimk* is the form most commonly used (personal communication). The *k* that appears at the end of *Se'tta'newimk* is a locative ending indicating "at"/"to"/"on." Throughout this book instances of "at"/"to" *Se't-ta'newimk* are often stated, which may appear redundant, but the prepositions "at"/"to" /"on" must be retained in English in compliance with proper grammatical expression and meaning. I have also seen *Se'tta'newimk* referred to as *setonewing*, which, according to my sources, is erroneous.

2. *Muin* or "bear" in Mi'kmaw society is a prominent symbol. The muin clan is associated with the surname of Sylliboy. Each summer a clan gathering is held in Eskasoni where all extended members of the muin clan gather for a communal feast.

3. This excerpt is taken from an article titled "The Micmac Indians: The Catholic Church in the Wilderness" in *The Irish Ecclesiastical Record* XLI, (February 1868). The author of the article is uncertain. However, the bibliographical information notes that the author is possibly Fr. Christian Kauder, who worked among the Mi'kmaq from 1856 to 1871.

4. The shrine of Sainte-Anne-de-Beaupré, located about 48 kilometres north of Quebec City, is a site of healing. Since the first documented miracle cure during the construction of the original church (1657–1662), thousands of pilgrims have been cured at the shrine. The crutches, walking canes, and wheelchairs left at the shrine are testimony to the healing powers of St. Anne. The current Basilica, dedicated in 1876, is the fourth church constructed on the site (Annals, Sainte-Anne-de-Beaupré, 1889: iii-iv).

5. Elizabeth Chute suggests that the missionaries took advantage of Mi'kmaw summer gathering places, and chapels built at these locations eventually became "foci for summer gift-giving, where French authorities distributed presents, medals and commissions to the assembled bands" (1992: 52). In

addition, anthropologists Wallis and Wallis describe St. Anne's Day celebrations as the Mi'kmaw " 'national holiday' which was the union of the aboriginal summer council with the feast of Ste. Anne" (1955: 283).

6. The Grand Council annual St. Anne's Day meetings and addresses to mission attendees by the Kji-keptin (Grand Captain) and Kji-saqamaw (Grand Chief) relate to Mi'kmaw social, political, and cultural concerns as well as religious matters. A comprehensive account of the duties and concerns of the Grand Council is provided in Leslie Jane McMillan's 1996 M.A. thesis titled *"Mi'kmawey Mawio'mi*: Changing Roles of the Mi'kmaq Grand Council from the Early Seventeenth Century to the Present."

7. Each year there are approximately one or two vacant positions on the council to be filled. Usually, vacancies arise if a member is either deceased or is too ill to carry out his/her duties; council members rarely resign their positions for any other reasons. Accepting a Grand Council membership is a serious undertaking, as these positions are considered to be for life.

8. The Putus holds the position of wampum reader/recorder. The traditional wampum that was worn by the Putus at Se'tta'newimk went missing some time in the 1960s. Some people say that it was offered for display during Canada's Expo '67 and was not returned to the Putus. Meanwhile, others claim that it may have been sold.

9. Significantly, the relationship between pilgrimage and the persistence of precontact traditions following missionization is documented in a number of other contexts in the Americas (Jarvenpa 1990: 198; Sallnow 1981: 176–80; Wolf 1958: 38).

chapter six

"We Are Born to Die": Death, Illness, and Grieving in Eskasoni

In spite of what the learned have said,
I still my old opinion keep;
The posture, that we give the dead,
Points out the soul's eternal sleep.
Not so the ancients of these lands–
The Indian, when from life released,
Again is seated with his friends,
And shares again the joyous feast.
His imagined bird and painted bowl,
And venison, for a journey dressed,
Bespeak the nature of the soul,
Activity, that knows no rest.

–Philip Freneau, *The Indian Burying Ground*

LEARNING OBJECTIVES

After reading this chapter, students should be able to:

- Distinguish among bereavement, grief, and mourning.
- Identify several culturally specific deathway rituals practised in Eskasoni.
- Identify and describe local responses to bereavement.
- Explain the significance of *apiksiktatimk* ("forgiving each other").
- Compare Mi'kmaw concepts of the soul with those found in other cultures.

INTRODUCTION

In Eskasoni, "years and years ago, before telephones and the like, if someone died, a man would stand in the doorway and shout 'It's a sacred time' [*alatsutmaykapo*] . . . Then the community would know that the person had passed on" (Fieldnotes, Book III: 389). Essentially, the thrice-repeated shout of *alatsutmaykapo,* literally "we are praying," was a summons to the community to gather at the home of the deceased. Alatsutmaykapo meant it was time to come together, to talk, to pray, and to keep the grieving family company. At the turn of the 21st century, the call of alatsutmaykapo is no longer heard in Eskasoni. However, within hours of the death of a Mi'kmaw person most people in the community are aware of the event. The news of death is still received as a summons.

In Eskasoni, the death of a community member is one occasion when the Mi'kmaw people are drawn together. Of course, in most face-to-face communities, death tends to bond people, but the degree to which the Mi'kmaq are collectively oriented is remarkable. The occurrence of death in Eskasoni is a time when the Mi'kmaq gather as a community to assist the family who has lost a loved one. It is also a time when political, religious, and personal differences are suppressed in the interest of providing a comforting and supportive atmosphere for those in mourning. One woman commented:

> When someone dies we forget about tensions and arguments. This is not the time and place for such things . . . What we do is allow people to grieve. They want for nothing. We give them food and comfort and they're allowed to grieve in their own way. This is how we show our strength. We have to be strong . . .

> *(Fieldnotes, Book II: 257)*

With few exceptions, deathways in Eskasoni tend to follow a well-established pattern. This pattern, as with many Mi'kmaw understandings relating to death and the afterlife, derives from a composite of Christian and non-Christian interpretative frameworks.

This chapter is primarily concerned with the ways Roman Catholic and non-Western cosmological (and ideological) beliefs and values inform various practices relating to Mi'kmaw illness, death, and grief. The material presented here offers one particular discourse about Mi'kmaw deathways, derived from the descriptions, beliefs, and opinions provided by adult members of the Eskasoni community. This particular group is the one that I came to know best during my fieldwork.

The initial focuses of my fieldwork did not include a detailed account of Mi'kmaw deathways. However, while formulating the themes for individual chapters to be included in this work, I became increasingly aware of the social and spiritual significance of Mi'kmaw funerary rituals, both for the family and the community. Unfortunately, I did not record certain aspects of Mi'kmaw deathways (such as specifics about private mourning). However, my frequent attendance at wakes, funerals, and postinterment gatherings provided me with sufficient experience to offer an informed commentary on Mi'kmaw responses to illness, death, and bereavement.

THEORETICAL APPROACHES TO THE STUDY OF DEATH

For most of the 20th century, anthropological theories relating to the study of deathways tended to focus either on Emile Durkheim's view that death rituals, as mechanisms of social control, elicit emotional responses during "life crisis" situations or on the alternative view that emotional responses guide the social construction of ritual practices.

Within the social sciences, analyses of death and deathways begin with Robert Hertz's study of secondary burial among the Dayak of Borneo. Hertz, a student of Durkheim's, proposes that conceptions of death and the emotions associated with death are socially constructed and as such can be studied as social facts. Hertz claims that mortuary rites and practices serve to organize and govern public and private emotions. He asserts that "death as a social phenomenon consists of a dual . . . process of mental disintegration" marked by the death of an individual and social reintegration, or "synthesis," which is achieved once specific mortuary rituals and a period of mourning have effectively "triumph[ed] over death" (1960: 86). Similarly, anthropologists Bloch and Parry note that in Hertz's analysis of deathways, "the reassertion of society manifested by the end of mourning and by the belief that the soul has been incorporated into the society of the dead" is mirrored by the way in which the "collective consciousness of the living has been settled by the funerary rituals" (1982: 4).

The term *communitas* was coined by anthropologist Victor Turner to refer to a "moment in and out of [ordinary] time," when the rules of social interaction do not apply (Turner 1995: 96–97). It is a stage when human relatedness, egalitarianism, and antistructure prevail. This stage pertains to the "transition" stage of Arnold van Gennep's tripartite model of *rites de passage* (Turner 1995: 94–96; van Gennep 1960: 11, 21). Van Gennep recognized that all rites of passage involve **rites of separation**, **rites of transition** (or liminality), and **rites of incorporation**. These rites are not developed to the same extent by all participants in every ceremony but vary according to the social-cultural contexts in which they are used. In *The Ritual Process* (1995), Turner identifies the stage of separation as "symbolic behaviour signifying the detachment of the individual or the group either from an earlier fixed point in the social structure, from a set of cultural conditions (a 'state'), or from both" (1995: 94). During the second phase, the transitional or liminal period, "the characteristics of the ritual subject (the 'passenger') are ambiguous; he passes through a cultural realm that has few or none of the attributes of the past or coming state" (1995: 94). In the final phase of incorporation (which he renamed "reincorporation"), the ritual subject "returns to a relatively stable state and is granted rights and obligations of a clearly defined and 'structural' type: he is expected to behave in accordance with certain customary norms and ethical standards binding on incumbents of social position in a system of such positions" (1995: 94–95).

CHANGING THEORIES ABOUT DEATHWAYS

More sophisticated theoretical frameworks for the study of ritual have emerged in the latter part of the 20th century. Anthropologist Renato Rosaldo argues that, historically, theoretical approaches to the study of deathways tended to privilege the role of ritual over and above emotional responses to death (1989). In his essay on Ilongot headhunting, Rosaldo observes that headhunting is a culturally and socially constructed idiom through which the rage associated with grief is acknowledged and expressed. For the Ilongot, headhunting is a primary means of coping with death. However, Rosaldo argues that, in the study of deathways, the considerable influence of emotional turmoil on the ritual process has always been overlooked by scholars. As a result, "social structure, not death, and certainly not bereavement" has become the primary object of study (Rosaldo 1989: 13). He suggests that social scientists tend to "mask the emotional force of bereavement by reducing funerary ritual to orderly routine" by fitting death "neatly into the author's view of funerary ritual as a mechanical programmed unfolding of prescribed acts" (Rosaldo 1989: 13).

In the following chapter, the various dimensions of funerary ritual in Eskasoni and my interpretation of people's emotional responses to death are discussed. The analysis of Mi'kmaw deathways presented in this chapter draws on van Gennep's tripartite model of *rites de passage* and Turner's concept of *communitas*. In particular, I draw attention to several rites of separation, transition, and incorporation that the Mi'kmaq closely associate with their cultural and social identity.

MI'KMAW DEATHWAYS

The idiom of healing associated with St. Anne's Mission can be broadly applied to various facets of Mi'kmaw deathways. For the Mi'kmaq of Eskasoni, the community solidarity sustained through close and frequent social contact is the means through which individual and collective healing takes place. The Mi'kmaq often say, "We try to do what is best for the community." However, "what is best for the community" often entails the emotional, physical, and spiritual well-being of individuals within Mi'kmaw society.

There is a proverb among the Mi'kmaq that "no one is born alone, and no one should die alone." In Eskasoni, the illness or death of any one of its residents is an occasion where members of the community are drawn together. The degree to which the Mi'kmaq are collectively oriented is remarkable. Many of the Mi'kmaw comments to follow stress this collective orientation. One Mi'kmaw woman told me, "We never leave the family alone. At the hospital when someone is dying, when they die, and when funeral arrangements are made. We get together for meals and share with each other" (Fieldnotes, Book II: 255). Upon hearing of a Mi'kmaw person's illness, family, friends, and acquaintances visit the sick person, offering prayers, food, and any assistance that may be required. Whether the sick person is in a hospital or at home is of little concern to the Mi'kmaq. Those who are ill are attended at all times, until either the person's health improves or the person dies.

Deathway Rituals

When a Mi'kmaw person is near death two specific rituals may be performed at the dying person's bedside. Both of these rituals are drawn from Mi'kmaw tradition and social convention. The first ritual to be performed is apiksiktatimk, or the act of mutual forgiveness. The second ritual involves the recitation of Christian prayers. With the exception of sudden or tragic death, the latter ritual is normally carried out. However, although a number of people mentioned apiksiktatimk to me, it is unclear to what extent this particular ritual is still widely practised. Apiksiktatimk was explained to me in the following manner:

> There is a ritual that we used to have and still do. When my uncle was dying the whole family went to him one at a time and asked him for forgiveness for any wrongs or hurts we had done to him. My uncle also asked each person for forgiveness.

(Fieldnotes, Book III: 387)

Apiksiktatimk is performed once the death of the sick person appears imminent. If a person is thought to be near death, it is common for family, friends, and all those present to engage in apiksiktatimk. Once requested, this mutual act of forgiveness is rarely denied. However, on occasion apiksiktatimk does not take place. I was present one evening when several people were discussing the deteriorating health of a friend:

> I'm disappointed because [Jess] and [Dan] didn't forgive each other ... It's [Jess's]'s, not [Dan]'s [problem]. She'll have to take it with her ... There's still quite a bit of anger. I wish they'd come to terms with this. [Jess] doesn't have much time left. She's had contact with the spirit world already. She's seen her father and others who have passed into the spirit world.

> *(Fieldnotes, Book V: 915)*

The failure to offer or grant apiksiktatimk is viewed as problematic both for the dying person and for surviving friends and family. Apiksiktatimk ensures that when a dying person leaves this world he or she does so with the best wishes of those around them. Performing this act benefits the living as well as the soon-to-be-deceased. Otherwise, survivors would have to carry unresolved problems with them for the rest of their lives. And the deceased would have to carry his or her problems into the next world. While apiksiktatimk allows for healing through the relieving of personal burdens, it is also an act of mutual respect that is an important aspect of Mi'kmaw culture. A refusal to offer mutual forgiveness is interpreted as a sign of disrespect for both the people involved and for basic Mi'kmaw social values.

In the final stages of illness, there is also a ceremony where the dying person is attended to by a Catholic Mi'kmaw prayer group. The prayer group sets up a vigil at the bedside of the afflicted person. It continually offers prayers, especially the rosary, to comfort the dying person and his or her family. Many Mi'kmaq consider this way of dealing with death and illness to be different from non-Aboriginal approaches. One Mi'kmaw woman proudly related to me the following:

> We deal with sickness and death different than non-Natives. If someone is sick in the hospital there might be as many as fifty people in the room praying and watching over the sick person. Mi'kmaw people are accepting of illness and death ... That's life.

> *(Fieldnotes, Book III: 387)*

In addition to the prayer ritual described above, neo-Traditionalists and Catholic-Traditionalists often perform sweats, prayer in the four directions, and sacred circles to aid in the healing process of those who are ill. In both the sweat and the two prayer circles that I attended, there was an emphasis on healing. In fact, the sweat was requested by the sister of a dying man, as was one of the sacred circles. At the sweat, the prayers offered were non-Christian and of a highly personal nature. Each person participating in the sweat was asked to make his or her own specific prayers to the Creator. In a number of cases, supplication was made to the Creator to ease the dying person's transition from the world of the living to the "land of the ancestors." The last sacred circle that I attended focused on healing. This particular ceremony was attended by several neo-Traditionalists, Catholic Traditionalists, and one Catholic. All of them were asked to offer personal prayers. On this occasion Christian prayers were included as part of the ceremony.

During the latter stages of illness, it is understood that prayers no longer assist in physical healing, but they do offer dying persons and their loved ones spiritual nourishment.

Catholic prayer rituals do not replace the prayers performed by a Catholic priest or the Church's ritual of anointing of the sick. Prayer rituals are, instead, a gesture of solidarity on the part of the Catholic community to pray with, and for, the family about to experience the loss of a loved one. Once the dying person is approaching death, the priest is immediately summoned to perform last rites (or anointing of the sick), after which the prayer group continues to hold vigil with the family.

After death occurs, the deceased is tended by members of the prayer group and relatives until arrangements are made to have the body prepared for burial. Preparation of the remains for burial is done professionally at a local funeral home in the nearby city of Sydney, after which the body is returned to Eskasoni for the wake, funeral, and interment. From the moment of death until interment, the preparation of the body is the only time that the deceased is untended by a family member. If a death occurs late at night or early in the morning, at least one family member will keep vigil over the body until it is taken under the professional care of a funeral director. The remains are kept at a funeral home in Sydney, while the community makes preparations for the wake, funeral, salite, and funeral feast. Once the deceased's body is returned to the community for the wake and burial, constant vigil is kept over the body until interment.

The Wake

A Mi'kmaw man once told me that "the best thing we can do for each other is offer food and friendship." The occurrence of death is a time when food and friendship are of central importance, and both are freely given. In Eskasoni, death is a social affair. Many hands are required to assist with the practical, social, and religious aspects of the funeral process. The event of death is also a time when almost every family in Eskasoni becomes either directly or indirectly involved in funerary preparations and the performance of funerary rites and rituals. Prior to and during the wake, the family home is the centre of activity. With few exceptions, wakes are hosted in the family home. The men in the community work day and night repairing, cleaning, and painting the interior and exterior of the home where the wake is to take place. Friends, neighbours, and the extended family help the mourners in any way they can. Accommodation is offered to visitors, money and sundry items are collected for the salite, and food is prepared to serve the mourners and their guests during the wake. More important, grieving family members are provided with spiritual and emotional support at all times. At no time during the wake, funeral, and salite is the family left alone.

The death of a Mi'kmaw person is considered to be one of the most important occasions for the Mi'kmaq. It is not unusual for extended family members and friends to travel long distances to attend funerals, wakes, and postinterment ritual gatherings (salites and funeral feasts). If a Mi'kmaw person dies outside of Eskasoni, residents of Eskasoni often travel to the community of the deceased to attend the wake or at least the funeral service and the salite. Likewise, Mi'kmaq from other communities throughout Mi'kmaki travel to Eskasoni when a death has occurred. Attendance at funerals, wakes, and postinterment ritual gatherings, while not compulsory, is considered a proper show of respect for the deceased and for the deceased's family.

Throughout Mi'kma'ki, there is a common understanding that those in mourning are in need of support. As a member of the Mi'kmaw community, one is expected to respond to this need. Interestingly, intracommunity distinctions of all kinds are subdued in the case of death. Although personal and social conflicts are evident in various other social situations, there was no evidence of such tensions at the funerals, wakes, salites, and funeral feasts that I attended. Instead, I witnessed a strong show of support for bereaved families despite existing political, social, and religious differences. While living in Eskasoni, I found this sense of community to be especially remarkable on two particular occasions. In the first instance Henry, a well-known politician from Eskasoni, was under investigation for several indictable offences. Many people in the community were aware that Henry's questionable activities had adversely affected most members of the community. Many residents were quite angry about the entire situation. A number of people had publicly criticized Henry and insisted that he be brought to justice under the full weight of the law. In the midst of this controversy, Henry lost a close member of his family in a tragic accident. Interestingly, I found the wake, funeral, and salite for Henry's deceased family member to be one of the most well-attended social functions that I witnessed in the community. I attended the wake with two of my closest friends, Jon and Dora, who, prior to the accident, had publicly criticized Henry. Both Jan and Dora admitted to feeling awkward about going to the wake, but put aside their personal differences and offered support to Henry and his family. Dora remarked to me, "It doesn't matter what the man did, this is different. I have to go [to the wake]. I'd feel a lot worse if I didn't" (personal communication).

While I was living in Eskasoni, another death occurred that illustrates the willingness of the Mi'kmaw people to put aside personal grievances when a death occurs. When Baxter, a man from a neighbouring Mi'kmaw community, was killed in a traffic accident, many family members, friends, and acquaintances attended the wake, funeral, salite, and funeral feast. Baxter was a noted anti-Catholic activist. Reportedly, at one time, he interrupted a Mass to renounce God and the Catholic faith in front of all those present. Many Mi'kmaw people, especially Mi'kmaw Catholics, were highly offended by such behaviour. Baxter came to be looked upon disfavourably within the Mi'kmaw community at large. However, upon Baxter's death, community members again showed their willingness to overlook personal differences by attending the various functions that marked Baxter's passing.

The numbers of people participating in wakes and other public functions vary in relation to how well known or socially important the deceased was. If the deceased person was prominent in the community, or worked in a public capacity that influenced the lives of many people, then acknowledgement of the deceased's contributions is reflected in the large number of people in attendance at the wake and other services. The number of children, grandchildren, and size of kinship network are also factors influencing how many people attend. Services for elders are particularly well attended. In addition to the immediate and extended family of the deceased elder, which is often quite large, many Mi'kmaq who are not blood relatives of the deceased make a special effort to attend functions honouring the person.

Mi'kmaw wakes are held over a period of three days, exclusive of the two- to three-day preparation period leading up to the event. Shortly before the return of the deceased's body to the community, close friends, loved ones, and immediate and extended family members gather at the home where the wake is to be held. The gathering is normally attended by a representative from the Sante' Mawio'mi (usually a prayer leader) and the parish priest, who conduct prayers once preparations for the viewing are complete. The funeral director from Sydney accompanies the body of the deceased to the family home and prepares a room in the home for visitation. The funeral director and his assistants quickly transform the room into a reception area replete with standard funerary accoutrements. Stands are supplied for floral tributes, guest books, and sympathy cards. A bier or stand upon which the casket rests is placed on one side of the room. Kneeling benches are placed along the exposed side of the casket for those who wish to offer personal prayers. Typically, there are abundant flowers, including wreaths in the shape of crosses and hearts. Some floral tributes are small, simple bunches of flowers pinned to the inner lining of the open casket.

The deceased usually wears regular clothing. A man is typically dressed in a suit or a shirt and dress pants. Women are usually clothed in a dress or blouse and skirt. On occasion there are departures from this standard attire. At a funeral for a strong promoter of Traditional Mi'kmaw culture that I attended, the deceased man's Mi'kmaw regalia (L'nu'ktat) symbolically reflected the personal philosophies he embraced. He was dressed in a ribbon shirt, choker, and headband, and a number of eagle feathers were placed in the casket by friends and family (Fieldnotes, Book V: 1008). The particular attire worn by the deceased is closely associated with Mi'kmaw identity. Typically, ribbon shirts, headbands, and chokers make up modern Mi'kmaw regalia, worn by Mi'kmaw men on special occasions such as weddings, powwows, St. Anne's Day, Treaty Day, and funerals. The wearing of regalia signifies the importance of the occasion and is an overtly symbolic means of expressing ethnicity and culture.

By the time the funeral attendants have completed the job of setting up the reception area, it closely resembles that of a typical visitation room at a funeral home. However, there are several differences distinctive to Mi'kmaw wakes. One remarkable difference is the prominent display of the Grand Council flag on the wall behind the casket. This tradition has been a part of local Mi'kmaw funerary practices for as long as people in Eskasoni can remember. Another distinctive feature involves a bowl or shallow dish placed directly on the casket, where money is collected for donation to the salite.

A number of the men appearing in the above photo are dressed in ribbon shirts. Note also that the male council members are wearing a sash over their left shoulder.
Photo: Angela Robinson, 1999

Immediately after arriving at the wake, guests proceed directly to extend condolences to the family members. Once condolences are offered guests advance to the visitation area, where most kneel to say a prayer over the body of the deceased. After the visitation, guests usually move to a different room in the house to socialize with the other visitors and mourners. While in the visitation area people are quiet and subdued in consideration of those who need time for personal reflection or prayers. However, the mood in the social areas of the house is in direct contrast to that of the reception area. Much like the salite, Mi'kmaw wakes are generally relaxed and vibrant social affairs. People talk, laugh, and exchange stories, usually humorous, about the deceased, while large amounts of tea, sandwiches, and sweets are consumed. A typical wake in Eskasoni usually accommodates a large number of guests, most of whom arrive throughout the afternoon and early evening. Wakes are never closed to the public, as family members and close friends keep vigil over the deceased throughout the night. These vigils are carried out for the duration of the wake.

The Funeral

In Eskasoni, funerals are usually held at 11:00 a.m. on the third day of the wake, but never on a Friday because it is considered bad luck to do so. Once again family members, close friends, and other loved ones gather at the home of the deceased for the "closing of the casket." A Catholic priest and a member of the Sante' Mawio'mi, usually a prayer leader, preside over the closing ceremony. Led by the priest, prayers and blessings are said over the body, after which those present are given the opportunity to have a private moment with the deceased. Normally, this is a very emotional time for those close to the deceased. People openly weep and comfort each other. The casket is then carried out to the hearse, which will transport the body to the church. The hearse heads up the procession, immediately followed by the limousine transporting the family. All other mourners follow close behind in their vehicles as the funeral procession makes its way to the church.

At the church, seats are reserved on the right side of the centre aisle for the deceased's family and on the left for members of the honour guard. Every Mi'kmaw funeral has an honour guard, comprising mostly members of the Grand Council and Aboriginal representatives of the local police force. Quite often the church is nearly full to capacity by the time the principal mourners and the deceased arrive at the church.

Funeral masses at Eskasoni are performed in compliance with Catholic liturgical practice, with the exception that, as at regular masses, most of the prayers and hymns are said in Mi'kmaq. However, at the request of family members, special poems or secular songs are sometimes performed at the service. I was informed that in some instances, Traditional practices, such as the burning of sweetgrass, drumming, and pipe ceremonies, are also integrated into the funeral service, but these innovations are exceptional. None of the 10 or more funerals that I attended included any Traditional rites or practices.

There is one remarkable funerary practice associated with interment. At the end of the funeral mass, the family and most of those in attendance proceed to the gravesite. At this time, the priest says a final prayer. The pall, which is invariably a Grand Council flag, is removed and given to the principal mourner. After the final prayer and the removal of the pall the casket is lowered into the ground, at which time each family member takes a piece of earth and tosses it onto the casket and then leaves the gravesite. Each person in the graveyard follows, replicating exactly the same gesture until everyone has left the graveyard. This poignant gesture of farewell symbolizes personal attachment to the deceased. It also

The Mi'kmaw national flag, or Grand Council flag, is used as a backdrop for caskets at wakes and as a pall during funerals.
Image courtesy of Helen Sylliboy

symbolizes a strong sense of community, as it is the community of mourners that sees one of its own committed to his or her final resting place.

Although some degree of tension exists between the various religious factions in Eskasoni, up until and including the turn of the 21st century there has been no incidence of religious conflict disrupting local funerary processes. It is possible that ritual disruption has been averted because the local rituals that foster positive social relations between community members are highly respected. However, in Eskasoni, there are several other overarching social, cultural, and religious factors informing Mi'kmaw deathways that limit the possibility of overt conflict concerning funerary rituals. First, none of those who promote the various neo-Traditionalist or non-Christian discourses are yet deceased. Therefore, to date the occasion of a neo-Traditional funeral has not arisen. Second, most Mi'kmaq have been baptized into the Catholic Church and are entitled to a Catholic burial. Third, in many cases the immediate and extended families of many neo-Traditionalists, and others who have left the Catholic Church, maintain close ties to the Catholic faith. Typically, funeral arrangements are made and carried out in compliance with the wishes of surviving family members rather than those of the deceased. Baxter's death, mentioned earlier, is a case in point. As noted, Baxter was a self-proclaimed anti-Catholic activist. However, upon his death Baxter was granted full burial privileges by the Catholic Church, including a funeral mass and interment in the local Catholic cemetery. All this was done at the request of his wife, who, despite her husband's wishes, remained a devout Catholic.

As mentioned, in Eskasoni standard funeral practices tend to conform to the procedures prescribed by the official Roman Catholic Church. However, since the Vatican II reforms and Pope John Paul II's 1990 encyclical, *Redemptoris Missio*, the Catholic Church has become more tolerant of incorporating traditional Aboriginal practices into Catholic liturgical celebrations. Jane McMillan suggests that Pope John Paul II not only encouraged this but, during his 1984 visit, also made a direct request of Kji-saqamaw Donald Marshall to "incorporate [the Mi'kmaw] belief system into the Roman Catholic system" (1996: 115). Although considered acceptable, Aboriginal religious expressions have not been integrated rapidly into funerals at Eskasoni. It wasn't until 1992 that the first pipe ceremony was conducted in the church during a general absolution ceremony. In 1993 the first smudge was performed during a funeral in Holy Family parish. However, very few such Aboriginal religious expressions have taken place since. As mentioned earlier, I was also told that on occasion drumming and the burning of sweetgrass have been included in a number of funeral services. However, I did not witness any of these practices at the funerals that I attended.

Salites and Funeral Feasts

Among the Mi'kmaq, grief associated with death of a community member is felt and acknowledged both collectively and individually. In Eskasoni, the profound emotions associated with individual and collective bereavement are mediated through two interconnected postinterment celebrations, the salite and the funeral feast. The salite and funeral feast, which occur directly after the interment of the deceased, are efforts on the part of the community to offer emotional, spiritual, and financial support to those in mourning. The social and cultural frameworks that underpin local postinterment ceremonies are informed by the basic Mi'kmaw values of equality, reciprocity, and sharing. Essentially, salites and funeral feasts involve the sharing of emotional loss, financial resources, and a communal meal. All of these supports will be reciprocated in turn to every family in its time of need.

Salites, or auctions, as described in chapter one, are "local" funerary practices that cannot be accommodated under the rubric of mainstream Roman Catholic practice. However, the salite and the accompanying funeral feast are considered by the Mi'kmaq to be among the most important features of their funerary rituals. The communal "feast and auction" are not simply a meal and an auction. They are events perceived to contribute to the well-being of both the deceased's family and their guests. Salites and funeral feasts are viewed as emotionally satisfying ways of dealing with communal and individual bereavement. Much like the Tanacross Athapaskan potlatch (Simeone 1991), the goal of the salite is "to transform grief into joy and reknit the bonds of community" (Simeone 1991: 157). However, unlike potlatches salites have an added financial dimension. Among the Mi'kmaq "no one [person] ever pays for a funeral" (Fieldnotes, Book III: 453). In potlatches, the manner in which goods/resources are dispensed by the aggrieved family is in direct contrast to the way that the salites relieve Mi'kmaw families of costs incurred for funerals. Although relatives and friends often contribute money and labour to the potlatch, Simeone's description also suggests that potlatches often impose financial burdens on the family of the deceased (Simeone 1991). In the Mi'kmaw communities throughout Cape Breton, grieving family members never have to bear the cost of the funeral alone. Salites are designed to relieve financial burdens just as they relieve the emotional burden of loss.

Salites and funeral feasts are generally festive occasions that celebrate the life more than the death of the deceased. As one person put it, "[at salites] you forget everything ... after everyone cries and is miserable [during the wake and funeral], everybody is laughing and you don't feel so bad anymore" (personal communication). In Turnerian terms, however, salites and funeral feasts are also complex ritual spaces in which rites of separation, transition, and reincorporation are combined. First, funeral feasts are considered to be the last gesture of the deceased for his or her people. As such, they mark the separation of the deceased from the temporal world and the transmigration (transition) of the soul to the afterlife (incorporation) (Turner 1995: 94–95). Funeral feasts and the accompanying salites also mark a period of transition for the bereaved, who experience a sense of communitas. Turner referred to this as a "moment in and out of [ordinary] time," when the rules of social interaction do not apply (Turner 1995: 96–97). Mi'kmaw postinterment rituals are performed without exception for all deceased community members, regardless of their status, notoriety, or religious affiliation. Essentially, these gatherings are social occasions where differences become neutralized, at least temporarily.

In Eskasoni, postinterment ceremonies are usually held at the Gabriel Centre in the basement of Holy Family Church. The family of the deceased is expected to stay for the duration of these events, which typically last for five to six hours, because family members are considered to be the official hosts of the celebration. In Eskasoni, salites and funeral feasts are open affairs. Anyone wishing to attend is welcome. Both ceremonies are normally well attended but are rarely overcrowded. Some guests leave while others arrive to replace them. The entire time that the salite and feast are in progress there is a relatively even flow of people to and from the building.

At the Mi'kmaw funeral feasts that accompany salites, people are seated at large tables on which the main meal (usually roast turkey or ham), desserts, and refreshments are provided for the hosts and their guests. The serving of meals and the order and manner in which people are served reflect certain honouring practices of the Mi'kmaq. The deceased's family members are given an elevated social position at this event in recognition of their dual role as hosts and honoured guests. They are assigned a special seating area and are the first to be served. The only other guests given special consideration are elders, who are also among the first to be seated and served at the feast. All remaining guests are treated equally, including children, who are seated at the tables alongside adults. Often there are too many people in attendance to be served at once, so as people finish their meals they leave the table to socialize or to attend to other matters. Some people leave the gathering, but may return later to participate in the salite.

Throughout the salite, people continually socialize, recalling memories and relating anecdotes about the deceased, most of which have an element of humour. Implicit in these social exchanges is the understanding that the life of the deceased was important to individuals and to the community. The relating of stories is a means of expressing this understanding. Amid the chatter and laughter, the voice of the auctioneer can be heard announcing items for bidding and the offers proposed. The articles auctioned at salites are donated by family and friends. In many cases, various personal possessions of the deceased are auctioned off. These items are often purchased by a close friend or family member, who will return the item to the family as a gift, or keep it as a memento of the deceased. The personal belongings of the deceased are viewed differently than the other items in the auction and usually fetch a selling price far beyond their actual material value. In effect, articles belonging to the deceased have an added emotional value because of their connection to the dead person. For instance, at the salite of a well-known musician one of his instruments was auctioned and sold for more than $400. At salites the large amounts of money paid for such items is an indication of the esteem in which the deceased and the family are held by the buyer (personal communication).

In some instances, newly purchased items have attached emotional value as well. For instance, at one salite a family member purchased and donated an expensive piece of jewellery, which was repurchased by the donor for a large amount of money. This item was given promptly to the mother of the deceased. In this instance the gift was given three times.

First, the item was bought as a gift to be donated to the auction. Second, it was repurchased by the donor for a price at least equal to its retail value at the auction, and the proceeds earned went to the deceased's family. Third, it was presented as a gift to one of the principal mourners. The significance of gift-giving of this type expresses, symbolically, at least three messages. First, the thrice-given gift is the donor's public and private acknowledgement of the grief felt by the mother of the deceased. Second, the gift acknowledges shared grief and expresses love and respect for the deceased and for the recipient of the gift. Third, the manner and context in which the gift was given exhibit family solidarity and exemplify the generosity valued among the Mi'kmaw people.

Gestures of gift-giving, such as the incident described in chapter one and the example provided above, are commonplace at salites. However, the significance of gift-giving associated with salites has many nuances of meaning far too diverse and complex to be fully treated here. In general, the act of giving, as a crucial part of salites and the bereavement process, can be seen as an aspect of funerary ritual that coincides with the basic Mi'kmaw social values of benevolence, reciprocity, and mutual respect. Salites and funeral feasts are also occasions that create a social space in which the ability and willingness of the Mi'kmaq to provide for those in need is exhibited. Community solidarity is expressed and maintained. As one man told me, "It's a good thing for us to do. It keeps the community together" (Fieldnotes, Book III: 453).

PUBLIC AND PRIVATE EXPRESSIONS OF GRIEF

Metcalf and Huntington note that "cultures vary widely in the ways in which they perceive and evaluate emotional states" (Metcalf and Huntington 1991: 5). Within certain cultures public expressions of grief—or mourning—are understood to indicate inner emotional states. In some cultures a failure to express emotions openly may be interpreted as a lack of attachment to the deceased. In Mi'kmaw society, however, a hesitancy to express one's inner emotional state is viewed differently. Among the Mi'kmaq excessive emotional displays are discouraged and therefore tend to be suppressed. Even though everyone is "allowed to grieve in their own way" (Fieldnotes, Book II: 257), public expressions of grief generally conform to a culturally specific pattern.

The results of studies on death rituals in a number of non-Western cultures show that the suppression of the emotions associated with grief is part of social convention among various cultures throughout the world. For instance, among the East Cree (Preston and Preston 1991) and the Tanacross Athapaskans (Simeone 1991) grieving behaviour is subject to social restrictions. Likewise, the Mi'kmaq value stoicism in the face of emotionally charged situations. Elation may be revealed by an irrepressible smile; excessive emotional pain may take the form of social detachment. Among the Mi'kmaq, most emotional situations, either joyous or distressing, are normally met with a firm grasp of the hand or a hug. In the case of acute grief, someone may simply state, "*Metua'lik*" ("I'm having a difficult time"). When people are coping with the death of a loved one, their lips may tremble, their eyes may fill with tears and voices may waver with emotion, but the Mi'kmaq tend not to give in to emotional extremes. Generally, for the Mi'kmaq equanimity and even-temperedness are considered the acceptable responses to bereavement. These are valued above public displays of despair and inconsolable grief.

Unlike the East Cree (Preston and Preston 1991) and the Tanacross (Simeone 1991), the Mi'kmaq do not consider prolonged grief and mourning to be damaging to the physical and emotional health of the survivor. Rather, the impetus behind the suppression of grief within Mi'kmaw society arises from the need to ensure the emotional and spiritual well-being of dying or deceased persons. Ruth, a woman from Eskasoni, told me of a concept called "letting the spirit go." She described this idea in the following manner:

> [My brother] was diagnosed with incurable cancer and was bedridden for well over a year... He had surgery around Christmas and a few months later had renal failure. They [his family] brought him to the hospital, but the doctors told them to take him home and keep him comfortable. He did OK on Sunday, Monday and Tuesday, but by Wednesday it was clear that he would die. On Wednesday at 11 o'clock at night, the family went to him ... His wife and children started crying when he stopped breathing, but he started breathing again. He opened his eyes and looked at us, but he was full of sadness because they were crying about him. His wife noticed how sad he was and told him, "It's OK, keep going wherever you're going." His son understood and said, "Yes, keep going." Shortly after he died with a smile on his face.

> *(Fieldnotes, Book III: 387–88)*

The notion of "letting the spirit go" as described by Ruth suggests that the purpose of restraining grief is to secure the emotional well-being of the dying person. However, several Mi'kmaq also told me that "letting the spirit go" also pertains to the spirit or soul of a deceased person. One woman explained to me that the "old people told us not to cry too much because the soul of the dead person turned back and they might not find their way to heaven" (Fieldnotes, Book II: 271). Significantly, anthropologists working in Asia and Europe have found similar prohibitions against excessive grieving at funerals, although the rationales behind these sanctions vary widely. Sherry B. Ortner notes that, among the Sherpa of Nepal, there is a "cultural/religious injunction against exhibiting strong emotions around death, which itself has several rationales." One is that "too much crying at a funeral will . . . cause a veil of blood to cover the eyes of the deceased, so that he or she cannot find 'the road,' the way to a good rebirth" (Ortner 1999: 139). Ortner also remarks that "women at funerals are often reminded by the lamas [religious leaders] to stop crying, as hearing such crying keeps the deceased attached to his or her previous life" (Ortner 1999: 139). Similarly, folklorist Anatole Le Braz recounts a legend, titled *Il Ne Faut Point Trop Pleurer l'Anaon* ("One Must Not Cry Too Much for Anaon") about a young woman from Coray, Brittany. The legend relates the experience of a daughter who became overwrought with grief upon the death of her mother. The mother appeared to the daughter and implored her to stop her persistent grieving because she was forced to carry the bucket of tears shed by her daughter until Judgement Day. This narrative also suggests that excessive grieving creates hardships for the soul of the deceased in the afterlife.

Many comments I heard among the Mi'kmaq suggest that prolonged or excessive grief is viewed as an undignified personal indulgence and a sign of immaturity or culture loss, or indicates a lack of personal strength. Lorna, a Mi'kmaw woman, repeated a recent conversation that she had with Martin, a man from Eskasoni:

> [Martin] looked at me and said, "I believe we're losing our culture. When my mother died I didn't take as much as an Aspirin, and when my brother died I did the same thing. That's the way I was taught. I had to take it. I had to deal with it. But today there was a man here who just lost his brother. He was so drugged up he could hardly talk. That's

not the way that we were brought up. The doctors are giving these people drugs and they're taking them. They're not facing the fact that they have to deal with death."

(Fieldnotes, Book III: 390–91)

According to Mi'kmaw social and cultural convention, then, one must "deal with death" in a manner consistent with Mi'kmaw values. Martin views indulgence in emotional extremes or excessive grieving as incompatible with the way the Mi'kmaq have traditionally confronted and managed their grief.

Emotional restraint is viewed by many Mi'kmaq as a characteristic that is acquired and is therefore primarily associated with maturity. For instance, after a wake one elder complained that she was unable to concentrate on praying. She said, "There's too much noise. All the young people, they don't handle themselves like older people do" (Fieldnotes, Book II: 270). Another woman who was present commented, "The young people are carrying on and crying. Crying too much" (Fieldnotes, Book II: 271). Implicit in the responses of these two women is the notion that young people who are "carrying on and crying . . . too much" have not been adequately socialized. They do not manage their grief in a responsible and mature manner consistent with that of the "older people."

The equanimity with which many adult Mi'kmaq confront grief should not be interpreted as reflective of inner states. It is better understood as a means to ensure the emotional and spiritual well-being of the dying or deceased person. Furthermore, excessive grief, rather than being seen as reflecting the individual's close relationship to the dying or deceased person, may be interpreted as a personal indulgence or lack of maturity that indicates an inability to "deal with death" in a dignified manner that is consistent with Mi'kmaw teachings.

MI'KMAW ATTITUDES, CONCEPTIONS, AND BELIEFS ABOUT DEATH AND DYING

The Mi'kmaw expression *Kisu'lkw tlite'lmHsk wskwijinuin*, meaning "It is the wish of the Creator that you should become a person," suggests that *being* exists before one actually becomes a "person." As a "wish" of the Creator,[1] life is a respected gift that is considered sacred. Similarly, death as a part of created life is also considered to be the will of the Creator. Most Mi'kmaq with whom I spoke believe that death is part of a preordained natural order. One Mi'kmaw woman explains it as follows:

It's a very odd thing, but our people seem to be comfortable with death. They are very accepting of death and as far as I can see they view it as a part of the natural process. Life and death are one, they're inseparable. I think this comes from our closeness with nature. We understand nature because we observe it. My father used to take us on walks. Along the way he would tell us the names of plants and trees. I forget them now, but I remember he knew all the names and taught them to us.

(Fieldnotes, Book III: 389)

Among the Mi'kmaq, death is not necessarily conceived of as a permanent state. Rather, it is understood as a stage or state of being that is inconsistent with life as we know it in this world. In the Mi'kmaw language, "the absentative case, indicated by the suffix *o'q*, suggests that a person is in a different state of consciousness" (personal communication, Bern Francis). Ruth Holmes Whitehead notes that, in Mi'kmaq, the "absentive [sic] case-ending 'conveys the idea of existence, though apart for the time.' It is used in speaking of an absent person or a dead one—each still animate, but now out of sight of the speaker" (1988:10; cf. Rand 1894: xxxvi). For example, to say *Anno'q* means that Ann is "away," that she has arrived but left again, or is either sleeping, in a comatose state, or deceased. The suffix *o'q*, then, suggests that Ann is absent or is in a state of being inconsistent with those who are speaking of her. When referring to a person who is deceased, *o'q* suggests that a person's spirit or soul, while not present in a worldly state, still exists. The person simply exists elsewhere:

> In Mi'kmaw tradition death is looked upon as a type of birth really. It's a journey that you've prepared for. The Mi'kmaw word for death, **nept**, means dormancy, death, sleep. So, if you look at it in this way, it [death] has a different meaning. It's something that we have to think about.

> *(Fieldnotes, Book III: 547)*

Box 6.1	Absentative Case

The suffixes *aq* and *o'q* are **absentative markers**. For instance, when I speak of my father (**nujj**), who is deceased, I would use the absentative form *aq*, thus in this case I would refer to my father as "*nujjaq*." For "Where is my daughter (**ntus**)?", I would say, "*ntusaq*?", or "*Ntusaq nepataq*," meaning "My daughter fell asleep." When a proper name is used, however, the absentative is *o'q*. For example, "Where is Jane?" would be "*Janeo'q?*" The two together would be as in the following: "*Nepataq ntusaq Janeo'q*," meaning "My daughter Jane fell asleep." In this case you see use of the two endings *o'q* for the proper name and *aq* for the personal pronoun (personal communication).

The state of existence implicit in the use of *o'q* and *nept* is central to understanding the Mi'kmaw concept of death. The deceased person is not here on earth with the living, but he or she still exists in another realm or in a different state of being. In this state, the deceased is still able to maintain connections with this world. Whitehead maintains this about Mi'kmaw myths about creation:

> [The] basic structures and the language in which they were told were in a continuous state of transformation . . . both Micmac language and Micmac tales have the same structure as the Micmac universe. As stories hold many levels of meaning, the cosmos holds many levels of existence.

> *(Whitehead 1988: 2–3)*

Generally, Mi'kmaw Catholics and non-Catholics believe that living people maintain communion with the dead, both in the temporal and other-worldly realms of existence. While I was living in Eskasoni, I was told several anecdotes about communications between dying people and the spirits of the dead. In the first case, mentioned earlier in this chapter, Jess, in the final stages of an advanced illness, was said to have "had contact with the spirit world already. [She's] seen [her] father and others who have passed into the spirit world" (Fieldnotes, Book V: 915). In this instance, Jess's close contact with the spirit world was interpreted as an indication that the spirits of the ancestors had come to guide Jess into the next world.

In a similar incident, Neil, a young man dying of an incurable disease, was said to have had an experience in which an elder, with whom he was unacquainted, spoke to him in a language he could not decipher. Although Neil was unable to converse with the elder, he could recall part of what was said and offered a description of the person. After hearing the description, Neil's mother determined that the "visitor" was her mother, whom Neil had never met and who had spoken to Neil "in old [archaic] Mi'kmaq." Neil's grandmother had died before he was born (Fieldnotes, Book III: 608). The event was interpreted by the family and others as a clear indication that Neil was soon to die. As in Jess's case, Neil's ancestor had come to guide him into the next world.

For Mi'kmaw Christians, the afterlife is most commonly referred to as heaven (*wa'so'q*), and among non-Christian Mi'kmaq it may simply be conceived of as a reunion with the ancestors. Mi'kmaw linguist Bern Francis supplied me with two phrases referring to the ancestral world that are no longer in common usage: ***Kniskamijinaq wskitqamumuow***, meaning "our ancestors' world" and ***Kniskamijinaq eimu'ti'tij***, which is less specific, meaning "where our ancestors are." According to Francis, *Naji-tkweiwatka kniskamijinaq* would be akin to "gone to another plane of existence" (personal communication). Neo-Traditionalists and other non-Christian Mi'kmaq claim that, prior to European contact, belief in another realm was a feature of Mi'kmaw **eschatology** (teachings about the final destiny of individuals, humanity, and the cosmos). For some Mi'kmaq the *Sk'te'kmujuawti* ("Ghost Road"), or what westerners call the Milky Way, "is the path that our people walk on with our ancestors after death" (personal communication). This belief is not unique to the Mi'kmaq. For example, the 17th-century Huron also held this view (Sagard 1939: 172).

Among the Mi'kmaq, contact with the spirits of the deceased is understood to be a two-way process of communication. For instance, at a relative's wake, Nora told me the following:

> The spirits of the dead go to heaven where the people who went before wait for them. I prayed to my mother and father this morning that the wake would be blessed. I believe they answered my prayers because everything is going well so far.
>
> *(Fieldnotes, Book II: 271)*

The fact that Nora prayed to her parents and feels she has received a response clearly indicates that communication is presumed to be sustained between the living and the dead. This notion that the living and the dead continue to have contact was a recurrent theme on several separate occasions, when different Mi'kmaw people told me that they either prayed or spoke to deceased family and friends. In some instances prayers or verbal appeals were made to the deceased, asking for their intervention in solving personal problems or relieving the illness of a sick friend or relative. Invocations to the deceased are made by Catholics, neo-Traditionalists, and Catholic Traditionalists alike. For Catholics, prayers are usually personal invocations rather than formalized prayers such as the Our Father or Hail Mary. Similarly, Catholic Traditionalists and neo-Traditionalists appeal to the deceased, especially ancestors, in the form of personalized prayers. Offerings to the deceased in sweats and prayer circles are sometimes prayers of thanksgiving.

The spirits of deceased loved ones, then, much like St. Anne, are appealed to for assistance in personal matters and for healing. Like St. Anne, the spirits of the deceased are believed to respond to the requests of the living.[2] Interestingly, among the Plains Cree it is also believed that "the spirits of the dead" assist the living (Young 1990: 21). In both the Cree and Mi'kmaq examples, it is the spirits and not the souls of the deceased that sustain contact with the living. I suggest that, at least for the Mi'kmaq, there is a fundamental difference between these two concepts.

One of the most notable distinctions in Mi'kmaw culture between the notions of soul and spirit is that the soul is often prayed *for*, while the spirit is prayed *to*.[3] While Catholic teachings promote the notion of the soul and an afterlife dependent on the state of the soul at death, Mi'kmaw understandings of the ***mjimaqmij***,[4] translated as "spirit" or "shadow," do not ascribe states of "sinfulness or sinlessness" to the spirit:

> The spirit in the Mi'kmaw sense of the word has nothing to do with sinfulness or sinlessness . . . it [the spirit] exists long before birth and will move on long after death. The concept of spirit is referred to as *"mjimaqmij,"* i.e., spirit or shadow.

(personal communication)

The notion of spirit and soul as they are conceptualized within Mi'kmaw society bear strong similarities to the Nunamiut (an Inuit group) notion of soul (*inua*) as described by Daniel Merkur[5]:

> [The Nunamiut of northern Alaska used] a single term [*inua*] to refer to both the indwellers in nature and to a type of soul . . . When it refers to a type of soul, *inua* is the life-force . . . The *inua* has no specific location in the body. Ordinarily conceived as it exists in life, its origin and afterlife are vague. It is usually assumed always to have existed and to exist forever in the future . . . [Another] sense in which the Nunamiut use the term *inua* pertains to the postmortem soul . . . the name-soul (i.e., the postmortem breath-soul) . . . functions as a guardian soul . . . After death, all people's *inua* are in communication with each other . . . A further type of soul concept is the *taganinga*, "shadow," which is conceived as a second self.

(Merkur 1991: 6–7)

The understanding of inua as it refers to indwellers in nature or life force bears similarities to the Mi'kmaw idea of spirit. The Nunamiut conception of the postmortem or name-soul is comparable to the Mi'kmaw notion of soul. As in the Mi'kmaw case, the Nunamiut postmortem soul "functions as a guardian soul." Significantly, the dualistic concept of soul/spirit found among the Nunamiut and the Mi'kmaq is markedly different from the concept of the single soul as it is commonly applied and understood within Western society.

The notion of sin for many Mi'kmaq, including devout Catholics, differs from standard Western conceptualizations. If a sin is committed by a Mi'kmaw person it is considered not so much an act against God or the Creator but a show of disrespect for the person who suffers because of the transgression. In most cases, the person who perpetrates the transgression is as adversely affected as the one sinned against. All Mi'kmaq are held responsible for their own actions and must come to terms with the inappropriateness of their behaviour.

Many behaviours deemed inappropriate by the Mi'kmaq are consistent with those defined as sins by the Church. However, as one woman told me, the biblical Ten Commandments are viewed by some Mi'kmaq as redundant teachings:

> I believe in my traditional roots. I no longer go to Confession and haven't for at least twenty-five years. God forgives me when I ask for forgiveness. No matter where I am God knows who I am. I'm not the only one. Natives [the Mi'kmaq] do not follow the Commandments. They are not necessary teachings. Like, "honour thy father and mother," this is not a necessary teaching because a Mi'kmaw person would not dishonour their parents. It's somethin' that they're taught from a very early age and is a part of Mi'kmaw consciousness. Most of the Commandments that are taught have no real meaning for the Mi'kmaq because they are already taught these things. The Mi'kmaq don't take everything in the Church as "Gospel." We have our own understanding of things.

(Fieldnotes, Book I: 204)

To openly defy, insult, or harm another person is considered an act inconsistent with basic Mi'kmaw beliefs and values. There is also a clear understanding that such inappropriate behaviour must be corrected. However, it is up to the individual to seek forgiveness from the one wronged, which may include God.

CONCLUSION AND DISCUSSION

In many ways, the simple statement "No one is born alone and no one should die alone" conveys an understanding of Mi'kmaw existence, which finds expression in the various rituals associated with the processes of death and dying. Apiksiktatimk, local wakes, funeral feasts, and salites, which ameliorate emotional hardship and foster reciprocity, empathy, and friendship, are literal and symbolic "identity markers" that represent key aspects of Mi'kmaw culture. Within Mi'kmaw society, the passage from this world to the next is distinguished by a series of rituals designed to assist at each stage of the death process. In this chapter, I have focused on the many dimensions of Mi'kmaw deathways and the several rites of separation, transition, and incorporation that reflect key Mi'kmaw beliefs and values.

Commenting on the funerary rituals of the Berawan of Borneo in the South Pacific, anthropologist Peter Metcalf notes that "death rites are the most compelling of community rituals. To constantly fail to attend them is to renounce membership in the community. Even when a person of little social standing dies, everyone should contribute something to the funeral" (Metcalf 2001: 21). The social importance that the Berawan attach to funerals can also be claimed for the Mi'kmaq. One of the most notable features of Mi'kmaw deathways is the degree to which community members are involved in ritual processes. Beginning with apiksiktatimk and ending with salites and funeral feasts, individual and collective participation in ritual processes associated with death and dying are obligations that are always anticipated and are continually met. The ritual of apiksitatimk is a gesture of mutual respect between dying people and survivors that allows for healing through the relieving of personal burdens of guilt and bitterness. This simple act of forgiveness also reinforces the value placed on the life of each individual community member. It is the community that extends its best wishes for the deceased and the fate of his or her soul after death. Apiksiktatimk not only helps survivors in this world but is also believed to ease the soul of the deceased in its transition from this world to the next.

Noteworthy also is the role of community members in preparing for the wake, funeral, and postinterment celebrations. As soon as a death is reported, male and female volunteers come to the assistance of the deceased's family. Anyone attending a Mi'kmaw salite and funeral feast will be immediately struck by the generosity of participants and the celebratory air of these two events. In Mi'kmaw postinterment rituals the grieving family and their guests reaffirm their ongoing mutual relationships through the sharing of resources and friendship. This exchange is significant in Mi'kmaw culture as it represents the deceased's "final act" here on earth. In addition, these ceremonies also indicate a willingness on the part of the community to share the burdens associated with bereavement, grief, and mourning. As "no one is born alone and no one should die alone," it is also believed that no one should mourn alone or bear the financial and emotional hardship resulting from the death of a loved one. Among the Mi'kmaq, implicit in the exchange of goods and friendship is the guarantee of reciprocity—a mainstay of Mi'kmaw social organization. People who extend their hand in a time of need are assured that in their own time of need, the helping hands of others will be extended.

Among the Mi'kmaq death is looked upon as an immutable fact of existence that must be faced in a practical, yet sensitive manner. In Eskasoni, bereavement associated with death is collectively felt and shared by the community. The rituals that accompany the death of a community member serve to reaffirm the continuation of Mi'kmaw society in the face of death. The Mi'kmaw experience of mourning tends to follow a specific pattern that is generally adhered to, notwithstanding individual political or religious convictions. Some features of this pattern are informed by Western ideological and institutional structures. However, other Mi'kmaw practices, such as salites, funeral feasts, and apiksiktatimk, involve specific occasions, beliefs, and values that are considered by most Mi'kmaq to be vital aspects of Mi'kmaw personal and collective identities.

CONTENT QUESTIONS

1. Which Mi'kmaw funerary practices and beliefs are culturally specific expressions of grief, mourning, and bereavement?
2. What is the significance of the salite and the funeral feast for the Mi'kmaq?
3. What is the significance of the suffix *o'q* as it is used by the Mi'kmaq?
4. Identify and discuss the different concepts of soul discussed in this chapter.

ENDNOTES

1. Among the Mi'kmaq, the terms *God* and *Creator* are often used interchangeably. The term *Niskam*, derived from *niskamij*—meaning "grandfather"—is translated as "God," whereas the term *Kisu'lkw* is translated as the "one who makes us," or "our Creator."

2. Similarly, anthropologist William Christian comments that a young priest in Spain once complained to him "that people have the false notion that they can pray to the souls in purgatory, instead of for them" (Christian 1989: 94). However, Christian points out that this notion was in fact inculcated by priests in the past. He remarks that, as in many cases, devotional practices that present-day clergy deem to be "folkloric or deviationist" are often practices that were taught by Church representatives in previous generations (Christian 1989: 94).

3. The historian Jacques Le Goff notes that "Christians seem to have acquired the habit of praying for the dead at a very early date. Le Goff argues that, in part, the development of purgatory in the late Middle Ages served to mark a distinction between the Christian concern for the souls of the deceased and the non-Christian tendency to appeal to the dead for protection: "But in order for the idea of Purgatory to develop, it was essential that the living be concerned about the fate of their dead, that the living maintain contacts with the dead, not in order to call on them for protection, but rather to improve their condition through prayer" (Le Goff 1981: 46).

4. "The initial 'm' is simply a marker telling us that the noun has not gone through declension: *Njijaqmij*, (my spirit); *kjijaqmij*, (your spirit); *wjijaqmijl*, (his/her spirit)" (personal communication).

5. Merkur draws on the work of Åke Hultkrantz, who observes that "the lowest common denominator" of traditional Inuit religion involves a dualistic concept of the soul: the life-soul, or breath soul and the free-soul (Hultkrantz 1953: 55–60, as quoted in Merkur 1991: 4).

chapter seven

Mi'kmaw Religion and Identity

The drumsong fills the air
I dance as my heart fills with happiness.
My joy I give to others in spirit
Who need but are unable to express.
The ban is still in place, put there long ago
Naming it pagan, they did not understand
My native word for God
Kisu'lkw (the One who made us)
I have had knowledge from the beginning.

Rita Joe, from "My Shadow Follows"

LEARNING OBJECTIVES

After reading this chapter, students should be able to:

- Identify various meanings of the term *traditionalism* as it is used among the Mi'kmaq.
- Trace the development of neo-Traditionalism among the Mi'kmaq.
- Discuss the cultural and social significance of the Eskasoni powwow.
- Outline the input of pan-Indian elements in the Eskasoni powwow.
- Identify the therapeutic aspects of neo-Traditionalist practices.

INTRODUCTION

On a warm, sunny afternoon in late June 1999, the Eskasoni powwow was in full swing. Voices rose in chant, dancers circled the dance ground keeping time with the rhythm and pace of the drums. Colours flashed, and beads, bone, and feathers twirled in the air and bounced against bodies caught up in the motion and drama of the dance. Suddenly, the sharp blow of a whistle brought the dancers to an abrupt halt. The chanting stopped, and silence replaced the beat of the drums. Several men formed a circle around an object lying on the ground. The master of ceremonies announced, "An eagle feather has been found in the dance circle. We have to find the owner." As he explained, the feather was now desecrated and must be "smudged" (purified) before the dancing could resume. I continued to watch as one of the dancers retrieved the feather from the ground, being careful not to touch it with his hands. A torch lit from the sacred fire was brought to purify the area where the feather had fallen. The owner was found, and the smoke was passed over him. My companion, Lynn, told me that the owner must now lose possession of the feather since he had been negligent in its care. Once the smudging was completed the owner of the feather selected a person whom he deemed worthy of receiving it. The feather was passed to Les, a man I recognized as a regular participant at St. Anne's Mission. Once the feather was in the possession of its new owner the drumming and chanting resumed, and the men began an honour dance, circling around Les to show respect and to acknowledge his new status as a feather bearer.

Lynn, a devout Catholic, brings her family to the powwow each year because she sees it as an opportunity to familiarize her children with "Native culture." Lynn explained that Les had participated in the powwow only for the past two years, and this was the first time he had received a feather—a notable event according to Lynn. Among Mi'kmaw neo-Traditionalists, the conferring of a feather bestows honour on the recipient. As Carrie, a Catholic-Traditionalist, commented to me, "The eagle feather is important to us because if we receive one we instantly earn pride and respect" (Fieldnotes, Book V: 887).

The event described occurred at the Eighth Annual Eskasoni Powwow, also referred to as the Eskasoni Mawio'mi (literally, the "Eskasoni gathering"). Powwows at Eskasoni normally run over a period of five days, usually beginning on a Thursday and ending on a Monday. The Eskasoni Mawio'mi is usually held over the weekend of the summer solstice. The powwow grounds are the locus of activity for the duration of the five-day event. However, among the local residents who come to participate in or to observe the powwow, there are diverse and often conflicting opinions about its importance and significance.

Chapter one of this book drew attention to the ways that the term *traditionalism* is variously interpreted by the Mi'kmaw people. Since I make frequent reference to these multiple interpretations throughout this chapter, it is necessary at this point to review them. For some, Mi'kmaq tradition, spirituality, and religion have very specific meanings. However, for others, Mi'kmaq tradition, spirituality, and religion are fluid concepts that are often interconnected and open to interpretation. In Eskasoni, the most commonly practised, immediately identifiable religious groups are Traditionalists—or neo-Traditionalists—Catholics, and Catholic-Traditionalists. For most Mi'kmaq, the term *Traditionalist* refers to those Mi'kmaq who subscribe to what are considered to be "authentic," pre-Christian religious practices exclusive of Catholicism. However, many Mi'kmaw Catholics understand a traditionalist as one who upholds Mi'kmaw culture and tradition but who retains Catholicism as a primary religious orientation.[1] Of these Mi'kmaw Catholics, those who consider themselves traditionalists maintain that because most of

The above photo was taken at the Eighth Annual Eskasoni Powwow. Note that the ceremonial dress worn by powwow participants is not Mi'kmaw in design. For instance, the young girl appearing on the right is wearing an Ojibwa Jingle Dress.
Photo: Angela Robinson, 1999

"authentic" Mi'kmaw religion has been irretrievably lost and because Catholicism is an ancestral religion, it is legitimately Mi'kmaq. The third group, Catholic-Traditionalists, accommodate elements of both religious affiliations in a variety of public and private devotional practices. Of the three groups, Catholic-Traditionalists are possibly the least criticized among the Mi'kmaq. It appears that individual religious expression is condoned by most Mi'kmaq as long as tradition, as it is broadly conceived, is upheld. Catholicism, along with other traditional beliefs, is respected.

Competing claims to "authentic" as opposed to "inauthentic" religio-cultural expression and beliefs are crucial for understanding the ways that identity is constructed and maintained. Participation in the Eskasoni Mawio'mi represents a specific type of neo-Traditionalism practised by only a small percentage of Eskasoni residents. Of the 200 to 300 participants in the Eskasoni powwow, I estimated that only 20 percent (approximately 1 to 2 percent of the population of Eskasoni) were from the host community. Most of the other performers/participants were from Newfoundland and Labrador, mainland Nova Scotia, Prince Edward Island, New Brunswick, or Maine. I was told that many of the visitors participating in the powwow actually "worked the powwow circuit" during the summer months, travelling in and around the Atlantic provinces and to specific destinations in the United States (personal observations). Although only a small percentage of the Eskasoni population participate, the powwow is a suitable starting point to launch a discussion of Mi'kmaw religion and identity. The dominant discourse about authenticity expressed by Mi'kmaw Catholics,

Catholic-Traditionalists, and neo-Traditionalists who do not participate in the powwow fundamentally challenges participants' claims that it is a culturally, spiritually, and/or religiously significant event.

This chapter presents a detailed ethnographic account of neo-Traditionalism in Eskasoni, including first-hand accounts by Traditionalists, Mi'kmaw Catholics, and Catholic-Traditionalists, who offer a number of diverse and often disparate views on the importance of neo-Traditionalism within the community. Here, I draw specific attention to the practice of neo-Traditionalism as a locus of dispute around which opposing discourses about Mi'kmaw identity are constructed, articulated, and openly challenged.

THE EMERGENCE OF NEO-TRADITIONALISM

During the early 1970s, anthropologist Tord Larsen recorded a number of Mi'kmaw "identity markers" that in his view best represented Mi'kmaw identity and nationhood at that period. Larsen includes the following in his list of items and occasions that are "distinctively Micmac": "native language, basketry, aboriginal legends, the game of waltes [a traditional dice game] and Indian dancing," all of which he classifies as "precontact." Larsen also lists the Micmac ideographic system (developed by the Catholic missionaries, Fathers Chrétien Le Clercq and Pierre Maillard), "customs such as *maomegisioltimk bousoubonananeouimk* ['we eat together and we wish each other a happy new year']" and the celebration of St. Anne's Mission as items that are "Catholic in origin, but heavily infused with Micmac content" (Larsen 1983: 111). By the beginning of the 21st century, however, the complexity of Mi'kmaw experience had rendered such a simplistic classification inadequate.

Throughout the last three decades of the 20th century, the Mi'kmaq, like many North American Aboriginal groups, experienced a period of cultural renaissance (Barker 1998; Churchill 2000; Goulet 1982; Grim 2000; Kidwell 2000). Part of this renaissance involves the revitalization of non-Christian Aboriginal belief systems. In Eskasoni, the rise of neo-Traditionalism is an emergent and recent phenomenon. Since the 1970s, there has been a slow but steady resurgence of Aboriginal Traditional ways. Some of these ways, such as powwows and sacred circles, are believed to derive from pan-Indian influences. "Tradition," as it is presented by Mi'kmaw Catholics, Catholic-Traditionalists, and neo-Traditionalists, involves strategically determined sets of values, beliefs, and institutions in which select aspects of "tradition" are emphasized while others are downplayed. For instance, most Mi'kmaq agree that rituals such as fasts, sweats, and the use of a sacred pipe have their origin in "authentic" Mi'kmaw practices. However, they fundamentally disagree about the original meanings of these practices and their relevance in present-day Mi'kmaw contexts.

The trend toward the revitalization of Aboriginal ways has its genesis in the American Indian Movement, which began in the late 1960s. Lori, one of the Catholic-Traditionalists with whom I spoke, was a member of this revolutionary movement, which sparked her interest in Aboriginal spirituality. Other neo-Traditionalists learned of Traditionalism while travelling to Aboriginal communities throughout the United States and Canada. Many Eskasoni residents became acquainted with neo-Traditionalism through association with local adherents and Aboriginal visitors who brought specific practices and beliefs to Eskasoni. One neo-Traditionalist told me that some Traditionalists in the community conduct sweats in the Sioux tradition. However, most neo-Traditionalists in Eskasoni attempt to follow Mi'kmaw traditions. This is often problematic because most precontact Mi'kmaw religious practices were passed on through experience and oral tradition and hence are difficult to trace. Moreover, with the inception and adoption of Roman Catholicism from the 17th century onward, many original religious practices fell into disuse. Elsie Clews Parsons observed that in the 1930s chanting and dancing were features of Grand Council activities at St. Anne's Mission. It is likely that when parish priests became the primary overseers of religious services in Mi'kmaw communities, their attempts to standardize Catholicism throughout Mi'kma'ki involved the subversion of religious practices, such as chanting, drumming, and dancing, that were formerly deemed part of Mi'kmaw Catholic tradition by the Grand Council. Significantly, Eskasoni has become one of the main centres in Nova Scotia where Aboriginals and non-Aboriginals alike congregate to participate in sweats, fasts, sacred circles, and other neo-Traditional practices.

For most Mi'kmaq, cultural creativity (or cultural revitalization) is associated with the struggle to achieve Aboriginal autonomy based on traditional Mi'kmaw beliefs and values that are independent of those promoted by Western ideologies and institutions. For many neo-Traditionalists, the struggle for autonomy includes a rejection of Roman Catholicism and a move toward Aboriginal ritual expressions found within specifically non-Western "spiritual" contexts. While this focus on the revival or re-creation of Aboriginal religious forms is celebratory for some Mi'kmaq, other community members are less enthusiastic about Traditional spirituality. However, as noted throughout this book, the rejection of Western influences by some Mi'kmaq does not necessarily make Mi'kmaw Traditionalism and Roman Catholicism mutually exclusive belief systems.

Since religion is considered by many Mi'kmaq to be of central importance in constructing and maintaining Mi'kmaw personal and social identities, it is also a forum for the articulation of conflict between Christian and non-Christian points of view. Divergent perspectives on the distant past, the recent past, and the present as they pertain to Mi'kmaw religious beliefs and expressions have given rise to internal conflicts at Eskasoni.

Reasons for adopting neo-Traditional practices are as diverse as the people who adopt them. However, there are three dominant themes that appear in the personal accounts related to me by practising neo-Traditionalists. First, powwows,[2] sweats, fasts, and participation in sacred circles are considered by most neo-Traditionalists to be religiously meaningful rituals through which individual and group spirituality is developed and maintained. Second, involvement in neo-Traditionalism is viewed by some Mi'kmaq as a means of counteracting the invasive and persistent encroachment of Western culture upon Aboriginal societies in general and upon Mi'kmaw society in particular. Third, aside from being politically and culturally relevant, the revival of Traditional ways also holds a therapeutic dimension. For many of its adherents, Traditionalism is perceived to provide a coherent and powerful therapeutic community within which a balance among the emotional, physical, and spiritual aspects of existence are facilitated and maintained. Numerous neo-Traditionalists have found non-Christian, more spiritually centred Aboriginal belief systems to be conducive to promoting physical and emotional healing and effective in helping to correct what are perceived to be imbalances in their lives.

THEORETICAL APPROACHES TO THE STUDY OF CULTURE AND TRADITION

Since the 1980s, anthropologists and other social scientists have come to the understanding that tradition and culture are not stable entities that have been inherited from the past. Anthropologist James Clifford remarks that there exists a "pervasive habit in the West of sharply distinguishing synchronic from diachronic, structure from change" (1988: 341). However, "as Marshall Sahlins (1985) has argued, these assumptions keep us from seeing how collective structures, tribal or cultural, reproduce themselves historically by risking themselves in novel conditions. Their wholeness is as much a matter of reinvention and encounter as it is of continuity and survival" (Clifford 1988: 341). Similarly, Lamont Lindstrom argues that tradition is "an attempt to read the present in terms of the past by writing the past in terms of the present" (1982: 317, cf. Hanson 1989: 890). The contemporary uses and interpretations of tradition within any given society largely depend upon who is doing the "reading." Edward Shils remarks that, in the process of transmission, traditions are prone to modification and reinterpretation by their users:

> Traditions are not independently self-productive or self-elaborating. Only living, knowing, desiring human beings can enact them and reenact them and modify them. Traditions develop because the desire to create something truer and better or more convenient is alive in those who acquire and possess them.

(Shils 1981: 14–15)

Frequently, however, the reality of tradition encountered "on the ground" (i.e., actual interactions with the people being studied) is at variance with the social scientific view of tradition that ethnographers take into the field. Richard Handler and Jocelyn Linnekin argue the following:

> "[T]radition" is at once a commonsense and a scientific category. The commonsense meaning presumes that an unchanging core of ideas and customs is inherited from the past. From the perspective of the social constructivist ethnographer, however, tradition is not "defined in terms of boundedness, givenness or essence. Rather, tradition refers to an interpretative process that involves continuity and discontinuity."

(Handler and Linnekin 1984: 273)

Handler and Linnekin observe that one inadequacy of this view of tradition is that it puts forward "a false dichotomy between the 'traditional' and 'new' as fixed mutually exclusive states." In actuality, "the ongoing reconstruction of tradition is a facet of all social life" that is symbolically constructed (1984: 273–76).

The "ethically problematic aspect" of the invention of tradition argument, according to Linnekin, is that it is perceived as being "politically revisionist and anti-native." It either implicitly or explicitly undermines the authority of Aboriginal peoples to claim cultural authenticity (Linnekin 1991: 446). In effect, the argument for the invention of culture relativizes claims to authenticity by rendering symbols, practices, and beliefs valid and authentic regardless of their genesis and the reasons for their incorporation into specific social and cultural matrices. For the ethnographer it is not problematic to give equal value to the different interpretations of tradition encountered in the field. However, for the Mi'kmaq of Cape Breton, whose very identity is at stake, discrepant claims to authenticity cannot be so easily accommodated. The personal narratives recounted in this chapter elucidate the ways that divergent religious discourses, based on specific views of tradition, are central to the debate concerning authenticity as they pertain to the formation of Mi'kmaw personal and social identity.

THE ESKASONI MAWIO'MI

The Eskasoni powwow grounds is a large open field located just off Denny's Lane. The central powwow area comprises a series of concentric circles. The inner circle, referred to as the *arbor*, is approximately 21 metres in diameter. This area is cordoned off by rope and has a roof that rises in the shape of a tepee. The arbor houses the drummers and chanters and is covered with a protective canvas tarpaulin to shelter the drums and the musicians from the elements. The middle circle, approximately 61 metres in diameter, is reserved for dance performances. Like the arbor, it is separated from the general powwow area by a rope fence. The dance circle and the arbor are considered sacred areas, meaning that entrance to both these areas is restricted to those who have been smudged by smoke from the sacred fire. This prohibition is lifted for general dances when members of the audience are invited to join in the dancing but is never lifted for the formal dances that are performed by registered dancers. The perimeter of the middle circle is the area allocated for the audience.

To the left of the dance circle and arbor is a large canvas tent where elders, honoured guests, and powwow participants share communal meals, or "feasts." Next to the food tent is the sacred fire, which is lit during a sunrise ceremony on the first day of the Eskasoni Mawio'mi. This fire is the source for all smudging ceremonies over the five days of the powwow. The fire is always attended by a "fire-keeper," who is responsible for its maintenance. Offerings of tobacco are continually added to the fire by powwow participants. The fire-keeper keeps watch to make sure that no other items are tossed into the pit.

Left of the sacred fire is the entrance to the powwow dance circle. Each day of the powwow, before the dancers enter the sacred area of the powwow grounds, officials smudge the dance ring, the arbor, and the drummers and their drums. As dancers arrive for the "Grand Entry," which marks the beginning of the day's ceremonies, they register with the master of ceremonies and proceed to the smudging area. As people are registered and smudged, they line up in single file at the entrance gate in the order in which they are registered. Once the powwow begins the master of ceremonies announces the dancer, states his or her community of origin, and announces the type of dance to be performed. Often, a person's dress indicates the type of dance performed by the wearer. The attire worn by a grass dancer varies greatly from that of a jingle dancer or fancy dancer. The origins of particular dance forms are also mentioned. For instance, the jingle dance is recognized as Ojibway, while the grass dance[3] is of Sioux origin. At the Eskasoni Mawio'mi, pan-Indian, or cross-cultural, content is acknowledged and duly noted by the master of ceremonies. In most cases, the significance of the dance is also publicly stated. At the Eskasoni Mawio'mi, it was announced that the Ojibway jingle dance is conducted for the purpose of healing. The original jingle dress, upon which present-day jingle dresses are modelled, is reported to have been made by an Ojibway man whose wife was ailing. My companion Lynn informed me that "the old man made the dress for his wife and said a prayer with each jingle that he put on the dress. There's supposed to be 365 jingles on the dress—one for each day of the year" (Fieldnotes, Book I: 162). Once the jingle dance is announced, people who are ill or those who wish to dance on behalf of a sick relative or loved one are invited into the ring. Lynn remarked that this dance always reminds her of St. Anne's Mission because "the sick are being prayed for" (Fieldnotes, Book I: 162).

Many of the dances included in the powwow celebrations are ceremonial, while others are simply for the demonstration of expertise and entertainment. Because "honour," or "ceremonial dances," are considered sacred performances, members of the audience are requested to refrain from taping, filming, or taking pictures while they are being performed.

Outside the sacred area of the powwow grounds is a large area reserved for vending booths. The booths are rented by individuals and groups offering a variety of items for sale. There are a number of stalls selling snack foods, such as ice cream, hotdogs, pop, and "four cents cake," a local type of flat bread. Venders at various other booths offer Aboriginal handicrafts for sale, including basketry, beaded accessories, dream catchers, and locally crafted items. Venders often sell raffle tickets on prize items. For instance, at one booth tickets were being sold for Aboriginal crafts to raise money for a local charity. In another instance, a woman wishing to go to the shrine of Sainte-Anne-de-Beaupré in Quebec sold tickets to raise travel money.

NEO-TRADITIONALISM AND IDENTITY

Like St. Anne's Mission, the Eskasoni Mawio'mi holds a number of different meanings for different people. For some Mi'kmaq, the powwow is a ritualized celebration of origins and symbolic artifacts that date back to a precontact past involving music, dance, regalia, and communal gathering as vital aspects of Mi'kmaw identity. Although particular features of the Eskasoni Mawio'mi may differ from precontact ritual occasions, it is the performance portion of the powwow that makes it a meaningful event for many Mi'kmaw participants. Claiming the Eskasoni Mawio'mi as a culturally significant and religiously meaningful ceremony is equivalent to appealing to ritual practices and beliefs that are believed to be derived from precontact ideologies and institutions. However, as mentioned, the predominant discourse shared by many Catholic and non-Catholic Mi'kmaq maintains that this particular performance genre holds little historical, religious, or cultural significance for most Mi'kmaq. Primarily, the powwow is viewed as a social occasion.

In many respects, the Eskasoni Mawio'mi is analogous to St. Anne's Mission. Like Se't-ta'newimk, the powwow is an occasion to gather and socialize. As with the spiritual or religious aspects of the mission, the Eskasoni Mawio'mi is symbolically ambiguous. The powwow can also be seen as the inverse of the mission. Catholic Mi'kmaq ascribe religious and spiritual significance to Se'tta'newimk, whereas many neo-Traditionalists view the mission as culturally and socially significant but religiously (though not necessarily spiritually) marginal. Conversely, some neo-Traditionalists view the powwow as a sacred occasion, while Mi'kmaw Catholics consider it to be religiously, but not necessarily spiritually, marginal. In Eskasoni, the multiple discourses on identity that arise in response to the event of the powwow are diverse and contradictory.

As mentioned, for some Mi'kmaq, especially those who are not involved in neo-Traditionalism, the Eskasoni Mawio'mi may be viewed as a social occasion with little or no cultural or spiritual significance. Rather, it is an occasion where features of pan-Indianism are displayed, most of which fall outside of "authentic" Mi'kmaw tradition. While most Mi'kmaq acknowledge that specific styles of drumming, chanting, and dancing[4] are Mi'kmaq in origin, they also recognize that many neo-Traditional practices are unfamiliar to most Mi'kmaq born in the 20th century. One visitor from a neighbouring Mi'kmaw community, a Catholic woman in her 80s, commented that her "parents never did anything like that." For some Mi'kmaq, many neo-Traditionalist practices are perceived as "invented" traditions that are unconnected to established Mi'kmaw convention. Other Mi'kmaq view specific aspects of Traditionalism, especially the various beliefs and expressions that have been imported through pan-Indianism, as threatening to "authentic" Mi'kmaw culture and tradition. Jonal, introduced in chapter one, is a middle-aged Catholic man who views tradition as attached to Mi'kmaw language and culture. He sees some neo-Traditional practices as abusive and threatening to "true" Mi'kmaw ways:

> Some of those people are angry and Traditionalism is a platform for venting their anger, but there are other groups who call themselves the "real" traditionalists—"true"

traditionalists who are devoted to what our ancestors believed. "Traditionalists" is a bad name for the others. They've abused the name. Many of them have been drug abusers. Some of them claim certain powers. You can't claim them just like that!

(Fieldnotes, Book IV: 728)

Explicit in Jonal's statement is the belief that Mi'kmaw beliefs and values have more cultural depth than the symbols associated with powwow "exhibitionism" and therefore must be upheld. For Jonal, the powwow is a gross oversimplification of Aboriginal traditions. It has little to do with Mi'kmaw ancestral practices but threatens to absorb them on some level. For Jonal, the events of the powwow are understood as a set of generic Aboriginal motifs that must remain separate from the elements of Mi'kmaw culture through which their "true" Mi'kmaw beliefs and values are expressed.

Len, a non-Christian Mi'kmaq, also negatively views the incorporation of non-Mi'kmaw traditions of any type into Mi'kmaw society. Len told me that he was concerned:

[T]hey're bringing in so-called spiritual leaders from other Native groups ... I've listened to these people and I attended some of the meetings that they conducted ... under the name of spirituality. I'm concerned about that because ... the question I keep asking myself is this, "Is it better to be bamboozled by non-Natives or is it better to be bamboozled by other Natives?"... My feeling is that it's worse when we get bamboozled by our cousins ... We don't need that anymore ... It's time now that we begin to look deeply at the Mi'kmaw culture and allow the culture to tell us the direction that we should go spiritually.

(taped interview)

For Len, adopting pan-Indian culture or relying on external religious influences is analogous to rejecting, or at least obscuring, "authentic" Mi'kmaw practices. From Len's perspective, Mi'kmaw identity and autonomy must necessarily be independent of all alien symbolic artifacts, including those of "other" Aboriginal cultures. For Len, it is imperative to discourage any attachment to non-Mi'kmaw influences that pose a potential threat to Mi'kmaw autonomy and identity.

ADOPTING NEO-TRADITIONALISM

As remarked throughout this book, neo-Traditionalism in Eskasoni is variously interpreted and practised. In most instances, the ideological and institutional aspects of traditionalism, such as the role of the Grand Council, and particular beliefs about the soul/spirit and the afterlife, which are believed to be authentically Mi'kmaq, have been incorporated into Mi'kmaw Catholicism. However, there is a group of neo-Traditionalists who question Catholic beliefs and teachings at a fundamental level. Matt, Mitch, and Gordon are neo-Traditionalists who are critical of Catholicism for a number of reasons. Matt and Mitch outrightly reject Catholicism, while Gordon holds a critical but more moderate view of the Church.

Matt, a man from Eskasoni in his 40s, became involved in neo-Traditionalism in the mid-1980s. Matt suggests that many of the forms of neo-Traditionalism currently practised in Eskasoni are not authentically Mi'kmaw:

There are different groups of Traditionalists here [in Eskasoni]—different factions. Sioux followers are here. There are Mi'kmaw Traditionalists and then there's these others. We call them "cowboys" because they want their booze, they want their drugs, they want their party and they want their sweat lodge. They do their stuff, but it's not right for me to go over there and tell them they're disrespectin' because they're doing that. It's not right for me to do that. I follow the Mi'kmaw way.

(taped interview)

Matt's account of the community's reaction to his adopting Traditionalism as his religion of choice gives us some indication of the importance Eskasoni residents attach to personal religious conviction:

Soon as I went Traditional, soon as I started going to ceremonies, people started coming. I'd get calls. It was a rough ride there for awhile. They let go [eventually]—they just stopped...I'm not sure if they feared it [Traditionalism] or [if] it was just me... My kids used to get beat up at the bus stop...They were beaten up at school. They [the community] turned around on me just because I wanted to be who I am. I'm L'nu. I'm Mi'kmaw. I don't need the Church...They [the community] would've liked it better if I stayed a Catholic and stayed drunk...[In Traditionalism] I was granted a healing...I realized, "there's something there!"

(taped interview)

Matt's account of the community's reaction to his turning Traditional seems to suggest a social bias against Traditionalism within the community. He believes that within Catholicism the Mi'kmaw people have developed a narrow cultural, religious, and spiritual focus. According to Matt, instead of acknowledging the therapeutic and positive aspects of Traditionalism the community continues to uphold faith in and allegiance to Mi'kmaw Catholicism. Conversely, Matt aligns his adoption of neo-Traditionalism and his subsequent rejection of Catholicism as essential to his identity as L'nu or Mi'kmaw. Matt feels that Western institutions, like the Church, retain little meaning for him as a Mi'kmaw person. He criticizes the Church as an institution because, in his view, it adds to social problems by imposing strict moral rules and by undermining Mi'kmaw culture and society.

For the most part, Matt's move away from Catholicism and subsequent involvement in neo-Traditionalism was prompted by his own personal dilemmas. Matt experienced a difficult childhood with an alcoholic father who repeatedly physically and mentally abused his family:

My father was one of my biggest critics...I was never man enough. I was never smart enough. I was never good enough. Nothing was ever good enough for him. When I started going Traditional that was another thing. I was gonna go to hell. "You're leaving the Church, what the hell's wrong with you, you dog-eater?" and all that bullshit.

(taped interview)

However, Matt also considers the Church to be as abusive and detrimental to his well-being as were his father's personal attacks. Matt claims that the Church fosters social problems by offering negative criticism and by failing to promote a positive Mi'kmaw image:

I had no belief at all. I attended church. I was a so-called good Christian that went every Sunday like clockwork. Take my family, go sit in the front—right in the front—sit there and listen to this priest. Well, he was always criticizin,' puttin' down the people when he spoke . . . He would read this gospel and then interpret it the way he thought it was and a lot of the time it was all negative. Like, I couldn't relate to that. Being a Native and being in school and listening to the nuns criticize us and put us down through school. I got married and I'm at church and I'm listening to the priest every Sunday puttin' our people down. Never once a positive message! I couldn't understand it . . . I know that some priests that were here were really racist priests. Hypocrites! I couldn't take it anymore. I couldn't go to that church anymore.

(taped interview)

In Matt's opinion, the Church and its representatives are quick to undermine Mi'kmaw culture and society, therefore encouraging negativity rather than actively working to resolve social problems within the community. He feels that prior to becoming a Traditionalist there was an excess of negativity in his life, partly brought on by Catholicism and partly the result of his family situation. Matt suggests that since he saw Catholicism as contributing to his problems, neo-Traditionalism became a viable means of alleviating his anger at himself and others:

I was a very angry man when I started. Through a lot of fasting and soul-searching I worked through all that anger . . . It's a tough road, the Traditional path. It's a very tough road 'cause you do a lot of soul-searching for the first few years. [It will] take you maybe seven years to really understand yourself . . . It took a long time just for that to sink in . . . To figure out how to forgive. How to forgive all these people who tormented me in my life.

(taped interview)

In Matt's view, his troubled family life was compounded by feelings of insecurity and inferiority resulting from religious and social marginalization. In Eskasoni, the negative views of neo-Traditionalism are fuelled, at least in part, by the fact that many of those who have found a healing within neo-Traditionalist practices are people like him who had previously been socially marginalized within the community. Matt admits to having been an abusive person with a drinking problem, who, at times, expressed his anger through physical acts of violence. Many, but not all, of the neo-Traditionalists with whom I spoke told me that they have been accused of different social transgressions, such as sexual abuse, physical abuse, alcoholism, drug abuse, and adultery. Such behaviours are perceived as the cause of serious social strife within the community. Most Eskasoni residents are very critical of them. However, many neo-Traditionalists believe that, at base, the Catholic Church is responsible for this type of moral outrage that results in the marginalization of community members. Most of the neo-Traditionalists with whom I spoke see the Catholic Church's imposition of strict moral codes as reinforcing a social hierarchy that encourages the demoralization of those who transgress those social and moral codes. That is, those who remain within the Catholic Church and follow its rules and regulations are looked upon as morally and socially superior, whereas those who do not follow Church teachings are perceived as being morally and socially inferior. Catholicism, then, is viewed by some Mi'kmaq as an institution that reinforces a hierarchical social order in a community that subscribes to an egalitarian ethos. In effect, for some Mi'kmaq neo-Traditionalism operates in opposition to the authority claimed by the Church and reinforced in the institution of the Grand Council.

In Mitch's case, it was ostracism by the community that forced him to leave the home where he had lived for nearly 40 of his 46 years. Mitch was born and raised in Eskasoni, and as a young man settled there with his wife and family. Now divorced and remarried to a white girl, Mitch works and lives in a nearby non-Aboriginal community. His reasons for leaving Eskasoni are many but are primarily connected to his separation from his first wife, his subsequent marriage to Marla, and his adoption of neo-Traditionalism. Mitch was always a "good" Catholic and regularly attended church from the time he was a young child until approximately eight years ago:

> I was a good Catholic, was involved in the Church and all that, but somehow it all seemed too hollow to me. Even when I was doin' these things I wasn't really into it ... I went from being a outstandin' citizen to being an outcast. It started a long time ago ... Eight or nine years ago when I was still married to my first wife rumours started that I was having an affair and eventually got to my [Catholic] prayer group who made trouble for me. It was very uncomfortable. It was after this that things started to change for me. I still went to Mass, but I started to get involved in Traditionalism. I went to a few sweats and started to pray in the four directions. The people in my [Catholic] prayer group found out about the sweats and asked me about it. I told them that I'd gone to sweats and found them helpful. One woman in the group started to make fun of Traditionalism ... Before I did the sweats I spent a lot of time in the Church, but I never thought I was truly spiritual. I went to church ... because it was habit, and it was expected of me. When I did sweats I still went to church and the [Catholic] prayer groups but some people didn't agree with what I was doing and told me so.

> *(Fieldnotes, Book V: 1001–1003)*

Mitch suggests that throughout his life he had always attempted to follow the rules of the Church and to live a good life. However, he told me that he had been unhappy in his marriage and only intended to stay married until his children were grown (Fieldnotes, Book V: 1001). Mitch also suggested that part of his dissatisfaction stemmed from an unfulfilled religious life. He claims that he did not feel spiritual as a practising Catholic but only found spiritual meaning within Traditionalism. Mitch's disillusionment with the Church and its followers increased when members of his prayer group began to ridicule his new spiritual leanings. Like Matt, Mitch feels that for many Mi'kmaw Catholics alternative religious orientations are rarely encouraged and, in some cases, are not tolerated. In Mitch's view, Catholicism imposes restrictive moral and social rules that prescribe a specific code of behaviour that leaves little room for error. Therefore, anyone who moves outside the parameters of the prescribed code to, for example, seek a divorce, live in a common-law relationship, or search for healing within an alternative spiritual community must be prepared to bear the brunt of ridicule and risk potential ostracism. For Mitch, adopting neo-Traditionalism met at least two of his personal needs. He was part of a therapeutic religious group that promoted spirituality and healing at a fundamental level, and he was part of a community that accepted his personal lifestyle choices.

Gordon, another Mi'kmaw man in his late 40s, became involved in neo-Traditionalism in the 1980s. As with Matt and Mitch, it was spiritual healing that Gordon sought and received through Traditionalism. Gordon considers neo-Traditionalist practice to be a difficult, but worthwhile, spiritual orientation. He remarks:

> My first experience with Traditionalism was incredible. The first time that I went to a praying circle and a sweat I prayed so hard that I didn't worry about anything. Really,

we were sacrificing ourselves. The feelings were so intense it terrified me. When I started out in the [sweat] lodge I almost had a heart attack. After I was there for awhile, I felt the spirit of my dead brother, my grandfather and my close family. It's hard to explain. You see, we [Traditionalists] don't go to heaven or hell, we go to the spirit world. Our tradition is here, it's not in another land . . . When we want to know things we fast. We do it by the heart. We don't lie about it. Traditionalists are very strict in their ways. You have to do it in person, you can't have someone do it for you. It is very beautiful though. Easy, and very powerful and tough at the same time.

(Fieldnotes, Book V: 664–65)

Although Gordon is critical of the Catholic Church, he does not renounce it. He explains that he left the Catholic faith for several reasons, and the reluctance of the Catholic community to accept Traditionalism figures prominently. Gordon also takes issue with the hierarchical structures reinforced by the Church as well as its fundamental tenets and beliefs about the ability of Jesus to provide salvation:

We [Traditionalists] don't renounce the Church, but we'd like to see changes. I don't like this whole idea that Jesus is going to save us. Jesus is a middleman. God is who we have to pay respect to—our Creator. I'd sooner take the more humble and more comfortable approach to being saved and that's through Traditionalism. I think Traditionalism is more in line with Jesus' teachings than what we hear in the Church . . . For Mi'kmaw [Traditionalists] there is no worship of idols, no churches, priests or nuns. Religion is a matter directly between the person and God—their Creator . . . I'm offended when people ridicule us when we're praying and sweating for our people . . . We go to funerals out of respect, but there's a lot of prejudice among our own people. Have you ever walked into a room full of men? Do you know how you feel then? Uncomfortable isn't it? Well, it's like that for me when I go to church. You're an Indian, but you feel that you're a disgrace to your people. There's lots of healers and freaks all over the place around here. That makes it difficult for us . . . What we do is offer tobacco, but you have to believe first in your heart. If you find yourself in a certain situation, say you are a drunk, you have to ask yourself why you are in this condition. It's a sickness and you have to look for purification and health. We don't emphasize glorification of a God and we don't want wealth—we only use tobacco. Our medicine people will help you if you offer tobacco and you're serious about your request . . . I go at least once a month. I feel better when I go, better than when I go to church. In the circle we're all one, no one is any better or any worse than the other.

(Fieldnotes, Book III: 663–65)

As with the two previous respondents, Gordon's experiences with neo-Traditionalism reveal a dimension of spirituality that he had previously not known. Gordon's critique of the Church suggests that its theological principles promote an indirect route to personal salvation through Jesus Christ that denies the supplicant direct experience of his Creator. Alternatively, Gordon proposes that the capacity of Mi'kmaw neo-Traditionalism to provide salvation and therapy comes from direct encounters with the spiritual world, which, rather than emphasizing life in the hereafter, addresses personal and immediate concerns of this life.

CATHOLIC-TRADITIONALISTS

Each year at the Eskasoni Mawio'mi, a lead dancer is chosen to oversee dance ceremonies. This task is a demanding one that requires a great deal of physical effort in leading several dances per day over a period of five days. In 1999 the lead dancer was Ross, a Mi'kmaw man from Eskasoni. Lynn told me that Ross had been a problem drinker before becoming involved in local powwows. She explained that "since he's been participating [in the powwows] he has cleaned up a bit." Lynn, like others in the community, believes that ceremonial dancing helps Ross with his drinking problem. She told me that "when [Ross] started to dance he had no regalia. He used cheap dime-store cotton scarves that he wrapped around his head, and his arms and legs. After that the people in the community got together and made him a rib-bon shirt—the one he's wearing now" (Fieldnotes, Book I: 165–66). Significantly, Ross also participates in St. Anne's Mission. He is not a member of the Grand Council and does not have any official capacity at Se'tta'newimk, although he often acts as a member of St. Anne's security.

Ross is a Catholic-Traditionalist, who, like many others in Eskasoni, participates in neo-Traditionalist practices but also maintains close ties to the Catholic Church. Among those who have adopted neo-Traditionalist practices without abandoning Roman Catholicism are Carrie and Lori. Carrie, a Catholic-Traditionalist, incorporates elements of Catholicism into neo-Traditionalist contexts. Lori privileges neither the Christian nor the Traditional aspects of her faith.

Carrie, an Eskasoni woman in her early 50s, is a devout Roman Catholic but has par-ticipated in the powwow for the past five years. Carrie recalls that she attended her first powwow with a great deal of trepidation but has since become involved in the event, par-ticipating annually. Like Piel (introduced in chapter one), Carrie interprets neo-Tradition-alism within the framework of Catholicism. Carrie does not view the powwow as a religious occasion per se but accepts it as a part of Aboriginal spirituality, identity, and culture. She explains that her appreciation for Mi'kmaw traditions evolved over a long period. She does not view taking part in the powwow as a challenge to her Roman Catholic roots:

> When I got older I began to understand Mi'kmaw traditions more and more. I came to see that it [tradition] is a spiritual and cultural thing that can't be found in other ways. Native people know that the world is alive around them. There's life in everything. Tra-ditionalism is part of a spiritual awakening. It shows that the spirit is alive and that we have values and cultural pride. It's important for people to speak out as Natives. Spir-ituality is complicated. We have to listen to others. The seed is there, but where is the seed going? Why are there choices? For me, whatever comes out as good is good—a person who is good is good . . . I was worried about "Traditionalism" at first. This is an all-Catholic community and I felt that this was something that I couldn't accept. When they started the powwows I didn't feel too good about it, but I decided to go see for myself. By the second night my toes were tapping. Many of my friends and fam-ily were there and some were involved in the powwow. I thought to myself, this is where it is. God wants me to join in. I just love it now. I can smile back at people. I have confidence in myself and my own Indian identity started coming out. I even camp out there now, even though I live in Eskasoni. But, I stay there, sleep there and my friends come by and have a cup of tea and something to eat. I really enjoy being there. I dance and dance and I love it. I feel free, but not as free as I want to. When I'm in the lit side of the arbor I take my time and I dance politely and when I'm on

the dark side I break out, I go crazy. So, I still hold myself back, but not as much as I used to. First I was really shy but now I can dance by myself if I want to.

(Fieldnotes, Book V: 831–32)

Carrie's suggestion that the powwow offers a spirituality and culture that "can't be found in other ways" implies that, for her, Catholicism is spiritually and culturally limited. Carrie's experiences at the powwow revealed a side of Mi'kmaw life that was previously unavailable to her. Like Piel, for whom the cultural and spiritual significance of neo-Traditionalism is made meaningful within a Christian frame of reference, Carrie draws a distinction between religion and spirituality. For Carrie, the powwow becomes spiritually meaningful only when Catholic elements are incorporated into the performance.

Carrie, however, is discriminating in her support of the powwow and other aspects of neo-Traditionalism. She believes that the Mi'kmaq must be cautious about the way in which they incorporate Aboriginal spirituality into religious practices:

We've got to be careful how we use our traditional ways. We have to understand our own Native spirituality before it's used freely. Many of the elders in our church didn't want those things introduced. They didn't want new things. They wanted to continue on the way we always did in the church. They were afraid for some reason. Maybe they didn't think it was right. We have to understand what's going on with drumming and dancing. The beat of the drum is like a heartbeat that wakes up mother earth. It wards off evil spirits. It makes you confident and gives you inner peace. When I dance, I dance for my Lord.

(Fieldnotes, Book V: 87–88)

Aside from connecting her to her Aboriginal roots, participation in the powwow also affords Carrie the freedom to worship the Lord in a specifically Aboriginal context. Interestingly, Carrie did not pursue neo-Traditionalism for the purpose of healing. Rather, it answers to her spiritual needs while reinforcing cultural integrity and Aboriginal identity.

Lori, another Mi'kmaw woman from Eskasoni in her 50s, also finds cultural and spiritual significance in neo-Traditionalism. Although Lori is actively involved in sacred circles, sweats, and fasts in Eskasoni and elsewhere on a regular basis, she does not see participation in the powwow as a necessary means of expressing her Traditionalism. However, she does not deny that the powwow is of benefit to some people. Like Matt and Mitch, Lori turned to neo-Traditionalism for healing. Lori recalls her negative experiences in the Shubenacadie residential school, which culminated in a lifetime of physical and emotional abuse. Lori finds that Roman Catholicism alone no longer answers her spiritual and emotional needs. She blames the Church for many of her personal problems. Lori does not reject the religion in which she was raised. She still attends church regularly and receives the sacraments. However, she feels that, to some degree, the Catholic Church denies her "Indianness." "I feel really good in Church," says Lori, "but there are times when I need something more. The Church just can't help me. Usually, it's when I start thinking about residential school and what happened there" (Fieldnotes, Book IV: 768). About her experiences at the Shubenacadie school Lori says the following:

I was a mess . . . I really thought that I had no spirituality left. I used to pray to understand. I'd get a rush of images and eventually the answers came . . . I needed to be

alone to heal myself. I found healing in Traditionalism . . . I wanted to pray like an
Indian. I wanted to be an Indian. I wanted to pray but my Catholic upbringing held me
back. An old woman told me to pray to the four directions. I didn't know how. So, I
asked the Creator and then I knew how to pray. I asked in Mi'kmaq.

(Fieldnotes, Book IV: 705, 709)

Lori, like Matt, Mitch, and Gordon, is a Mi'kmaw who felt that the help she needed to
repair her life could not be found within Catholicism. It is significant that most of the neo-
Traditionalists that I interviewed have found spiritual fulfilment and emotional healing
within neo-Traditional religion.

CATHOLICISM AND NEO-TRADITIONALISM

The idiosyncratic nature of neo-Traditionalist practices draws attention to discrepancies
between individual autonomy and social convention. For many Mi'kmaq, neo-Traditionalism represents a break from contemporary Mi'kmaw social convention. In Eskasoni, dominant definitions of acceptable moral behaviour are informed by the beliefs and values
associated with Mi'kmaw Catholicism. For instance, in Eskasoni, views on common-law
unions and divorce are fundamentally consistent with Roman Catholic teachings. It is commonly accepted in Eskasoni that if you are "shackin' up"—that is, living in a common-law
relationship—then you are unable to receive the sacrament of communion. This prohibition
is not part of Church law but is a social restriction generally upheld by the Mi'kmaq themselves. Likewise, Mi'kmaw views on divorce are similar to those held by the Catholic Church.
As we saw in Mitch's case, his divorce and subsequent remarriage caused him to be socially
marginalized within the community.

As noted throughout this book, Mi'kmaw Catholicism is important to the majority of
Mi'kmaq. However, some Mi'kmaq argue that Western ideologies and the institutions that
embody them encourage negative responses to neo-Traditionalism. The Mi'kmaq, like most
North American Aboriginal groups, have yet to escape from the negative impact of a colonial racism that maintains an invisible but very real barrier between them and their non-
Aboriginal neighbours. For many Mi'kmaq, especially Mi'kmaw Catholics, along with the
development of and continued involvement in non-Christian Aboriginal religions, there is
the attendant fear of being labelled *pagans*, *heathens,* or *nonbelievers* by non-Aboriginal
Christians. Among Mi'kmaw Catholics, one defensive strategy against such labelling is
social and ideological distancing that finds expression in a critique and a concomitant marginalization of neo-Traditionalism. Once, when I asked a Mi'kmaw elder what he thought
about Mi'kmaw Traditionalists he responded, "Who, the born-again savages?" At the time
I was taken aback by his answer, but as my fieldwork progressed I began to understand his
reaction to my question. Pan-Indian movements and the rise of neo-Traditionalism have
been widely disparaged by Mi'kmaw Catholics who believe that the Catholic Church is a
fundamental part of existing Mi'kmaw culture and society. As mentioned earlier, apologists
for Mi'kmaw Catholicism argue that Catholicism is more traditional than many of the pan-
Indian or neo-Traditionalist practices and beliefs that have been adopted by some Eskasoni
residents since the 1970s. Associated with the practice of Mi'kmaw Catholicism is the notion
that the Mi'kmaq are a "civilized" people who, prior to European contact, "knew God."
According to this perspective, the acceptance of Catholicism among the Mi'kmaq is a means

through which indigenous belief is upheld. Similarly, several Mi'kmaq assured me their ancestors were never "sun worshippers," as the Catholic missionaries supposed. The Mi'kmaq understood the natural world and saw the sun as necessary to the process of creation. Within this particular discourse the sun was seen as the source of all life but was not deified (taped interview, January 2000).

In addition, as discussed earlier, there is a strong attachment in Eskasoni to the Catholic faith, especially among the middle-aged and elderly. James, a man in his early 60s who comes from a devoutly Catholic family, told me that "in the final stages of his life, my father made a simple request. He said 'When I die don't let them throw tobacco at me and get on with their noise. I don't want any of that'" (Fieldnotes, Book III: 699). James's father belonged to a generation that is generally skeptical about neo-Traditionalist practices. When I asked James how he felt about the Traditionalists he said:

> I don't mind them. They do their own thing. Sometimes they come to the church on certain occasions. When the Traditionalists started they butted into things. Now they have the good sense to ask people what they want. If someone is sick and dying they'll ask the family if they want drumming and chanting. They didn't do that at first.
>
> *(Fieldnotes, Book III: 699)*

A similar position is taken by Ron, a middle-aged Mi'kmaw from Eskasoni. Ron is a Catholic who is not involved in neo-Traditionalism, but he normally attends the annual Eskasoni Mawio'mi. Aside from being a social occasion, Ron views the powwow as having little value for Mi'kmaq:

> The powwow is the Traditionalists' attempt to be spiritual, but they have no real leadership. There's no one with the fortitude to lead "those things." It's a time for them [Traditionalists] to "do their thing," whatever that may be. People involved in the powwow are those who haven't made an impression on us in our everyday lives. These are people who made mistakes in their own lives. There's an outward appearance of restitution, but inwardly there's no change. It's like those people walked into a different room because most of us believe that they haven't really changed. If you walk into another room you're only changing places. The powwow is an attempt to prove that they're renewed people. We don't see ourselves following the people who make a show of drumming, chanting and dancing. Other Mi'kmaq besides the Traditionalists do go to the powwow, but this is a social thing and doesn't have anything to do with any real belief in what's going on. The Mi'kmaw people have made judgements about the Traditionalists, but they are not good ones.
>
> *(Fieldnotes, Book I: 11)*

For Ron, the drumming, dancing, and chanting performed at the powwow is not objectionable. Rather, it is the context and manner in which these practices are carried out that he calls into question. In Ron's opinion, to "make a show" of one's beliefs is exploitative and distances the experience from a profoundly felt spirituality or a genuine appreciation for Mi'kmaw culture. Ron sees powwows as occasions where specific neo-Traditionalist agendas are set and as social settings where culture, religion, and spirituality are taken out of their original context and used for purposes for which they were not intended. Ron's suggestion that the powwow has a political dimension is supported by one specific "sin of omission" at the Eighth Annual Eskasoni Mawio'mi. Each previous year the local parish priest was invited to say Sunday Mass at the powwow grounds. At the Eighth Annual Eskasoni Mawio'mi, however, powwow organizers did not extend an invitation to the local priest, and no Mass took place. Some Mi'kmaw Catholics saw this as a retaliation against the Grand Council, which had refused to allow a powwow to be performed at Potlotek during the St. Anne's Mission (Fieldnotes, 1997).

For some community members, Traditionalist practices are closely aligned with spirituality and culture but must be distinguished from religion. In addition, there is the understanding that neo-Traditionalists are often indiscriminate in the expression of their spirituality, as Mara, a Catholic woman in her early 50s from Eskasoni, commented:

> Traditionalists are those who have discovered their spirituality. You have to see the difference between spirituality and religion. Some grab onto whatever they can get, but we try to live our culture and spirituality everyday—it's the Mi'kmaw way. It's easier for people of my generation because we know our language. It's not so easy for others. It's harder for them to grasp . . . You have to apply Traditionalism to the individual. It's an individual thing and not all people present it in a favourable light. [For instance, Mark] is not a good role model. He's a rapist and people don't like that. When they want to teach Traditionalism at the school for whatever reason, they won't ask [him] because too many parents don't want him [there].

(Fieldnotes, Book IV: 728)

Mara's comments about spirituality, religion, and Traditionalism exhibit some deeply held convictions about Mi'kmaw society and culture that have been touched upon throughout this book. Mara believes that people like her, who grew up speaking the Mi'kmaw language and were socialized in Mi'kmaw culture, hold a privileged position within Mi'kmaw society. She does not endorse neo-Traditionalism because she perceives it as a feeble attempt by those who do not "live our culture and spirituality everyday . . . to grab onto whatever they can get." Like many people from Eskasoni, Mara believes that Mi'kmaw culture, religion, and identity are maintained by speaking and thinking in the Mi'kmaw language and by living in accordance with the "Mi'kmaw way."

CONCLUSION AND DISCUSSION

During the 1970s and early 1980s, for those Mi'kmaq who had been born and raised within the Catholic faith neo-Traditionalism was an unfamiliar religious orientation. However, since the 1990s the increased interest in neo-Traditionalism among a certain sector of Mi'kmaw society has led to a general familiarity with neo-Traditionalist practices. This acceptance may result in part from Pope John Paul II's publication of *Missio Redemptoris* in 1991, which called for the incorporation of Traditional rituals into the Roman Catholic liturgy. At the turn of the 21st century there are many Mi'kmaq who view neo-Traditionalism as spiritually meaningful and culturally relevant. However, as mentioned in chapter one, many Catholic Mi'kmaq can accept neo-Traditionalism as spiritually meaningful only as long as it is practised in accordance with, and not exclusive of, the Catholic faith. I use the term *spiritually* here, because although I consider neo-Traditionalism a religious orientation according to Geertz's (1973) definition of religion, Mi'kmaw practitioners of neo-Traditionalism and Mi'kmaw Catholics alike rarely refer to neo-Traditionalism as a religion. They almost exclusively refer to it as a form of spirituality. This reluctance to classify neo-Traditionalism as a religion may be grounded in popular understandings of the definition of the term. In common usage, *religion* is often used as a referent for institutionalized practices, which, of course, excludes noninstitutionalized religious orientations like neo-Traditionalism. Furthermore, some neo-Traditionalists may be reluctant to assign the Western category of religion to a non-Western faith.

Throughout this chapter, I have presented the ways that neo-Traditionalists perceive their religious choice(s) and the responses to these choices within the community at large. Neo-Traditionalism has two specific consequences for the Mi'kmaq of Eskasoni. First, involvement in neo-Traditionalism provides its practitioners with an alternative therapeutic community in which healing takes place and in which equality of social status and personal self-worth is reaffirmed. Second, the practice of neo-Traditionalism is a contentious issue around which divergent views on what constitutes "authentic" Mi'kmaw tradition emerge and are called into question.

I have suggested in previous chapters that the negotiation of personal and collective Mi'kmaw identities ultimately rests on the ways in which religion, spirituality, tradition, and culture are constructed and maintained within Mi'kmaw society. Catholic Mi'kmaq subsume Mi'kmaw Catholicism under the rubric of tradition, while most non-Catholic Mi'kmaq challenge this claim to "authenticity." For non-Catholic Traditionalists, "authentic" Mi'kmaw practices and beliefs originate within a pre-Christian past. In addition, the argument promoted by many neo-Traditionalists, including Catholic-Traditionalists, that Catholicism is culturally and spiritually limiting is circumvented by the Mi'kmaw Catholics who claim that spirituality and religion are discrete categories that should not be confused.

In this chapter, I have also provided a number of possible explanations for the prominence of anti-Traditionalist statements expressed by Catholic Mi'kmaq. First, as noted above, many Catholics clearly distinguish Traditionalism from spirituality. Conversely, many Mi'kmaw Catholics view neo-Traditionalism, not as a legitimate religion, but as a form of spirituality. Second, in North America the persistence of negative colonial attitudes continues to desacralize indigenous religions, contributing to their continued marginalization even within the Aboriginal communities in which they are practised. Third, the move toward neo-Traditionalism is viewed by some Mi'kmaq as a contravention of commonly accepted Mi'kmaw social and cultural norms and values.

In summary, the rise of neo-Traditionalism in Eskasoni, and local opposition to it, is one of the internal struggles with which the Mi'kmaq, like many other Aboriginal groups in North America, are forced to contend. The competing discourses that emerge from such struggles, the "politics of identity" that they embody, and the claims to "authenticity" negotiated within these divergent views become manifest in complex local religious expressions that remain culturally meaningful and historically emergent.

CONTENT QUESTIONS

1. What is meant by neo-Traditionalism?

2. What are some of the main reasons for the adoption of neo-Traditionalism as a meaningful religious orientation?

3. How is neo-Traditionalism therapeutic?

4. What is the connection between neo-Traditionalism and identity?

5. Discuss the nature and implications of "invented" versus "authentic" tradition in the Mi'kmaw context.

ENDNOTES

1. In reference to Catholic and non-Catholic religious orientations, and in accordance with oral tradition, keep in mind that many Mi'kmaw beliefs and values held to be pre-Christian bear close similarities to those of Roman Catholicism. Therefore, it becomes difficult to attribute certain beliefs to either Roman Catholic teachings or to pre-Christian Mi'kmaw understandings. There is an abundance of oral and written documentation supporting this claim, aspects of which will be discussed in the following chapter.

2. Powwows are perhaps the exception in this list since not all neo-Traditionalists accept them as a traditional Mi'kmaw practice. However, neo-Traditionalists consider a combination of fasts, sweats, and sacred circles essential to Traditionalism (personal observations).

3. Grass dancers wear brightly coloured clothing adorned with long fringes around the legs and arms and across the front of the garment. At the Eskasoni Mawio'mi, it was announced that traditionally grass dancers were the first dancers to enter the dance ring because as they navigated the circle they would pick grass and stick it into the seams of their garments as a way of preparing the ring for subsequent dancers. By the time the grass dancers had finished their dance the circle would be picked clean of grass. However, grass dancers no longer perform this service, and the former grass fringes are now made from brightly coloured yarn that adds to the drama of the garment (Fieldnotes, Book I: 162).

4. Interestingly, some Mi'kmaw songs that were ritually performed have survived intact. At present, surviving songs are performed in traditional style by Mi'kmaw drummers and chanters at powwows and other functions, such as Treaty Day. Although I have managed to obtain cassette tapes of some of these songs, I must refrain from publishing the lyrics in written form. The Mi'kmaq enforce strict prohibitions on committing orally transmitted texts to paper (personal observations).

chapter eight

Conclusions

Meaning resides in the journeying, not the destination, and the authenticity of ethnographic knowledge depends on the ethnographer recounting in detail the events and encounters that are the grounds on which the very possibility of this knowledge rests.

–Michael Jackson, from *At Home in the World* (1995)

LEARNING OBJECTIVES

After reading this section students should be able to:

- Outline the main arguments and thesis of this book.
- Identify the predominant forms of religious expression among the Mi'kmaq.
- Explain the diversity and creativity of Mi'kmaw religious expression.
- Discuss the significance of religion in the lives of the Mi'kmaq.
- Outline the complex relationship between Mi'kmaw personal and social identity and religious orientation.

In his 1966 account of the Mi'kmaq of Restigouche, Quebec, anthropologist Philip K. Bock claims the following:

> There is general agreement that for more than two hundred years, virtually all Micmac were devoted Roman Catholics ... The aboriginal faith is dead: any survivals are better treated as fragments of folklore (ref. Wallis and Wallis, 1953). Until recently there has been no serious "rival doctrine": many people are apparently "firm in their faith."

(Bock 1966: 55–56)

Bock's description of Catholicism and the "dead" Aboriginal faith is indicative of the way that Mi'kmaw religion typically has been portrayed by scholars. This image of Mi'kmaw religion may appear to be somewhat dated. However, at the beginning of the 21st century most discussions of Mi'kmaw religion continue to resemble the views expressed by Bock. Generally, academic discourse on Mi'kmaw belief systems tends to centre either on the primacy of Catholicism among the Mi'kmaq or deals exclusively with what Bock refers to as the "aboriginal faith." Accordingly, 19th- and 20th-century scholarship commonly refer to the Mi'kmaq as Roman Catholic. However, in the latter part of the 20th century Mi'kmaw religion could not be categorized so succinctly (Campbell 1998; McMillan 1996; Reid 1995).

The preceding chapters argued that the specific categories ascribed to local belief and practice, such as Roman Catholicism and Traditionalism, are reductionist terms that obscure the variety and complexity of Mi'kmaw belief systems. Mi'kmaw religious expression can be likened to the diverse forms of popular or local Roman Catholicism studied by anthropologists and historians elsewhere (Badone 1990; Brandes 1990; Stirrat 1992). Like these "intricately patterned and highly elaborated" forms of popular Roman Catholicism, Mi'kmaw religion did not emerge from a fixed pattern. It developed, and continues to develop, "in response to an infinite variety of social, economic, political and cultural circumstances" (Brandes 1990: 185).

I also argued against the dominant scholarly notion that there exists a "passive acceptance" of Roman Catholicism among the Mi'kmaq (Bock 1966: 56). Historically, scholarship relating to Mi'kmaw Catholicism tends to treat the Mi'kmaq not as autonomous human agents who contribute to the basic ideological and philosophical principles that help shape their lives. Rather, they are portrayed as having little control over the construction of cultural meaning and religious significance in their communities. In many cases, the persistence of Catholicism among the Mi'kmaq is attributed to the efforts of the missionaries (Bock 1966; Johnston 1960; Krieger 1989). For instance, Bock suggests that by translating prayers, hymns, and catechisms into the Mi'kmaw language and by encouraging particular devotions, "especially to St. Anne," the missionaries Le Clerq and Maillard initiated and sustained "a version of Catholicism ... suitable to the Indians"[1] (Bock 1966: 55). Bock, however, makes no mention of the roles played by the Sante' Mawio'mi (Grand Council) and the Mi'kmaq generally in constructing and maintaining Mi'kmaw Catholicism. This ethnography offers evidence that suggests that, through time, the Mi'kmaq were reflective members of the religious community to which they belonged. They continually made choices and took action based on their assessment of the various sets of circumstances that made past and existing (re)constructions of Mi'kmaw religion possible. Local interpretations of Christian and non-Christian religious orientations are expressed in diverse ways. These include Mi'kmaw Catholicism, existing and emergent hybridized forms of Catholicism and neo-Traditionalism, and locally defined ritual performances such as salites and St. Anne's Mission (Se'tta'newimk) observances.

Finally, I suggest that for many Mi'kmaq, notions of autonomy and cultural identity are closely associated with religious affiliation. My research indicates that the primary concern for many Mi'kmaw people is the continued survival of the Mi'kmaq as a socially and culturally distinct group. While most Mi'kmaq are unified in this cause, responses vary regarding the role of the Catholic Church in achieving this goal. For many Catholic conservatives, being Mi'kmaw and being Catholic are synonymous. From this perspective the Catholic Church, in addition to being an institution that is historically, socially, and culturally significant, is seen as the only viable religious orientation for the Mi'kmaq. The strongest opponents of Mi'k- maw Catholicism are those whose primary goal is to rid Mi'kmaw culture and society of all perceptible Western influences. Most dissenters from the Catholic faith view the Church's ide- ological structure and institutional authority as a persistent threat to both Mi'kmaw autonomy and the preservation of "authentic" Mi'kmaw culture and society. As this book has illustrated, in addition to the Mi'kmaq who have rejected the Catholic Church on philosophical bases, others voice opposition to the Church for personal reasons. For instance, some former stu- dents of the residential schools claim that the emotional, sexual, and physical abuse suffered while at the schools makes it difficult for them to remain Catholics.

This book has outlined the distinctive features of Mi'kmaw Catholicism in particular and has also drawn attention to the complexity and diversity of Mi'kmaw belief systems in gen- eral. In addition, the book has addressed the tensions between conservative, moderate, and rejectionist views of Mi'kmaw Catholicism. The introductory chapter presented the book's main points and introduced several Mi'kmaq whose voices express key aspects of Mi'k- maw Catholicism, Catholic-Traditionalism, and neo-Traditionalism. Chapter two illustrated various ways that the Mi'kmaq have been, and continue to be, culturally, religiously, eco- nomically, and socially marginalized. Chapter three delineated Mi'kmaw lifeworlds and cul- ture and offered a number of perspectives on the Mi'kmaw ethos as it is understood by devotees of Catholicism, Catholic-Traditionalism, and non-Catholic religious orientations. Chapter four centred on Mi'kmaw perceptions of the Catholic Church and the role of the Church within Mi'kmaw society. In chapter five, the significance of St. Anne, Se'tta'newimk (St. Anne's Mission), and Potlotek was discussed. Chapter six explored approaches to death and dying in Eskasoni and other Mi'kmaw communities with specific emphasis on the salite and funeral feast as central features of local Mi'kmaw funerary practice. Chapter seven was primarily concerned with neo-Traditionalism as a religious choice and presented diverse responses to that choice within the Mi'kmaw community.

This book has paid particular attention to the transformative effects of cross-cultural exchange on religious beliefs and expressions. These findings contribute to theoretical per- spectives that resist the notion that indigenous peoples are "presumed to be *either* primitive and untouched, *or* contaminated by progress" (Clifford 1997: 157). Commenting on the Wahgi of Papua, New Guinea, as presented in an exhibit at the Museum of Man in London, James Clifford observes that the Wahgi are "both tribal and modern, local and worldly. They cannot be seen as inhabitants of an enclosed space, either past or present, a paradise lost or preserved" (Clifford 1997: 157). In the Mi'kmaw case, as with the Wahgi, "we are thrown into the midst of transformations" in which present-day realities cannot be "portrayed on a before/after axis, with a 'traditional' baseline preceding the arrival of 'outside' influences" (Clifford 1997: 154). Instead, we are faced with "hybrid productions" wherein perceived "pre-contact" artifacts, motifs, and rituals interact with those of the present (Clifford 1997: 154–57).

As well, the introductory chapter drew attention to the fact that, in the Mi'kmaw case, rigid boundaries cannot be sustained between Western and non-Western frameworks of meaning and significance. All boundaries, real or imagined, have holes. Currently, many

Mi'kmaq use modern communication devices such as satellite dishes, motor vehicles, televisions, and the Internet. However, in the midst of all that is "modern," there is also a perceived need to establish and maintain a certain amount of community insularity, whereby the community becomes a tool for the preservation of Aboriginal culture and society. Anthropologist Tord Larsen wrote about the Mi'kmaq in the mid-1980s:

> Indians employ elements in their universe—among other things, elements of their aboriginal culture, the history of Indian/White relations, the ways in which they see themselves different from whites—in order to construct a statement which is intended to make whites see things differently. In doing so, Indians give new import to old facts, juxtapose ideas that have not been related previously and endow forgotten events with new significance.

> *(Larsen 1983: 39)*

However, the "elements" of which Larsen speaks are not necessarily confined to "authentic" aspects of a precontact Mi'kmaw "universe." Instead, these elements are prone to the "processes of selective appropriation and change" (Clifford 1997: 152–53). They may be drawn from many different historically based artifacts, motifs, and occasions. My research clearly shows the ways that multiple and simultaneous influences of two divergent, but apparently reconcilable, belief systems appear in hybridized forms. For instance, Eva, a middle-aged Catholic woman, claims that the Mi'kmaq were "a nation of cross-bearers" prior to contact and had an awareness of Jesus and the Christian God. Eva suggests that by following Christianity, the Mi'kmaq are not abandoning "authentic" Mi'kmaw beliefs. They are preserving them.

Beginning in the 1960s, a cultural renaissance ushered in changes that have prompted renewed pride and interest in Mi'kmaw language, culture, and history. However, with this period of revitalization a number of contentious issues have arisen relating to notions of identity and authenticity. In Eskasoni and throughout Mi'kma'ki, conflicts arising from different perceptions of the role of the Catholic Church are symptomatic of the ongoing process of (re)constructing national and personal identities.

This ethnography emphasizes the role of religion as it pertains to constructing Mi'kmaw identity primarily because religious and spiritual views help shape subjectivity and the social environment. Within Mi'kmaw society and culture specific religious orientations and their respective ideologies and expressions both shape and are shaped by personal and social identities. The reciprocal nature of this relationship between religious affiliation(s) and individual and collective identities is evident in the varied perceptions of culture, spirituality, and religion found within Mi'kmaw society.

For some Mi'kmaq, spirituality finds its expression in the lived immediacy of day-to-day existence. This may or may not include religious observances. For instance, Jonal claims the following:

> You can be spiritual without being religious ... spirituality is how you live your life and religion is just one way of making contact [with] or praying to the Creator. You can be spiritual without being religious. You really don't need religion, but spirituality is a completely different matter. You must be able to strike a balance between mind, spirit and body and too much of any one is no good ... I go to church ... because it is part of my upbringing and there are good points to the church.

> *(Fieldnotes, Book I: 199)*

Clearly, for Jonal, spirituality is closely aligned with a society's ethos, whereas religion is not. Jonal's conditional acceptance of the Church rests on its pragmatic function within Mi'kmaw society. He does not see it as being a necessary part of spirituality. Spirituality for Jonal is essentially a means through which the balance between "mind, spirit and body" is maintained. However, among Mi'kmaw Catholic conservatives, spirituality is perceived differently and is often equated with religion and culture. As chapter three illustrated, many devout Mi'kmaw Catholics view Catholicism as an institution that helped to preserve and protect Mi'kmaw culture during a period when the Mi'kmaw people and their way of life were under serious threat. However, this particular view is vehemently opposed by others. These people are critical of Catholicism. They claim that the Church, as an institution, enacted "cultracide" on the Mi'kmaq. It subverted original Mi'kmaw beliefs and values and replaced them with conceptions of the world that are alien to the "true Mi'kmaw mind."

Anti-Catholic arguments, like those proposed by Bern and Tanas in chapter three, suggest that the Catholic Church has historically promoted and continues to promote a world view and ethos that is inimical to precontact Mi'kmaw beliefs and values. Arguments for the primacy of language in revitalizing authentic Mi'kmaw systems of thought and expression, free from Western bias, claim that etymological analysis of the Mi'kmaw language can uncover seminal precontact beliefs and values. Bern and Tanas suggest that the very structure of the Mi'kmaw language provides insight into Mi'kmaw lifeworlds. Bern maintains that Mi'kmaw culture and society is firmly embedded within a language that is characteristically fluid and adaptable. He argues that because the Mi'kmaw language is verb-based, it exhibits a flexibility that can readily accommodate change. It reflects the Mi'kmaw understanding that the universe is active and ever-changing. He contends that this fluidity and adaptability also convey a particular cosmology along with the spiritual philosophies and patterns of culture that emerge from such a view. According to Bern and Tanas, this view runs counter to the teachings of the Roman Catholic Church, which rely on noun-based conceptions of God, creation, and the universe. Clearly, those who consider Catholicism a threat to Mi'kmaw autonomy and identity fear their culture will be so eroded by Western influences that the Mi'kmaq will lose their distinctiveness as a group.

The ongoing process of negotiating identity and establishing autonomy is not restricted to the Mi'kmaq of Nova Scotia. It is a common experience for the majority of Aboriginals. Take for example the Wampanoag of Mashpee, Massachusetts. Clifford points out that, as they sought to validate their legal status as a tribe through a lengthy court case, the process of documenting "certain underlying structures governing the recognition of identity and difference" was really an "experiment in translation, part of a long historical conflict and negotiation of 'Indian' and 'American' identities" (1988: 289). As Clifford documents, the court's insistence that the key factors of race, territory, community, and leadership must be continuously present (1988: 333–34) to legitimate Wampanoag claims is an externally imposed constraint that undermines Wampanoag autonomy and identity. It endorses the notion that "Native American societies" cannot "by definition be dynamic, inventive, or expansive" (Clifford 1988: 284). Mashpee Aboriginals do not follow specific codes of dress and behaviour that are consistent with non-Aboriginal stereotypes of "Indianness." Therefore, Wampanoag identity is questioned. The court required that Mashpee Aboriginals conform their political, social, and cultural identity to its narrow prescription of "Indianness."

Paradoxically, the essentialist views that Clifford attributes to dominant North American culture bear close similarities to the perspective of those Mi'kmaq who wish to discredit Catholic influences in order to revitalize "authentic" Mi'kmaw culture and society. The politics of identity that emerge in both the non-Aboriginal enterprise of distinguishing between "them" and "us" (Fabian 1983) and the Mi'kmaw project of re-establishing integrity, autonomy, and culture are similar. They both focus on identity characteristics deemed to be socially and culturally distinctive. For instance, the performance portion of the powwow, while not originally Mi'kmaw, does involve a specific style and content that is definitively non-Western. As such, it is often recognized and mistakenly understood by many non-Aboriginals (and some Aboriginals) as a typical Aboriginal religio-cultural performance. Although some Mi'kmaq are actively involved in promoting and performing in the powwow, most Mi'kmaq look upon the occasion as a form of entertainment. Most Mi'kmaq recognize that the dominant society's views of the Mi'kmaw people are cast in terms of stereotypes broadly attributed to Aboriginals. These stereotypes show little regard for regional, cultural, and social variations among Aboriginal groups. The Mi'kmaq who wish to revitalize "authentic" Mi'kmaw culture and society are specifically concerned with establishing Mi'kmaw distinctiveness from all other groups, both Aboriginal and non-Aboriginal. However, most Mi'kmaq, whether Catholic, Catholic-Traditionalist, or neo-Traditionalist, agree that the type of pan-Indianism promoted by occasions such as the powwow has little to offer in terms of (re)establishing distinctively authentic Mi'kmaw beliefs and values.

In contrast to the Wampanoag case, among the Mi'kmaq, discussions relating to the constitution of authentic Mi'kmaw identity are internally generated. Discussions about authentic versus inauthentic Mi'kmaw constructions of identity take place primarily with reference to ongoing dialogues and negotiations among the Mi'kmaw people themselves rather than with representatives from "mainstream" North American society. For many Mi'kmaq, debates on autonomy and identity revolve around perceptions of how Catholicism has transformed "authentic" Mi'kmaw beliefs and values. Among Mi'kmaw Catholics, the Church is seen as a vehicle for transmitting Aboriginal culture and as an institution that, historically, has granted power and autonomy to the Mi'kmaw people. However, the power structure introduced by the Church and adopted by the Mi'kmaw people (as witnessed in the role of the Sante' Mawio'mi) is seen by critics of Catholicism as reinforcing unwarranted social and cultural change. Critics of Catholicism, including some Mi'kmaw Catholics and Catholic-Traditionalists, voice disapproval of the "Westernized" structure of the council. Some Mi'kmaq assert that the original form of the Grand Council emphasized the equality of all Mi'kmaq. However, in its revised role in partnership with the Catholic Church it has adopted aspects of the hierarchical structure of the Church. It does not give fair representation to all Mi'kmaq, especially women, non-Catholics, non-Christians, and neo-Traditionalists. Therefore, some Mi'kmaq perceive the Sante' Mawio'mi as an elitist group. They believe that in conjunction with the structures of power and authority ceded through the Catholic Church the Sante' Mawio'mi serves to undermine Mi'kmaw society and culture. Moreover, for many non-Catholic Mi'kmaq, the introduction of Roman Catholic hierarchical structures into Mi'kmaw society is considered antithetic to Mi'kmaw autonomy and to the principles of equality inherent in Mi'kmaw culture.

Adaptability and fluidity as features of "authentic" Mi'kmaw ethos and language are also reflected in the recontextualization and transformation of certain aspects of Catholicism and neo-Traditionalism. This is particularly evident among Catholic-Traditionalists, who integrate elements from one set of rituals and beliefs with those drawn from another set. Catholic-Traditionalism is a highly innovative and individualistic religious orientation. Diverse and competing religious discourses are accommodated in many forms. Essentially, Catholic-Traditionalists participate in combinations of neo-Traditionalist and Mi'kmaw Catholic practices of their own choosing. For example Piel, introduced in chapter one, is a Mi'kmaw man who compares prayer in the four directions with "praying the [Christian] cross." For Piel, Aboriginal practices are only made meaningful within a Christian context. Conversely, in Eskasoni, using "our Creator" as a substitute for "God" or "Father" can be construed as interpreting a Christian concept within a neo-Traditionalist framework.

Most Mi'kmaw religious expressions cannot be pigeonholed into the neat analytical categories of Catholic or neo-Traditional. Rather, religious practices are hybridized forms involving each of these two foundational systems. This is exemplified in one of the most religiously complex and socially significant occasions in the Mi'kmaw calendar, the annual Se'tta'newimk at Potlotek. This is one event that most Mi'kmaq, regardless of religious affiliation, attempt to attend. Se'tta'newimk is often perceived as a religious event. However, to refer to it exclusively as such obscures the many reasons that people participate in the gathering. People attend Se'tta'newimk for a combination of purposes, including the veneration of St. Anne, offering prayers to St. Anne for special favours, showing respect for present and past ancestral traditions, or community bonding and socialization.

As noted in chapter five, the Potlotek gathering comprises a dual interpretation of sacredness that has given rise to conflicts between Catholic and non-Catholic Mi'kmaq. Because Potlotek is recognized as a precontact annual gathering site, pilgrimage to the island can be viewed as an enactment of, and a statement of respect for, long-standing Mi'kmaw religious traditions that have their origins outside of Mi'kmaw Catholicism. On the other hand, the performance of St. Anne's Day observances and rituals is considered by many Catholic Mi'kmaq and Catholic-Traditionalists as maintaining legitimate ancestral religious traditions.

Culturally, Se'tta'newimk and Potlotek retain meaning and significance for the Mi'kmaq in a number of ways. As mentioned, Potlotek is historically relevant and traditionally meaningful because, purportedly, it has continuously operated as a Mi'kmaw gathering site since precontact times. In addition, although many of the religious observances performed during Se'tta'newimk were introduced by representatives of the Roman Catholic Church,[2] that most of the liturgies, hymns, and prayers are said in the Mi'kmaw language is a culturally significant marker of identity. For those Mi'kmaq who reside outside Mi'kmaki or on reserves where English is the main language, Se'tta'newimk may be the only time during the year that many Mi'kmaq hear their language so widely spoken. It may also be one of the few occasions when a large group of Mi'kmaq are publicly addressed in the Mi'kmaw language. Furthermore, specific rituals associated with the mission, including *Lapa'tko'tewimk*—the annual Grand Council meeting and public address—the bathing of St. Anne's statue, and the dispensing of blessed cloth are understood by the Mi'kmaw people to be practices unique to Se'tta'newimk.

Se'tta'newimk is also a time when the Mi'kmaw people come together to discuss matters of political and social importance.[3] Although these matters are not central to Se'tta'newimk religious celebrations, they are discussed formally in Grand Council meetings and informally on a social level. The multidimensional aspect of St. Anne's Mission contributes to its status as an important event for most Mi'kmaq. At Potlotek itself, there is also a tangible sense that the various conflicts about the significance of the annual gathering and about issues of identity, authority, and authenticity are neutralized by the sense of communitas encouraged within the ritual context of the occasion.

The death of a community member constitutes another notable social context where political, religious, and personal differences are held in abeyance. Among the Mi'kmaq, locally held funeral feasts and salites parallel Se'tta'newimk celebrations as a time when social and familial relationships are highlighted. While many aspects of Mi'kmaw deathways involve rituals based in Roman Catholicism, community solidarity and the offer of "food and friendship" are also at the centre of Mi'kmaw funerary observances. As observed in chapter six, there are several overarching social, cultural, and religious factors informing Mi'kmaw deathways that act against the overt contestation of funerary rituals. More so than at Se'tta'newimk, there is general agreement that differences between individuals, families, and social factions are to be overlooked in the event of death. Among the Mi'kmaq is the expectation that community members, regardless of age, socio-economic status, political stripe, or religious affiliation, will attend local wakes, salites, and funeral feasts. With very few exceptions, this expectation is met.

In Eskasoni, the profound emotions associated with bereavement are mediated through the postinterment ceremonies of the salite and funeral feast. Essentially, the postinterment ceremonies reflect an attempt on the part of the community to provide emotional, spiritual, and practical support to the family and friends of the deceased. The communal feast and auction (salite) are ways of collectively healing a community of mourners. Of all Mi'kmaw events, postinterment gatherings and Se'tta'enewimk are considered by community members to be among the most expressive of Mi'kmaw beliefs and values. For most Mi'kmaq, these occasions, although formally linked to Catholicism, derive their significance and meaning from non-Christian contexts that are believed to have their genesis in precontact ritual observances. As such, they are believed to represent "authentic" Mi'kmaw culture and social organization.

In describing Mi'kmaw deathways, I have also drawn attention to several terms, concepts, and understandings, including *apiksiktatimk* (an act of mutual forgiveness), "letting the spirit go," Mi'kmaw distinctions between spirit and soul, Mi'kmaw understandings of sin, and Mi'kmaw concepts of the afterlife.

The local practices of apiksiktatimk and "letting the spirit go" help to promote the emotional well-being of survivors and the dying person. Apiksiktatimk relieves feelings of remorse and acrimony. The acts of mutual forgiveness and "letting the spirit go" have a similar function. They facilitate the transition of the deceased's spirit into the afterlife free of personal burdens and unencumbered by the grief of surviving family members and friends.

Many Mi'kmaq understand the concept of death, or *nept,* as moving into a different state of being that is not necessarily permanent. Conceptually, nept is best understood as dormancy or a state of existence inconsistent with life as we know it. Some Mi'kmaq also believe that it is possible to maintain communication with the dead. Many Mi'kmaw Catholics, neo-Traditionalists, and Catholic-Traditionalists appeal to deceased family members and friends for assistance in personal matters and in healing, much like invocations to St. Anne. And, like St. Anne, the deceased are believed to respond to the requests of the living. In effect, it is the "spirits" not the "souls" of the deceased that commune with the living. This suggests that, for the Mi'kmaq, there is a clear distinction between the concepts of soul and spirit.

Also discussed in this chapter is the notion of sin. For most Mi'kmaq, sin is not so much an act against God/our Creator as it is a reflection of personal failings and/or a transgression against others. In most cases, the person who acts irresponsibly (or sins) is as adversely affected as the person(s) sinned against. Mi'kmaw socialization stresses the idea that individuals are free agents who must bear responsibility for their actions. Interestingly, most behaviours deemed inappropriate within Mi'kmaw society tend to coincide with transgressions of the biblical Ten Commandments. However, many Mi'kmaq argue that basic precontact Mi'kmaw beliefs and values render the Commandments redundant.

Although many pro-Catholic Mi'kmaq emphasize commonalities between Roman Catholicism and precontact belief systems, anti-Catholic Mi'kmaq accentuate the differences between the two. At base, the respective arguments for or against the legitimacy of neo-Traditionalism and/or Mi'kmaw Catholicism ultimately rest on claims of authenticity. Most Mi'kmaw Catholics and Catholic-Traditionalists hold that Mi'kmaw Catholicism is a legitimate Mi'kmaw tradition. Conversely, many non-Catholic Mi'kmaq insist that "authentic" Mi'kmaw practices and beliefs are drawn from traditions that originate within a pre-Christian past.

Among the Eskasoni Mi'kmaq, the dominant discourse on issues of religious validity promotes the primacy of Catholicism and embraces an anti-Traditionalist rhetoric. Chapter six discusses a number of possible explanations for the negative assessment of neo-Traditionalism in the community. First, Mi'kmaw Catholics and Catholic-Traditionalists, the principal religious groups in the community, tend to view Traditionalism not as a religion but as a form of spirituality. Second, throughout North America the persistence of negative colonial attitudes continues to desacralize precontact religions. This contributes to their continued marginalization even within the Aboriginal communities in which they are practised. Third, some Mi'kmaq view the move toward neo-Traditionalism as a contravention of commonly accepted Mi'kmaw social and cultural conventions, including appropriate lifestyle choices.

The contested ground of authentic as opposed to inauthentic Mi'kmaw religious expression is simply one dimension of the relationship between Christian and non-Western religious beliefs and values as they are articulated and experienced among the Mi'kmaq of Eskasoni. Mi'kmaw belief systems are diverse and complex phenomena through which various cultural, political, spiritual, and existential concerns (which are not necessarily at variance) are mediated.

While the research materials presented here are based on my own fieldwork, the work of previous scholars informs my analysis of the data collected in the field. The following discussion contextualizes the contributions my work may make to the study of Native American religion, hybridized forms of religious expression, "local" religious practices, and the influence of colonialism on Mi'kmaw religion.

Generally, this ethnography adds to our knowledge base about religions in Canada. More specifically, it contributes to the growing field of scholarly literature on Aboriginal belief systems. In the latter part of the 20th century, studies of Aboriginal religion, notably by Alan Morinis (1992) and Kenneth Morrison (1981, 1990), have advanced the notion that, rather than being passive recipients, Aboriginals have influenced the ways that Western ideologies and institutions have been accepted into Aboriginal social contexts. Alan Morinis observes that among the Plains Indians the practice of sacred journeying (or pilgrimage) has been continually enacted "through eras of cultural and social upheaval" (1992: 101). Morinis notes that although recent contexts for pilgrimage centre on Christian shrines, ritual gathering has always been "an important feature of [Plains] cultural tradition" (1992: 111). Likewise, ethnohistorian Kenneth Morrison (1990) maintains that although the 17th-century Montagnais accepted

Catholicism they did so within the context of traditional religious understandings. Morrison concludes that by innovatively combining key aspects of traditional religion and Jesuit teachings the Montagnais accommodated Euro-American religious ideologies and practices while maintaining their own values and perceptual orientations (1990: 418). Morinis and Morrison offer critical perspectives that shed light on the ways that Native North American religions have emerged. The Mi'kmaw voices that appear in this ethnography and the complexity and diversity of Mi'kmaw belief systems that I have presented further substantiate the idea that, rather than being a people who were "acted upon," Aboriginal peoples have always actively negotiated the social, cultural, and religious aspects of their lives. Moreover, this study also promotes the idea that the "perceptual, cognitive, and value orientations" (Morrison 1981: 257) of Aboriginal peoples did not systematically disappear. They are at least partially a foundation for the existing and emergent traditions initiated by colonialism.

Moreover, this ethnography draws on and contributes to a reinterpretation of the role of Aboriginal peoples in colonialist situations. This follows, among others, James Axtell's work on the "contest of cultures" in colonial North America (1985), Jean and John Comaroff's treatment of the impact of Christian missionization on the Tshidi of South Africa (1990), Åke Hulkrantz's commentary on northern Algonkian eschatology (1979), and Sergei Kan's studies of the Tlingit of Alaska (1985, 1991).. My research indicates that, as with many indigenous belief systems (see Goulet 1982; Gualteri 1984; Morinis 1992; Morrison 1981, 1990), the colonial encounter has had a remarkable and irrevocable influence on Mi'kmaw religious expression. As social phenomena, Mi'kmaw religious beliefs and expressions speak to the social-cultural milieux from which they emerge, often appearing as hybridized forms of Roman Catholicism and indigenous knowledge. Here, I have demonstrated the ways that diverse personal and collective religious practices act as media through which multiple interpretations of Mi'kmaw culture and society are articulated and evaluated.

This ethnography also draws on the work of anthropologists studying the interaction between forms of popular and official religion. Scholars such as Lila Abu-Lughod (1993a), Caroline Brettell (1990), and William Christian (1981a, 1985, 1996) suggest that ongoing conflicts between the religious experiences of ordinary people and the religious practices sanctioned by officials of religious institutions are relatively common. Writing about the Islamic case, Abu-Lughod observes that scholars have tended to devalue local religious practices by drawing distinctions between "popular and orthodox religion, local and universal belief and practice . . . or, in the worst case, between ignorance and the knowledge of true religion" (1993a: 189). She states further that anthropologists are astutely aware of these distinctions and normative claims and now examine "without judgement the interaction of the complex of practices" that make up religious contexts (1993a: 189). Similarly, William Christian comments that in order to understand the intricacies and complexities of contemporary Catholic practice, it is necessary to understand the distinctions between "religion as practised" and "religion as prescribed" (formal church dogma) as they exist in local contexts (1981a). Much of Christian's work is concerned with the ways that the religion of the people is at variance with official Catholic Church teachings (Christian 1981a, 1985, 1996). From a slightly different vantage point, Caroline Brettell recognizes that the rootedness of local Catholic practice is "such that manifestations of religious practice (embodying both belief and behaviour) are neither of the orthodox institution (represented by its priests) nor totally of the people. They are, more often than not, an accommodation between the two"

(1990: 55–56). In line with these perspectives, I argue that many of the devotional observances and occasions discussed in this book depart from mainstream Catholic traditions and are more in keeping with "local" Mi'kmaw religious expression.

This book deals with the key phenomenological and theoretical aspects of Mi'kmaw religious beliefs and expression as they have been presented to me and as I understand them. Of necessity, my study has concentrated on "local" religion and has not dealt with Aboriginal religion on a North American level. Nor does it offer an in-depth comparison of Mi'kmaw Catholicism with hybridized forms of indigenous religion in global contexts. A more elaborate examination of hybridized forms of Aboriginal religious expression in Canada, and abroad, would require resources beyond the scope of this present work. However, illuminating comparisons can be drawn between contemporary Mi'kmaw religious expressions and those of other groups throughout the Americas, Africa, and Asia, where colonial elements have had an impact upon existing precontact philosophical, ideological, and institutional structures (Abu-Lughod 1993; Kan 1991; Stirrat 1992).

In closing, I would like to reintroduce Piel, a middle-aged Mi'kmaq who considers himself a Catholic-Traditionalist. Piel insists that although he has respect for and a strong devotion to Catholicism he also sees "value in material and traditional things" (Fieldnotes, Book IV: 803). Piel is very active in church administration at the local level and regularly attends Catholic functions. However, Piel is also a pipe-carrier. As such, he is often called upon to perform Traditional ceremonies in the Catholic Church and elsewhere.

Piel maintains that his devotion to the Catholic faith does not detract from his respect for non-Christian Mi'kmaw traditions but actually enhances their significance and meaning. Piel's "selective appropriation" of diverse elements of religious meaning and expression reconciles Catholicism with non-Christian beliefs and practices. For instance, Piel associates prayer in the four directions with the Christian cross. He also suggests that Catholicism is an important and necessary factor in maintaining a balance between spirituality, material goods, and tradition.

I asked Piel about his views on neo-Traditionalism:

I can see why people become fanatics about their traditional culture. I'm a Traditionalist, but I'm not a fanatic. I try to strike a balance between culture, religion, and the material aspect [of culture]. I have all three . . . Our people have prayed and meditated for thousands of years and we had our colours and the cross. When you think about it, when you bless yourself you pray in the four directions. We are a very spiritual people. Many times others [non-Natives] ask us to pray for them because [they think] our prayers are stronger, and in a way they are—we've been praying longer . . . I support the Church, but material things and traditions are also important . . . My people are like the salmon going up river to spawn . . . The river has changed, and the salmon are confused and disoriented. It is ingrained in the salmon to return to certain red [spawning] areas, but if the environment is changed, they can't return there because they are confused . . . Our people are like the salmon. We are attached to the earth and a certain way of life. It is ingrained in us just like the salmon, but things interfere with this . . . We can't go back five hundred years, we have to adapt to what exists . . . We really can't go back.

(Fieldnotes, Book IV: 801–803)

Although Piel's analogy evokes an image of the Mi'kmaq as a displaced, "confused and disoriented" people, his key message is not one of loss and despair. Rather, it is one of hope and possibility. Like Piel, most Mi'kmaq are aware that they "really can't go back," that the past can never be faithfully recovered. Nevertheless, most Mi'kmaq also have faith that a confluence of the past and the present continues to flow into newly recreated "ways of believing."

CONTENT QUESTIONS

1. Identify the main arguments and thesis of this book.
2. Identify the predominant forms of religious expression among the Mi'kmaq.
3. Discuss the diversity and creativity of Mi'kmaw religious expression.
4. What are the key elements of the relationship between Mi'kmaw personal and social identity and religious expression?

ENDNOTES

1. Ironically, this statement contradicts Bock's observation that the general Mi'kmaw attitude toward Catholicism "seems to be one of passive acceptance" (1966: 56).

2. Many of the ritual observances performed at Se'tta'newimk in honour of St. Anne are consistent with similar types of celebrations found throughout North America and Europe because a number of these celebrations are arguably local, a- or pre-Christian in origin. (See Badone, ed. 1990).

3. At the annual meeting of the Grand Council, many political, social, and economic concerns are taken up, but these meetings are closed to the general public. Individual concerns brought to the attention of district Keptins are discussed at council meetings by the Keptins and other Grand Council officials.

Glossary

Glossary of Mi'kmaw Terms and Expressions

alasutmuo'kuomk: at the church, or literally "at the praying wigwam."

alatsutmaykapo: commonly translated as "It's a sacred time." Used historically to announce a death in the community.

ankweyulkw: "she/he/it who is looking over us."

apiksiktatimk: a formal act of forgiving each other.

Glotjeioie Aogtigtog: Stations of the Cross.

Inua: an Inuktitut term for the concept of soul.

jikeyulkw: "she/he/it who is watching over us."

ki'ju: a common term for "grandmother."

kisu' lkw: "she/he/it who creates us."

Kisu'lkw tlite'lmHsk wskwijinuin: literally means "It is the wish of the Creator that you should become a person," suggesting that *being* exists before one actually becomes a "person."

kjijaqmij: "your spirit."

Kji-keptin: literally translates as "Grand Captain."

Kji-kinap: literally translates as "Great Power."

Kji-mntu: literally translates as "Great Spirit," referring to God.

Kji-saqamaw: literally translates as "Grand Chief."

Kniskamijinaq eimu'ti'tij: where our ancestors are.

Kniskamijinaq wskitqamumuow: meaning "our ancestors' world."

Lapa'tko'tewimk: Mi'kmaw reference to the annual Grand Council meeting at Potlotek on

Pentecost Sunday. The word is derived from the French *le Pentecôte*.

L'nu: according to oral tradition, the proper referent for the Mi'kmaw people.

L'nu'ktat: translated means "s/he is wearing Mi'kmaw attire."

L'nu'sinej: "let's speak L'nu (Mi'kmaq)."

luskinikin: a local type of soda bread usually served with butter and molasses.

maomegisioltimk bousoubonananeouimk: "we eat together and we wish each other a happy new year" (Larsen 1983:11).

Mesgig Alames: High Mass.

Metua'lik: loosely translates as "I'm not doing very well" or "I'm having a difficult time."

Mi'kma'ki: refers to Mi'kmaw territory, which includes lands within the Atlantic provinces of Newfoundland, Nova Scotia, New Brunswick, Prince Edward Island, and parts of Quebec.

Mi'kmaq: believed by many to be derived from *No'kmaq*, meaning "all my relations," but was taken by Europeans to be the name for the whole group.

Mi'kmaw: the singular form of Mi'kmaq.

Mi'kmaw Mawio'mi: literally the "Mi'kmaw gathering," referring to the annual powwows held at Eskasoni.

mjimaqmij: translates as "spirit" (no declension).

muin: bear

Naji-tkweiwatka kniskamijinaq: "gone to another plane of existence" (personal communication).

na'ku'set: the sun.

negm: refers to the third person singular: s/he.

nept: literally means "dormancy," "sleep," or a state inconsistent with a personal awareness of this world. Usually translated into English as "death."

netukulimk: literally means "we hunt in partnership," referring to the Mi'kmaw principle of recognizing the reciprocal relationship between humans and flora and fauna.

Niskam: "God."

niskamij: "grandfather."

njijaqmij: "my spirit."

ntio'mel: Frederick Johnson translates this term as "spiritual agents" (Johnson 1943: 66). However, I have been unable to find present usage of the term.

ntus: my daughter.

nujialasutma'jik: literally meaning "those who pray," applying to prayer leaders assigned by the Sante' Mawio'mi.

nujj: father.

Nujjinen: Mi'kmaw term for the "Our Father."

pako'si: a traditional root taken from the "cow lily" plant, usually prepared as an infusion to be taken orally (*Wi'katikn Iapjiwewey*, 1990: 61).

pa'tlia's: the Mi'kmaw word for a Catholic priest.

puo'in (or buo'in): currently, generally taken to mean "evil spirit" or "devil." Frank Johnson (1943: 66) refers to *buo'in* simply as a spirit, which, according to oral tradition, is closer to the precontact meaning of the word.

Putus: wampum keeper.

salite: refers to auctions held to raise money for the family of someone who has died.

Sante' Mawio'mi: refers to both the Grand Council and the annual "sacred gatherings" of the Grand Council held on Pentecost Sunday and Se'tta'newimk at Chapel Island.

Sagamore/Saqamaw: both translate roughly as "chief."

Se'tta'newimk: literally, "at St. Anne's Mission."

Sk'te'kmujuawti: literally, "Ghost Road," or what westerners call the Milky Way, and "is the path that our people walk on with our ancestors after death."

ta'n ninen telo'ltiek: translates as "the way we [the Mi'kmaw] are."

tekweyulkw: "she/he/it who is with us."

tepkunaset: the moon.

tu's: literally means "daughter," but is often used as a term of endearment.

Unama'ki: general Mi'kmaw term used to refer to Cape Breton. It is often translated as "land of the fog," but some Mi'kmaq dispute this interpretation.

waltes: a traditional game involving a bowl, six dice, and 55 counting sticks.

wa'so'q: the five-pointed star shape appearing on the Grand Council flag. This star in Mi'kmaw hieroglyphics represents heaven.

wela'lin: literally, "you do me well." Commonly used as an equivalent for the English "thank you."

wjijaqmijl: "his/her spirit."

wjipoti: refers to the medicine bag.

wkutputim: the carrier used in the St. Anne's Day procession to carry the statue of St. Anne.

English Glossary

absentative: a linguistic term that refers to verb endings in Algonquian languages.

assimilationist: a model in which it is presumed that a minority culture will become culturally like the dominant culture until there are essentially no differences between the two.

Catholics (Mi'kmaw): used in distinction from Catholic-Traditionalists and (neo-)Traditionalists to refer to Mi'kmaq who practise Catholicism as the Mi'kmaq have for centuries, with and without the presence of priests.

Catholic-Traditionalists: used in distinction from Catholics and (neo-)Traditionalists to refer to Mi'kmaq who incorporate non-Catholic features, such as the sacred circle, into their religious practices and beliefs.

communitas: refers to the egalitarian, communal ideology, behaviour, and social relations said to often accompany liminality.

contested: refers to the fact that not everyone who belongs to a culture agrees as to the meaning, significance, or role of some aspect of a culture.

emergent: means that a discussion of a culture emerges or develops out of a particular people who either belong to or are outside of the culture and who participate in that discussion. It is the participants themselves, who, in cooperation with the author, lend intricacy, complexity, and breadth to ethnographic research and writing.

existential: In this context, it refers to the basic concerns of day-to-day living or life in general.

eschatology: teachings about the final destiny of individuals, humanity, and the cosmos.

implicated: refers to the fact that those representing or explaining the culture, both insiders and outsiders, have a personal or individual effect on or influence the resulting description of the culture.

lifeworld: anthropologist Michael Jackson refers to lifeworlds as a domain of the basic everyday existence of a culture and the understanding that comes from that existence.

liminality: refers to the in-between stage of a rite of passage.

monologic: refers to using only one form of knowledge production or thinking (i.e., the Western scientific model).

multivocality: including many voices or viewpoints in anthropological research.

Other: the people being studied who are other than or different from the Western (usually male) researchers.

phenomenology: an approach that attempts to derive an understanding of elements in a culture from within the present-day experience inside that culture, rather than from its past or

from a terminology and understanding from outside the culture.

pipe-carrier: in Mi'kmaw culture, refers to a person who, through a process including prolonged fasting and intensive sweats, has progressed through sufficient devotional levels to have acquired a sacred pipe.

prayer in the four directions: an important feature of most ritual ceremonies, including smudges, sweats, sacred circles, and sunrise ceremonies. While there are differences in content, the form remains much the same: prayer is offered first to the east, then, moving in a clockwise direction, the one offering the prayer directs it to the south, next to the west, and ends with a prayer to the north.

reflexive: an approach where the social location of the researcher (e.g., gender, race, age, position of power) is included in a discussion of how knowledge is produced.

rites of incorporation: the ritual subject "returns to a relatively stable state and is granted rights and obligations of a clearly defined and 'structural' type: he is expected to behave in accordance with certain customary norms and ethical standards binding on incumbents of social position in a system of such positions" (Turner 1995: 94–95).

rites of separation: "symbolic behaviour signifying the detachment of the individual or the group either from an earlier fixed point in the social structure, from a set of cultural conditions (a 'state'), or from both" (Turner 1995: 94).

rites of transition: "the characteristics of the ritual subject (the 'passenger') are ambiguous; he passes through a cultural realm that has few or none of the attributes of the past or coming state" (Turner 1995: 94).

smudge: the practice of "bathing" in the smoke of burning sweetgrass, sage, or some other sacred material as a form of spiritual purification.

sweat: a ceremony using the sweat lodge, which in physical effects is very much like a sauna.

temporal: any statement about a given culture might be true only for a specific time.

(neo-)Traditionalists: used in distinction from Catholics and Catholic-Traditionalists to refer to people who draw upon Mi'kmaq (and other Aboriginal) traditions other than Mi'kmaw Catholicism in their personal religious beliefs and practices.

world view: a term typically used in traditional anthropology to refer to a relatively coherent system of cultural beliefs and values shared by members of a culture. It differs from *lifeworlds* in tending to be conceived in more global or large-scale terms rather than in day-to-day terms.

References

Works Cited

Abbott, Walter M., ed. 1966. *The Documents of Vatican II: Introduction and Commentaries by Catholic Bishops and Experts. Responses by Protestant and Orthodox Scholars.* Joseph Gallagher, trans. New York: American Publishing.

Abu-Lughod, Lila. 1993a. "Islam and the Gendered Discourses of Death." In *International Journal of Middle Eastern Studies.* 25: 187–205.

———. 1993b. *Writing Women's Worlds: Bedouin Stories.* Berkeley and Los Angeles: University of California Press.

Addelson, Kathryn Pyne 1990. "Philosophers Should Become Sociologists (and Vice Versa)." In *Symbolic Interaction and Cultural Studies.* Howard S. Becker and Michal M. McCall, eds. Pp. 119–147. Chicago: University of Chicago Press.

Angroisino, Michael V. 1994. "The Culture Concept and the Mission of the Roman Catholic Church." *American Anthropologist.* 96: 824–32.

Appadurai, Arjun. 1988. "Introduction: Place and Voice in Anthropological Theory." *Cultural Anthropology* 3:16–20.

Asad, Talal. 1991. "Afterword: From the History of Colonial Anthropology to the Anthropology of Western Hegemony." In *Colonial Situations: Essays in the Contextualization of Ethnographic Knowledge.* George W. Stocking, ed. Madison, Wis.: University of Wisconsin Press.

———. 1993. *Genealogies of Religion: Discipline and Reasons of Power in Christianity and Islam.* Baltimore: Johns Hopkins University Press.

Assembly of First Nations, *Towards Linguistic Justice for First Nations,* Ottawa, 1990.

Axtell, James. 1982. "Some Thoughts on the Ethnohistory of Missions." *Ethnohistory* 29: 35–41.

———. 1985. *The Invasion Within: The Contest of Cultures in Colonial North America.* New York: Oxford University Press.

Badone, Ellen. 1989. *The Appointed Hour: Death, Worldview and Social Change in Brittany.* Berkeley: University of California Press.

———. ed. 1990. *Religious Orthodoxy and Popular Faith in European Society.* Princeton: Princeton University.

———. 1991. "Memories of Marie-Thérèse." In *Coping With the Final Tragedy: Cultural Variation in Dying and Grieving.* David R. Counts and Dorothy A. Counts, eds. Pp. 213–29. Amityville, NY: Baywood Publishing.

———. 1995. "Anthropological Perspectives on Pilgrimage." Paper prepared for the Dept. of Religious Studies Departmental Colloquium on Pilgrimage in Diverse Religious Traditions. McMaster University, March 1995.

Barker, John. 1998. "Tangled Reconciliations: the Anglican Church and the Nisga'a of British Columbia." *American Ethnologist* 25(3): 433–51.

Basque, Will. 1995. "Uniquely Micmac: Three Important Treaties." In *Maliseet and Micmac: First Nations of the Maritimes.*

Robert M. Leavitt, ed. Pp. 273–77. Fredericton, NB: New Ireland Press.

Bateman, Rebecca. 1997. "Comparative Thoughts on the Politics of Aboriginal Assimilation." *BC Studies* 114: 59–83.

Battiste, Marie. 1997a. "Nikanikinu'tmaqn." In *The Mi'kmaw Concordat* by James Youngblood Henderson. Pp. 13–20. Halifax: Fernwood Publishing.

———. 1997b. "Mi'kmaq Socialization Patterns." In *The Mi'kmaq Anthology*. Leslie Choyce and Rita Joe, eds. Pp. 145–61. Lawrencetown Beach, NS: Pottersfield Press.

Behar, Ruth. 1990. "The Struggle for the Church: Popular Anticlericalism and Religiosity in Post-Franco Spain." In *Religious Orthodoxy and Popular Faith in ... European Society*. Ellen Badone, ed. Pp. 76–112. Princeton: Princeton University.

———. 1997. *Ritual: Perspectives and Dimensions*. New York: Oxford University Press.

Bell, Catherine. 1992. *Ritual Theory and Ritual Practice*. New York: Oxford University Press.

Bennett, Gillian. 1989. "'Belief Stories': The Forgotten Genre." *Western Folklore* 48: 289–311.

Blanchard, David. 1982. "To the other side of the sky: Catholicism at Kahnawake, 1667–1700." In *Anthropologica* 24:77–102.

Bloch, Maurice and Jonathan Parry, eds. 1982. *Death and the Regeneration of Life*. Cambridge: Cambridge University Press.

Bock, Philip K. 1966. *The Micmac Indians of Restigouche: History and Contemporary Description*. Ottawa: National Museum of Canada.

Bowden, Henry Warner. 1981. *American Indians and Christian Missions: Studies in Cultural Conflict*. Chicago: University of Chicago Press.

Brandes, Stanley. 1976. "The Priest as Agent of Secularization in Rural Spain." In *Economic Transformations and Steady-State Values: Essays in the Ethnography of Spain*. Joseph B. Aceves, Edward C. Hansen, and Gloria Levitas, eds. Pp. 22–29. Flushing, NY: Queen's College Press.

———. 1990. "Conclusion: Reflections on the Study of Religious Orthodoxy and Popular Faith in Europe." In *Religious Orthodoxy and Popular Faith in European Society*. Ellen Badone, ed. Pp. 185–99.

Princeton, New Jersey: Princeton University Press.

Brettell, Caroline. 1990. "The Priest and His People: The Contractual basis for Religious Practice in Rural Portugal." In *Religious Orthodoxy and Popular Faith in European Society*. Ellen Badone, ed. Pp. 55–75. Princeton: Princeton University Press.

Bromley, Walter. 1822. *An Account of the Aborigines of Nova Scotia Called the Micmac Indians*. London.

Brooks, Katherine J. 1986. "The Effect of the Catholic Missionaries on the Micmac Indians of Nova Scotia, 1610–1986." In *The Nova Scotia Department of Agriculture, Recreation and Fitness*. Halifax: PANS 106–107(1).

Brown, Doug. 1991. "From Traditional Mi'kmaq Government to Now: Changing Those Who Did Not Need To Be Changed." In *Paqtatek: Policy and Consciousness in Mi'kmaq Life*. Halifax: Garamond Press.

Brown, Jennifer S. H. 1996. "Reading Beyond the Missionaries, Dissecting Responses." *Ethnohistory* 43 (4): 713–20.

Brown, Jennifer S. H. and Elizabeth Vibert, eds.

1996. *Reading Beyond Words: Contexts for Native History.* Peterborough: Broadview.

Brusco, Elizabeth and Laura Klein, eds. 1994. *The Message in the Missionary: Local Interpretation of Ideology and Missions Personality.* Williamsburg, VA: College of William and Mary.

Campbell, Robert. 1998. "Bridging Sacred Canopies: Mi'kmaq Spirituality and Catholicism." In *The Canadian Journal of Native Studies.* (2)18: 301–11.

Christian, William A. Jr. 1981a. *Local Religion in Sixteenth-Century Spain.* Princeton: Princeton University Press.

———. 1981b. *Apparitions in Late Medieval Renaissance Spain.* Princeton: Princeton University Press.

———. 1983. "'Us' Catholics and 'Them' Catholics in Dutch Brabrant: The Dialectics of a Religious Factional Process." *Anthropological Quarterly* 56: 167–78.

———. 1985. "Popular Devotions, Power and Religious Regimes in Catholic Dutch Brabrant." *Ethnology* 24: 215–20.

Christian, William A. Jr. 1987. "Folk Religion: An Overview." *The Encyclopaedia of Religion*, Mircea Eliade, ed. v. 5. Pp. 370–74. New York: Macmillan.

———. 1989. *Person and God in a Spanish Valley.* Revised edition [1972]. Princeton: Princeton University Press.

———. 1991. "Secular and Religious Responses to a Child's Potentially Fatal Illness." In *Religious Regimes and State-Formation: Perspectives in European Ethnology.* Eric R. Wolf, ed. Pp. 163–80. Albany, NY: State University of New York.

———. 1992. *Moving Crucifixes in Modern Spain.* Princeton: Princeton University Press.

———. 1996. *Visionaries: The Spanish Republic and the Reign of Christ.* Berkeley: University of California Press.

Churchill, Mary C. 2000. "Purity and Pollution: Unearthing an Oppositional Paradigm in the Study of Cherokee Religious Traditions." In *Native American Spirituality: A Critical Reader.* Lee Irwin, ed. Pp. 205–35. Lincoln: University of Nebraska Press.

Chute, Jane Elizabeth. 1992. "Ceremony, Social Revitalization and Change: Micmac Leadership and the Annual Festival of St. Anne." *Papers of the Twenty-Third Algonquin Conference.* William Cowan, ed., Pp. 45–62. Ottawa: Carleton University Press.

Clifford, James. 1988. *The Predicament of Culture: Twentieth-Century Ethnography, Literature and Art.* Cambridge: Harvard University Press.

———. 1997. *Routes: Travel and Translation in the late Twentieth Century.* Cambridge: Harvard University Press.

Clifford, James and George E. Marcus, eds. 1986. *Writing Culture: The Poetics and Politics of Ethnography.* Berkeley: University of California Press.

Clifton, James A. 1989. "Pioneer Advocates of Methodism Among the Lake Superior Chippewa." In *Being and Becoming Indian: Biographical Studies of North American Frontiers.* James A. Clifton, ed. Pp. 115–32. Chicago: Dorsey Press.

Coleman, Simon and John Elsner. 1995. *Pilgrimage Past and Present in the World Religions.* Cambridge: Harvard University Press.

Comaroff, Jean. 1985. *Body of Power, Spirit of Resistance: The Culture and History of a South*

African People. Chicago: University of Chicago Press.

Comaroff, Jean and John Comaroff. 1990. "Christianity and Colonialism in South Africa." In *Customs in Conflict: The Anthropology of a Changing World*. Frank Manning and Jean-Marc Philibert, eds. Pp. 222–50. Peterborough, ON: Broadview Press.

Conkling, Robert. 1974. "Legitimacy and Conversion in Social Change: The Case of French Missionaries and the Northeast Algonkian." In *Ethnohistory* 21 (1): 1–23.

Counts, David R. and Dorothy A. Counts, eds. 1991. *Coping With the Final Tragedy: Cultural Variation in Dying and Grieving*. New York: Baywood Publishing.

Danforth, Loring. 1982. *The Death Rituals of Rural Greece*. Princeton: Princeton University Press.

———. 1989. *Firewalking and Religious Healing: The Anastenaria of Greece and the American Firewalking Movement*. Princeton: Princeton University Press.

Davies, J. G. 1988. *Pilgrimage Yesterday and Today: Why? Where? How?* London: SCM Press.

Davis, Natalie Z. 1974. "Some Tasks and Themes in the Study of Popular Religion." In *The Pursuit of Holiness in Late Medieval and Renaissance Religion*. Charles Trinkaus and H. A. Oberman, eds. Pp. 307–36. Leiden: E. J. Brill.

Davis, Stephen A. 1991. *Peoples of the Maritimes: Micmac*. Tantallon, NS: Four East Publications.

Dedam, Alex. 1997. "Native Spirituality and Christianity." In *Maliseet and Micmac: First Nations of the Maritimes*. Robert M. Leavitt, ed. Pp. 114–15. Fredericton, NB: New Ireland Press.

Delâge, Denys and Helen Hornbeck-Tanner. 1994. "The Ojibwa-Jesuit Debate at Walpole Island, 1844." *Ethnohistory*. 42(2): 295–321.

Denny, Alex. 1997. "Ekinámuksikw aq Kelutmalsewusíkw." In *The Mi'kmaw Concordat* by James Youngblood Henderson, ed. Pp. 9–11. Halifax: Fernwood Publishing.

Denys, Nicholas. 1908. *The Description and Natural History of the Coasts of North America (Acadia)*. Toronto: Champlain Society.

Dickason, Olive P. 1984. *The Myth of the Savage and the Beginnings of French Colonialism in the Americas*. Edmonton: University of Alberta Press.

Drewal, Margaret. 1992. *Yoruba Ritual: Performers, Play, Agency*. Bloomington; Indianapolis: Indiana University Press.

Dubisch, Jill. 1995. *In a Different Place: Pilgrimage, Gender, and Politics at a Greek Island Shrine*. Princeton: Princeton University Press.

Dundes, Alan. 1980. *Interpreting Folklore*. Bloomington: Indiana University Press.

Dusenberry, Verne. 1962. *The Montana Cree: A Study in Religious Persistence*. Stockholm: Almqvist and Wiksell.

Eade, John and Michael Sallnow, eds. 1991. *Contesting the Sacred: The Anthropology of Christian Pilgrimage*. London: Routledge.

"Encyclical Letter *Redemptoris Missio*: On the Permanent Validity of the Church's Missionary Mandate (Excerpts)." In *International Bulletin of Missionary Research*. Vol. 15, No. 2, April 1991: 49–52.

Fabian, Johannes. 1983. *Time and the Other: How Anthropology Makes its Object*. New York: Columbia University Press.

Francis, Daniel. 1992. *The Imaginary Indian: The*

Image of the Indian in Canadian Culture. Vancouver: Arsenal Pulp Press.

Freeman, Susan Tax. 1978. "Faith and Fashion in Spanish Religion: Notes on the Observation of Observance." *Peasant Studies* 7 (2): 101–23.

Frères Mineurs Capucins. 1910. *Souvenir d'un IIIe Centenaiare en Pays Micmac.* Trois-Rivières: André-Albert de Saint-Germain.

Frideres, James S. 2001. *Aboriginal Peoples in Canada: Contemporary Conflicts.* Sixth edition. Toronto: Prentice-Hall Canada.

Friesen, John W. 1997. *Rediscovering the First Nations of Canada.* Calgary: Detselig Enterprises.

Furniss, Elizabeth. 1995. *Victims of Benevolence: The Dark Legacy of the William's Lake Residential School.* Revised edition [1992]. Vancouver: Arsenal Pulp Press.

Geertz, Clifford. 1973. *The Interpretation of Cultures.* New York: Harper Collins Publishers.

Gill, Sam. 1987. *Mother Earth: An American Story.* Chicago: University of Chicago Press.

Goulet, Jean-Guy. 1982. "Religious Dualism Among Athapaskan Catholics." *Canadian Journal of Anthropology* 3(1): 1–18.

Grant, John Webster. 1984. *Moon of Wintertime: Missionaries and the Indians of Canada in Encounter Since 1534.* Toronto: University of Toronto Press.

Grim, John A. 2000. "Cultural Identity, Authenticity, and Community Survival: The Politics of Recognition in the Study of Native American Religions." In *Native American Spirituality: A Critical Reader.* Lee Irwin, ed. Pp. 37–60. Lincoln: University of Nebraska Press.

Guemple, Lee. 1994. "Born-Again Pagans: The Inuit Cycle of Spirits." In *Amerindian Rebirth: Reincarnation and Belief Among North American Indians and Inuit.* Mills, Antonia and Richard Slobodin eds. Pp. 107–22. Toronto: University of Toronto Press.

Guha, Ranajit. 1983. *Elementary Aspects of Peasant Insurgency in Colonial India.* Delhi: Oxford University Press.

Hanson, Allan. 1989. "The Making of the Maori: Culture Invention and Its Logic." In *American Anthropologist,* 91: 890–902.

Handler, Richard and Jocelyn Linnekin. 1984. "Tradition, Genuine or Spurious?" In *Journal of American Folklore.* [No. 385] Pp. 273–90.

Henderson, James Youngblood. 1997. *The Mi'kmaw Concordat.* Halifax: Fernwood Publishing.

Hertz, Robert. 1960. *Death and the Right Hand.* Rodney and Claudia Needham, trans. of 1907 Essay. New York; Aberdeen: Free Press and Aberdeen University Press.

Hoffman, Bernard G. 1946. "The Historical Ethnography of the Micmac of the Sixteenth and Seventeenth Centuries." Ph.D. dissertation in Anthropology, University of California, Berkeley.

Honko, Lauri. 1964. "Memorates and the Study of Folk Beliefs." *Journal of the Folklore Institute* 1: 5–19.

Hornborg, Anne-Christine. 2001. *A Landscape of Left-Overs: Changing Conceptions of Place and Environment Among Mi'kmaq Indians of Eastern Canada.* Lund: Religionshistoriska avdelningen, Lunds universitet.

Hulkrantz, Ake. 1953. *Conceptions of the Soul Among North American Indians: A Study in Religious Ethnography.* Stockholm: Ethnographical Museum of Sweden.

————. 1979. "The Problem of Christian Influence on Northern Algonkian Eschatology." *Studies in Religion* 9(2): 161–83.

Jackson, Michael. 1989. *Paths Toward a Clearing: Radical Empiricism and Ethnographic Inquiry.* Bloomington: Indiana University Press.

————. 1995. *At Home in the World.* Durham; London: Duke University Press.

————. 1998. *Minima Ethnographica: Intersubjectivity and the Anthropological Project.* Chicago: University of Chicago Press.

Jackson, Michael, ed. 1996. *Things As They Are: New Directions in Phenomenological Anthropology.* Bloomington; Indianapolis: Indiana University Press.

Jaenen, Cornelius J. 1976. *Friend and Foe: Aspects of French-Amerindian Culture Contact in the Sixteenth and Seventeenth Centuries.* Toronto: McClelland and Stewart.

Jasen, Patricia. 1995. *Wild Things: Nature, Culture and Tourism in Ontario 1790–1914.* Toronto; Buffalo: University of Toronto Press.

Jarvenpa, Robert. 1990. "The Development of Pilgrimage in an Inter-cultural Frontier. In *Culture and the Anthropological Tradition: Essays in Honor of Robert F.*

Spencer. Robert H. Winthrop, ed. Pp. 177–203. Lanham, MD: University Press of America.

Johnson, Frederick. 1943. "Notes on Micmac Shamanism." In *Primitive Man: Quarterly Bulletin of the Catholic Anthropological Conference.* vol. XVI (3-4): 53–84.

Johnston, Angus A. 1960. *A History of the Catholic Church in Eastern Nova Scotia.* Volume 1. Antigonish, NS: St. Francis Xavier University Press.

————. 1972. *A History of the Catholic Church in Eastern Nova Scotia.* Volume 2. Antigonish, NS: St. Francis Xavier University Press.

Kan, Sergei. 1985. "Russian Orthodox Brotherhoods Among the Tlingit: Missionary Goals and Native Response." *Ethnohistory* 32:196–223.

————. 1989. *Symbolic Immortality: The Tlingit Potlatch of the Nineteenth Century.* Washington: Smithsonian Institution Press.

————. 1991. "Modern-Day Tlingit Leaders Look at the Past." *Ethnohistory* 38: 363–87.

Kastenbaum, Robert J. 1998. *Death, Society and Human Experience.* Sixth edition. Boston: Allyn and Bacon.

[Kauder, Christian?] 1868. "The Catholic Church in the Wilderness." In *The Irish Ecclesiastical Record.* 41: 238–54.

Kaufert, Joseph and John O'Neil. 1991. "Cultural Mediation of Dying and Grieving among Native Canadian Patients in Urban Hospitals." In *Coping With the Final Tragedy: Cultural Variation in Dying and Grieving.* David R. Counts and Dorothy A. Counts, eds. Pp. 231–53. New York: Baywood Publishing.

Kidwell, Clara Sue. 2000. "Repatriating the Past: Recreating Indian History." In *Native American Spirituality: A Critical Reader.* Lee Irwin, ed. Pp. 195–204. Lincoln: University of Nebraska Press.

Knockwood, Isabelle. 1992. *Out of the Depths: The Experiences of Mi'kmaw Children at the Indian Residential School at Shubenacadie, Nova Scotia.* Lockeport, NS: Roseway.

Krech, Shepard III. 1994. *Native Canadian Anthropology and History: A Selected Bibliography.* Revised edition. Winnipeg: Rupert's Land Research Centre.

————. 1999. *The Ecological Indian: Myth and History.* New York and London: W. W. Norton & Company.

Kreiger, Carlo J. 1989. "Ethnogenesis or Cultural Interference? Catholic Missionaries and the Micmac." In *Actes du Vingtieme Congres des Algonquinistes*. William Cowan, ed. Pp. 193–200. Ottawa: Carleton University.

Larsen, Tord. 1983. "Negotiating Identity: The Micmac of Nova Scotia." In *The Politics of Indianness: Case Studies of Native Ethnopolitics in Canada*. Adrian Tanner, ed. Pp. 37–136. St. John's: ISER.

Leavitt, Robert M. 1995. *Maliseet and Micmac: First Nations of the Maritimes*. Fredericton, NB: New Ireland Press.

Le Braz, Anatole. 1928. *La légende de mort chez les Bretons armoricains*. Fifth ed. 2 vol. Paris: Honoré Champion.

LeClercq, Christian. 1968. *New Relations of Gaspesia, with the Customs and Religion of the Gaspesian Indians*. William F. Ganong, trans. Reprint of 1910 ed. New York: Greenwood Press.

LeGoff, Jacques. 1981. *The Birth of Purgatory*. Arthus Goldhammer, trans. Chicago: University of Chicago Press.

Lehman, Arthur C. and James E. Myers, eds. 2001. *Magic, Witchcraft and Religion: An Anthropological Study of the Supernatural*. Fifth edition. Mountain View, CA: Mayfield Publishing.

Lenhart, John. 1932. *History Relating to Manual of Prayers, Instructions, Psalms and Hymns in Micmac Ideograms used by Micmac Indians of Eastern Canada and Newfoundland*. Sydney: Cameron Print.

Lieber, Michael D. 1991. "Cutting Your Losses: Death and Grieving in a Polynesian Community." In *Coping With the Final Tragedy: Cultural Variation in Dying and Grieving*. David R. and Dorothy A. Counts, eds. Pp. 169–90. New York: Baywood Publishing.

Lindstrom, Lamont. 1982. "Leftamap Kastom: The Political History of Tradition on Tanna, Vanuatu." *Mankind* 13: 316–29.

MacPherson, D., Rev. 1910. "Third Centenary of the First Baptism Among the Micmac Indians." In *Souvenir d'un IIIe Centenaire en pays Micmac*. Fréres Mineurs Capucins, eds. Pp. 46–61. Trois-Rivières: André-Albert de Saint-Germain.

Manning, Frank and Jean-Marc Philibert, eds. 1990. *Customs in Conflict: The Anthropology of a Changing World*. Peterborough, ON: Broadview Press.

Marcus, George E. and Dick Cushman. 1982. "Ethnographies as Text." *Annual Review of Anthropology*. 11: 25–69.

Marcus, George E. and Michael M. J. Fischer. 1999. *Anthropology as Cultural Critique: An Experimental Moment in the Human Sciences*. Second edition. Chicago: University of Chicago Press.

Marshall, (Chief) Donald Sr., Alexander Denny and Putus S. Marshall. 1989. "The Mi'kmaq: The Covenant Chain." In *Drumbeat: Anger and Renewal in Indian Country*. Boyce Richardson, ed. Pp. 71–104. Toronto: Summerhill.

Marshall, Joseph B. 1991. "Hunting and Fishing Rights of the Mi'kmaq." In *Paqtatek: Policy and Consciousness in Mi'kmaq Life*. Halifax: Garamond Press.

Marshall, Murdena. 1995. "Chapel Island: Mi'kmaq and Christian Spirituality." In *Maliseet and Micmac: First Nations of the Maritimes*. Robert M. Leavitt, ed. Pp. 109–11 Fredericton, NB: New Ireland Press.

McGee, Henry Franklin Jr. 1974. "Ethnic Boundaries and Strategies of Ethnic Interaction: A History of

Micmac-White Relations in Nova Scotia." Ph.D. dissertation in Anthropology. Southern Illinois University.

————. 1984. *The Native Peoples of Atlantic Canada: A History of Indian-European Relations*. Ottawa: Carleton University.

McMillan, Alan D. 1995. *Native Peoples and Cultures of Canada: An Anthropological Overview*. Second edition. Vancouver: Douglas and McIntyre.

McMillan, Leslie J. 1996. "*Mi'kmawey Mawio'mi*: Changing Roles of the Mi'kmaq Grand Council From the Early Seventeenth Century to the Present." M.A. thesis in Anthropology. Dalhousie University, Halifax, NS.

Merkur, Daniel. 1991. *Powers Which We Do Not Know: The Gods and Spirits of the Inuit*. Idaho: University of Idaho Press.

Metcalf, Peter. 2001. "Death Be Not Strange." In *Magic, Witchcraft and Religion: An Anthropological Study of the Supernatural*. Arthur C. Lehman and James E. Myers, eds. Fifth edition. Pp. 332–35. Mountain View, CA: Mayfield Publishing.

Metcalf, Peter and Richard Huntington, eds. 1991. *Celebrations of Death:*

The Anthropology of Mortuary Ritual. Second edition. Cambridge: Cambridge University Press.

Miller, Jay. 1997. "Old Religion Among the Delawares: The Gamwing (Big House Rite)." *Ethnohistory*, 44(1): 113–34.

Miller, Virginia P. 1980. "Silas Rand, Nineteenth Century Anthropology Among the Micmac." *Anthropologica*, 22: 235–50.

————. 1982. "The Decline of the Nova Scotia Mi'kmaq Population, A.D. 1600–1850." *Culture* 2, 3 : 107–20.

————. 1995. "The Micmac: A Maritime Woodland Group." In *Native Peoples: The Canadian Experience*. R. Bruce Morrison and C. Roderick Wilson, eds. Pp. 347–74. Second edition. Oxford: Oxford University Press.

Milliea, Mildred. 1989. "Micmac Catholicism in my Community: Miigemeoei Alsotmagan Nemetgig." In *Actes du Vingtième Congrès des Algonquiniste*s. William Cowan, ed. Pp. 262–66. Ottawa: Carleton University Press.

Mills, Antonia and Richard Slobodin, eds. 1994. *Amerindian Rebirth: Reincarnation Belief Among North American Indians and Inuit.*

Toronto: University of Toronto Press.

Morinis, Alan. 1992. "Persistent Peregrination: From Sun Dance to Catholic Pilgrimage Among Canadian Prairie Indians." In *Sacred Journeys: The Anthropology of Pilgrimage*. Alan Morinis, ed. Pp. 101–13. London: Greenwood.

Morrison, Kenneth G. 1981. "The Mythological Sources of Abenaki Catholicism: A Case Study of the Social History of Power." *Religion: Journal of Religion and Religions* 11: 235–36.

————. 1990. "Baptism and Alliance: The Symbolic Mediations of Religious Syncretism." *Ethnohistory* 37: 416–37.

Narayan, Kirin. 1989. *Storytellers, Saints and Scoundrels: Folk Narrative in Hindu Religious Teaching*. Philadelphia: University of Pennsylvania Press.

Ortner, Sherry B. 1999. *Life and Death on Mt. Everest: Sherpas and Himalayan Mountaineering*. Princeton: Princeton University Press.

Pacifique, F., Rev. 1910. "Excerpts From F. Pacifique's Address." In *Souvenir d'un IIIe Centenaiare en Pays Micmac*. Fréres Mineurs Capucins, eds. Pp. 62–66.

Trois-Rivières: André-Albert de Saint-Germain.

Parkhill, Thomas. 1997. *Weaving Ourselves into the Land: Charles Godfrey Leland, "Indians," and the Study of Native American Religions*. New York: State University of New York Press.

Parsons, Elsie Clews. 1926. "Micmac Notes: St. Anne's Mission on Chapel Island, Bras D'Or Lake, Cape Breton Island." In *Journal of American Folklore* 39: 460–85.

Paul, Daniel N. 1993. *We Were Not the Savages: A Micmac Perspective on the Collision of European and Aboriginal Civilization*. Halifax: Nimbus Publishing.

———. 1996. "The Twentieth Century and the Failure of Centralization: A Micmac Perspective." In *Out of the Background: Readings in Canadian Native History*. Ken S. Coates and Robin Fisher, eds. Second edition. Pp. 320–52 Toronto: Copp Clark.

Peacock, James L. 1986. *The Anthropological Lens: Harsh light, Soft Focus*. Cambridge: Cambridge University Press.

Pearce, Roy Harvey. 1988. *Savagism and Civilization: A Study of the Indian and the American Mind*. Revised edition.

Berkeley: University of California Press.

Pflüg, Melissa A. 2000. "*Pimadaziwin*: Contemporary Rituals in Odawa Community." In *Native American Spirituality: A Critical Reader*. Lee Irwin, ed. Pp. 121–44. Lincoln: University of Nebraska Press.

Pieris, Aloysius. 1988. *An Asian Theology of Liberation*. Maryknoll, NY: Orbis Books.

Pinker, Stephen. 1995. *The Language Instinct: How the Mind Creates Language*. New York: Harper Perennial.

Pratt, Mary Louise. 1986. "Fieldwork in Common Places." In *Writing Culture: The Poetics and Politics of Ethnography*. James Clifford and George E. Marcus, eds. Pp. 27–50. Berkeley: University of California Press.

Preston, Richard J. 1987. "Catholicism at Attawapiskat: A Case Study of Culture Change." In *Papers of the Eighteenth Algonquian Conference*, William Cowan, ed. Pp. 271–86. Ottawa: Carleton University.

Preston, Richard J. and Sarah C. Preston. 1991. "Death and Grieving Among Northern Forest Hunters: An East Cree Example." In *Coping With the Final Tragedy: Cultural*

Variation in Dying and Grieving. David R. Counts and Dorothy A. Counts, eds. Pp. 135–56. New York: Baywood Publishing.

Prins, Harald E. L. 1996. *The Mi'kmaq: Resistance, Accommodation and Cultural Survival*. New York: Harcourt Brace College Publishers.

Pritzker, Barry M. ed. 2000. *A Native American Encyclopedia: History, Culture and Peoples*. New York: Oxford University Press.

Rahner, Karl. 1966. *The Church After the Council*. Montreal: Palm Publishers.

Rand, Silas Tertius. 1888. *Dictionary of the Language of the Micmac Indians, Who Reside in Nova Scotia, New Brunswick, Prince Edward Island, Cape Breton and Newfoundland*. Halifax: Nova Scotia Printing Company.

Reid, Jennifer. 1995. *Myth, Symbol, and Colonial Encounter: British and Mi'kmaq in Acadia, 1700–1867*. Ottawa: University of Ottawa Press.

Rieglhaupt, Joyce. 1973. "*Festas* and *Padres*: The Organization of Religious Action in a Portuguese Parish." *American Anthropologist* 75: 835–51.

Rosaldo, Renato. 1989. "Grief and a Headhunter's Rage." In *Culture and Truth: The Remaking of Social Analysis*. Pp. 1–21. Boston: Beacon Press.

Sallnow, Michael J. 1991. "Pilgrimage and Cultural Fracture in the Andes." In *Contesting the Sacred: The Anthropology of Christian Pilgrimage*. John Eade and Michael Sallnow, eds. Pp. 137–53. London: Rutledge.

Sallnow, Michael J. 1981. "Communitas Reconsidered: the Sociology of Andean Pilgrimage." *Man* (New Series), 16: 163–82.

Sapir, Edward. 1985. *Selected Writings of Edward Sapir in Language, Culture and Personality*. David G. Mendelbaum, ed. Reprint. Berkeley: University of California Press.

Saussure, Ferdinand de. 1959. "Course in General Linguistics." In *Critical Theory Since 1965*. Hazard Adams and Leroy Searle, eds. Pp. 645–59. Tallahassee: Florida State University.

Schmidt, David L. and Murdena Marshall. 1995. "Introduction." In *Mi'kmaq Hieroglyphic Prayers: Readings in North America's First Indigenous Script*. David L. Schmidt and Murdena Marshall, eds. and trans. Pp. 1–15. Halifax: Nimbus Publishing.

Shils, Edward A. 1981. *Tradition*. London: Faber and Faber.

Simeone, William E. 1991. "The Northern Athapaskan Potlatch: The Objectification of Grief." In *Coping With the Final Tragedy: Cultural Variation in Dying and Grieving*. David R. Counts and Dorothy A. Counts, eds. Pp. 157–68. New York: Baywood Publishing.

Slaney, Frances M. 1997. "Double Baptism: Personhood and Ethnicity in the Sierra Tarahumara of Mexico." *American Ethnologist* 24(2): 279–310.

Smith, Michael French. 1988. "From Heathen to Atheist on Karuru Island." In *Culture and Christianity: The Dialectics of Transformation*. George R. Saunders, ed. Pp. 33–46. New York: Greenwood Press.

Stahl, Sandra Dolby. 1989. *Literary Folkloristics and the Personal Narrative*. Bloomington; Indianapolis: Indiana University Press.

Steckley, John. 1978. "The Soul Concepts of the Huron." MA thesis, Memorial University of Newfoundland, St. John's, NF.

———. 1992. "The Warrior and the Lineage: Jesuit Use of Iroquoian Images to Communicate Christianity." *Ethnohistory* 39 (4): 478–509.

Stewart, Omar C. 1980. "The Native American Church." In *Anthropology on the Great Plains*. Raymond Wood and Margot Liberty, eds. Pp. 188–96. Lincoln: University of Nebraska.

Stirrat, Robert L. 1992. *Power and Religiosity in a Post-Colonial Setting: Sinhala Catholics in Contemporary Sri Lanka*. Cambridge: Cambridge University Press.

Tanner, Adrian, ed. 1983. *The Politics of Indianness: Case Studies of Native Ethnopolitics in Canada*. St. John's: ISER.

Tedlock, Dennis. 1983. *The Spoken Word and the Work of Interpretation*. Philadelphia: University of Pennsylvania Press.

Tuck, Richard. 1979. *Natural Rights Theories: Their Origins and Development*. Cambridge: Cambridge University Press.

Turner, Victor W. 1974. *Dramas, Fields, and Metaphors: Symbolic Action in Human Society*. Ithaca, NY: Cornell University Press.

———. 1995. *The Ritual Process: Structure and*

Anti-Structure. Revised 1969 edition. Chicago: Aldine Publishing.

Turner, Victor and Edith Turner. 1977. "Death and the Dead in the Pilgrimage Process." In *Religious Encounters with Death: Insights from the History and Anthropology of Religions.* Frank E. Reynolds and Earl Waugh, eds. Pp. 24–39. Pennsylvania: Pennsylvania State University Press.

———. 1978. *Image and Pilgrimage in Christian Culture. Anthropological Perspectives.* New York: Columbia University Press.

Thwaites, Reuben Gold, ed. 1896. *The Jesuit Relations and Allied Documents.* 73 vols. Cleveland: Burrows Brothers. Volumes I–III.

Upton, Leslie F. S. 1979. *Micmacs and Colonists: Indian-White Relations in the Maritime Provinces, 1713–1867.* Vancouver: University of British Columbia Press.

van Gennep, Arnold. 1975. *The Rites of Passage.* Monika B. Vizedom and Gabrielle L. Caffee, trans. Reprint. Chicago: University of Chicago Press.

von Gernet, Alexander 1994. "Saving the Souls: Reincarnation Beliefs of the Seventeenth-Century Huron." In *Amerindian Rebirth: Reincarnation Belief Among North American Indians and Inuit.* Antonia Mills and Richard Slobodin, eds. Pp. 38–54. Toronto: Toronto University Press.

Wallace, Anthony F. C. 1956. "Revitalization Movements." *American Anthropologist* 58: 264–81.

Wallenkamp, Jane C. 1991. "Fallen Leaves: Death and Grieving in Toraja." In *Coping With the Final Tragedy: Cultural Variation in Dying and Grieving.* David R. Counts and Dorothy A. Counts, eds. Pp.113–34. New York: Baywood Publishing.

Wallis, W. and R. S. Wallis. 1955. *The Micmac Indians of Eastern Canada.* Minneapolis: University of Minnesota Press.

Warkentin, Germaine. 1996. "Discovering Radisson: A Renaissance Adventure Between Two Worlds." In *Reading Beyond Words: Contexts for Native History.* Jennifer S. H. Brown and Elizabeth Vibert, eds. Pp. 43–70. Peterborough: Broadview Press.

Watanabe, John M. 1990. "From Saints to Shibboleths: Image, Structure, and Identity in Maya Religious Syncretism." *American Ethnologist* 17 (1): 131–50.

Weaver, Sally M. 1981. *Making Canadian Indian Policy: The Hidden Agenda, 1968–70.* Toronto: University of Toronto Press.

Weiner, A.B. 1985. "Inalienable Wealth." *American Ethnologist* 12: 210–27.

Weiser, F.X. s.j. (Society of Jesuit [Jesuit]). 1972. *Kateri Takakwitha.* Caughnawaga, QC: Kateri Centre.

Whitehead, Ruth Holmes. 1980. *Elitekey: Micmac Material Culture from 1600 AD to the Present.* Halifax: Nova Scotia Museum.

———. 1988. *Stories From the Six Worlds: Micmac Legends.* Halifax: Nimbus Publishing.

———. 1991. *The Old Man Told Us: Excerpts from Micmac History 1500–1950.* Halifax: Nimbus Publishing.

Whorf, Benjamin Lee. 1956. *Language, Thought and Reality; Selected Writings.* Cambridge: Technology Press of Massachusetts Institute of Technology.

Wolf, Eric R. 1958. "The Virgin of Guadalupe: A Mexican National Symbol." *Journal of American Folklore,* 71(1): 34–39.

Index

Names that appear in bold are members of the Mi'kmaw people.

Literary Credits

Chapter opening poem extract, p. 31; Battiste quotations, pp. 37–39: "Mi'kmaq Socialization Patterns." In The Mi'kmaq Anthology. Leslie Choyce and Rita Joe, eds. pp. 145–161. Lawrencetown Beach, NS: Pottersfield Press.

Chapter opening poem extract, p. 48: the quotation from "Church Going," by Philip Larkin, is reprinted from *The Less Deceived* by permission of The Marvell Press, England and Australia.

Chapter opening poem extract, p. 109: Joe, Rita. 1999. "My Shadow Follows." in *We Are the Dreamers: Recent and Early Poetry*. Wreck Cove, NS: Breton Books. .